CW00558138

The ISI War Crimes and Murder of Civilian Culture of Intelligence in Pakistan

The ISI War Crimes and Murder of Civilian Culture of Intelligence in Pakistan

Musa Khan Jalalzai

Vij Books India Pvt Ltd

New Delhi (India)

Published by

Vij Books India Pvt Ltd
(Publishers, Distributors & Importers)
2/19, Ansari Road
Delhi – 110 002
Phones: 91-11-43596460, 91-11-47340674
Mobile: 98110 94883
e-mail: contact@vijpublishing.com
www.vijbooks.in

ISBN: 978-93-90917-61-7 (Hardback)
ISBN: 978-93-90917-69-3 (Paperback)
ISBN: 978-93-90917-93-8 (ebook)

Contents

Introduction

The ISI War Crimes and Murder of Civilian Culture of Intelligence in Pakistan

Terrorist groups in Afghanistan have killed and tortured innocent civilians, and destroyed National Critical Infrastructure with the military and financial support of Iran and Pakistan. Terrorism has now become a profitable business across the globe, while terrorist groups are free to traffic narcotics drugs, and smuggle arms to finance their war against states. Despite massive expenditure by the US governments over the past two decades in Afghanistan, its security forces only achieved shame, championship of war crime, and genocide. Pakistan's interference and war crimes further exacerbated the pain of Afghans civilians. Having unmasked transmogrified face of his country's army, Prime Minister Imran Khan uncovered the US-Pakistan collaboration and fraternization against Afghanistan: "We have trained them to fight against a foreign occupation. It was a holy war, a jihad," he said. And with the Americans invading, Pakistan was telling the same people that "a fight against the Americans was terrorism. So, they turned against us. They called us collaborators... here were insider attacks against the Pakistani army, who had trained the mujahedeen," he said. "There were two suicide attacks on General Musharraf from within the army." Prime Minister Imran Khan said.

On 15 August 2021, before Taliban entered Kabul, their units were already committing atrocities, including summary executions of government officials and security forces members, raping, and kidnapping women and girls. In Kabul alone, they raided homes of journalists and activists, women, and dissidents who criticized their illegal operations in Afghanistan. They killed a pregnant woman police officer in Kandahar, tortured journalists and protesters. More than 900 Afghans were killed by the ISI-led Taliban. The Times of London (Hugh Tomlinson, Humayoon Babur-05 Aug 2021) reported the killing of 1000 innocent people by the Taliban and the ISI death squads after they entered Kandahar. BBC News reported (Yogita Limaye-31 August, 2021) extrajudicial killings. However, Former IG Police,

1

Mr. Tadin Khan, authenticated the killing of more than 800-900 people in Kandahar. The Daily Mail London (05 August 2021) reported the killing of 900 people as Taliban overran Kandahar.

On 16 June 2021, in Daulatabad, more than twenty-two unarmed Afghan Special Forces Commandos were executed while attempting to surrender to the Taliban forces. A video of the event circulated widely and was broadcasted by CNN. In July 2021, in Kandahar, the ISI-led Taliban extra judicially executed critics and people thought to have been members of province-level governments and their relatives. In early July 2021, in Malistan District, Taliban killed civilians, looted their houses, and destroyed homes in order to ethnically and religiously divide Afghan society. On 6 August 2021, Taliban claimed responsibility for the 5 August 2021 assassination of Dawa Khan Menapal, head of the government media and information Centre in Kabul. On August 21, 2021, a video showing Haji Mullah Achakzai, the ex-police Chief of Badghis province, was blindfolded and restrained before he was shot to death by the ISI-led Taliban at close range. The Pakistan army and Taliban have been known for their war crimes and sexual exploitation in Afghanistan and Pakistan. Its military units raped and killed women and girls in Waziristan and Balochistan.[1] Arie Perliger (August 18, 2021), in his analysis noted that 'the speed and efficiency with which Taliban forces were able to complete the occupation of most of Afghanistan, as well as the quick collapse of the Afghan government, has led to criticism of President Joe Biden's decision to end U.S. military presence in Afghanistan.[2]

For Afghan politicians and Taliban leadership, it is time to define their tangible enemy. The Islamic State (ISIS), the US army and NATO forces killed Afghans in their homes, markets, schools, and on roadways by drones, and their criminal militias. On 24 October 2019, Pakistan's former Ambassador to Afghanistan, Rustam Shah Mohmand in his article noted hardship, suffering, mental and physical diseases, and displacement of Afghans inside their own country at the hands of Taliban, Daesh, US army and NATO forces. In September 2019, in Helmand province, a wedding party was turned into a massacre after a commando raid by the U.S. and NDS killer Unit-02. Over 40 people were brutally killed. These attacks were justified in the name of fighting terrorism. The UNAMA report noted US army airstrikes on so-called drug laboratories in Farah province on 05 May 2019, which caused at least 39 civilian casualties. The casualties included 14 children and one woman. Apart from the adverse effects of causing civilian casualties, as pointed out by SIGAR, "the airstrikes in themselves appear to go squarely against international humanitarian law".

On 14 September, 2021, Global Times reported criticism of Chinese envoy in his UN speech against the United States war crimes in Afghanistan, and demanded investigation into its army's human rights abuse in the country. "Ambassador Chen Xu the Chinese envoy to the UN at Geneva called for an investigation into alleged crimes including torture and killing of civilians committed in Afghanistan by military personnel from the US and its allies in a speech at the 48th session of the UN Human Rights Council, and asked the US to reflect on its mistakes and address serious human rights abuses. "We express our deep concern that the United States and its allies have conducted military intervention in Afghanistan for 20 years, which severely undermined the sovereignty and territorial integrity of Afghanistan, compromised its economic and social development, and violated the human rights of Afghan people". Global Times reported. Ambassador Chen noted the killing Global Times, April 2020), 470,000 Afghan civilians killed in the war waged by the US and more than 10 million Afghan people were displaced. Chen also expressed deep concern about chronic human rights issues in the US, such as how the US, possessing the most advanced medical equipment and technologies, suffered the largest number of COVID-19 cases and deaths in the world. Mr. Chen warned.

On 29 August, 2021, the US army committed war crime by killing innocent children in Kabul. General Kenneth Mckenzie said: "As the combatant commander, I am fully responsible for this strike and its tragic outcome, it was believed that the target was militants trying to attack US forces and the evacuees at Kabul airport. This strike was taken in the earnest belief that it would prevent an imminent threat to our forces and the evacuees at the airport, but it was a mistake," McKenzie said. However, on 18 September, 2021, the US Defense Secretary Lloyd Austin also apologized and offered condolences for the families of the civilians who were wrongfully killed in the strike. General Kenneth McKenzie shamelessly by ordering the drone airstrike in Kabul's residential area. Moreover, the Pentagon also apologized after admitting drone strike in Kabul killed 10 civilians. More than 71,000 Afghan and Pakistani civilians have died directly from the war launched by the United States. Family members of the August 29 drone raid victims told Al Jazeera after the attack that the 10 people killed ranged in age from two to 40 years old. "They were innocent, helpless children," Aimal Ahmadi, whose nieces and nephews were killed in the attack, told Al Jazeera at the time.

The U.S. abrupt abandonment, betrayal and desertion of Afghanistan, failure of CIA and MI6 to inform their management on time, and the abrupt collapse of the Afghan artificial state and government put the so-called superpower's credibility in question. President Biden shamelessly said that withdrawal of US forces from the country was his upstanding decision, but allies will no longer trust the American leadership due to its selfishness and egocentrism. Analyst Joshua D. Kertzer, (September 2, 2021) noted "The Biden administration's withdrawal from Afghanistan will affect these calculations the next time the United States commits to an extraordinarily costly venture in a place not vital to the country's core security interests, but it is unlikely to sabotage U.S. credibility". Having dismantled all transport and military plans by the US army in Kabul Airport, world leaders condemned the Joe Biden government. President Putin (02 September-2021) in his comment on the Americans credibility and Biden's illegal and unethical demonstrations said: "The U.S. military intervention in Afghanistan had achieved nothing but tragedy and loss of life on all sides and showed it was impossible to foist foreign values on other nations. He said 20 years in the country only brought tragedies and loss of life".

On August 03, 2021, *The Kabul Times* noted the US army failure to confront ISI over its proxy war in Afghanistan. Ever since, US President Joe Biden announced that his country would pull out troops from Afghanistan by the end of August 2021, Pakistani Prime Minister Imran Khan were sermonizing about the shortcomings of US policy in the region"[3] In his article, former Canadian Ambassador to Afghanistan, Mr. Alexander noted; that Afghanistan needed one thing, a peace settlement with Pakistan." He also described Imran Khan as being "one of the Taliban's most vociferous backers".[4] However, Modern diplomacy in its 29 August, 2021 commentary noted some aspects of deteriorating security situation in Afghanistan:

"A crisis of incredible proportions is unfolding in Afghanistan as conflict combined with drought and COVID-19, and is pushing Afghans into a humanitarian catastrophe. Meanwhile, since the beginning of the year 2021, conflict and insecurity have driven more than 550,000 Afghans from their homes as some 70,000 displaced people have converged from across the country into the capital, Kabul.[5] Moreover, on August 14, 2021, Afghanistan Times reported the deteriorating security situation in Afghanistan as thousands of people fled their homes and were seeking resettlement in the capital Kabul and some major cities. They lacked access to humanitarian services, food and medical stuff. The whole world turned its back to Afghanistan-forgetting the fact that the chaos and destabilization of Afghanistan would leak to the world's powerful countries, even the west.[6] On August 08, 2021, Afghanistan Times also reported the forsakenness and immoderation of the people of Afghanistan by world community: "Situation in Afghanistan is becoming much grimmer with each passing day. The offensive heightened after the announcement of the withdrawal of foreign troop's withdrawal. Indeed, the US messed up in Afghanistan as its war on terror went in vain and moreover, its irresponsible withdrawal plan caused the militant outlets to start daydreaming of military victory. The international community, including the regional countries, were not happy with what the Taliban were doing at the moment. These countries backed negotiated settlement to the Afghan conflict and openly supported the Afghan peace process[7]."

The United States forces have finally been safely transported to Pakistan by the Taliban after they completed secret talks with the CIA Director in Kabul. The US forces will return to Afghanistan accompanying the commando force of NATO and the British army by the end of this year. Amit Chaturvedi, of *Hindustan Times* in 31 August, 2021 quoted the *Daily Mail* letter narrating the presence of those in the court who committed crimes: 'The Taliban used this tactic of issuing threats using the letters in villages when they were in power in Afghanistan more than 20 years ago. But this time, they are now widely circulated in cities. This shows that the governing style of the insurgent group has hardly changed from its last rule, despite Taliban leaders portraying the group as moderate.[8] However, Research Fellow of the Institute for Conflict Management-India, Ajit Kumar Singh noted fear and anxiety of Afghans in major cities; 'though just two weeks have passed since the Taliban returned to power in Kabul, fear among masses, as expected, has spread like wildfire across Afghanistan, forcing thousands to run towards the Hamid Karzai International Airport in Kabul, to escape a dreaded future. Unsurprisingly, the Kabul Airport and its surroundings have since become the epicenter of violence'[9].

The ISI-led Taliban military units killed 900 people as they overran the Afghan province of Kandahar, the *Times of London* (06 August 2021) noted.[10] The Taliban Death Squad was reportedly pulling people from their homes and executing them as they step up the hunt for anyone who helped the US and UK military operations. This was just a pretext they were on a revenge mission. Translators and other staff were living in fear with many attempting to desperately flee Afghanistan after the Taliban seized power in Kabul.[11] A leaked UN document said; 'the Taliban were intensifying the search for anyone who may have worked with the US or NATO'. However, the report–provided by UN threat-assessment advisers, said; 'the ISI-backed group had a "priority list" of individuals it wanted to hunt. Major targets of the ISI units included those who had central roles in the Afghan military, police and intelligence services–carrying out "door-to-door tours" across Afghanistan. Family members of those on the list were also at risk'.[12]

When the Taliban military units were dragging more than 900 Afghans out of their houses-blindfolded, and killed one by one with impunity, where were stashing Amnesty International and Human Rights Watch defenders to tell the world about their atrocities, killing and dumping? When their units killed all 900 Afghans in Chaman district and Kandahar, and put their wives and girls under lock and key for sexual exploitation, at what place were Amnesty International, and the British so-called human right organizations to investigate these war crimes.

Reverting to intelligence war between the ISI and the IB in Pakistan, I want to thoroughly investigate the murder of civilian culture of intelligence, and dematerialization of Intelligence Bureau (IB). Pakistan was established in 1947, and the ISI was established in 1948, but with the demise of Muhammad Ali Jinnah, things shaped differently. From Governor General Ghulam Muhammad (Sir Malik Ghulam Muhammad was a Pakistani politician who served as the third Governor-General of Pakistan, appointed in 1951 until being dismissed in 1955 due to health conditions) to Field Marshal Muhammad Ayub Khan (An army general who seized the presidency from the first president Skander Mirza in a coup in 1958), Intelligence Bureau (IB) of Pakistan led policy makers on right direction, and played a positive role in bringing democratic politicians and military establishment to a close[13]

Before the Soviet invasion of Afghanistan, the ISI never demonstrated and manifested in a professional course of action. As a weak, dematerialized agency, its intelligence reports, analysis, social and political relationship with policy makers were deeply underwhelming. However, in 1971, its counterfeit approach to the war, and its direct link with armed forces was not so friendly. Consequently, the country was dismembered due to the ISI's weak intelligence and geographical vision. For all these failures, the ISI is entirely responsible. The perception and brain-wave that ISI is a number-one intelligence agency, is totally uncorroborated and baseless. The ISI is expert of politics and alliance making. The achievement of the agency in 1965 and 1971 has been disenchanted and shameful, for the reason that neither ISI was proficient to counter Indian RAW, nor was competent to led policy-makers in right direction. Former Indian IB officer and present National Security Advisor in the Prime Minister Modi government, Mr. Ajit Doval has been spying on Pakistani leadership, the ISI, IB, and military establishment for seven years in Lahore Pakistan. The No-one agency was at a loss and unable to identify him. The fact of the matter is, on 03 December 1971, India and Pakistan entered into a full-fledged war after a long period of conflict and strife between East and West Pakistan, but the ISI was not prepared to use propaganda machines against India. The 1971 war had become an international event, in the use of media technology, making it an image-driven war covered by international documentary and photographers. Although, Zulfiqar Ali Bhutto tried to strengthen the ISI's role in domestic politics, but the agency kept a watchful eye on the Bhutto family whilst they were in Pakistan or when they were abroad in political exile in places like London.[14]

Research Scholar and expert, Jyoti M. Pathania in her research paper, (ISI in Pakistan's Domestic Politics: An Assessment-CLAWS Journal 2020) noted General Ayub Khan and Yahya Khan's attempted to strengthen the ISI, while the agency was affixed behind the Bhutto family in and outside the country. Prime Minister Zulfikar Ali Bhutto, further expanded the ISI's political role by creating political cell to monitor his political opponents: "Hence, the policies and strategies adopted by Ayub Khan and Yahya Khan made ISI the most powerful intelligence agency within Pakistan, with its primary and specific functions becoming more and more blurred as well as enlarged. Even the civilian leaders did not hesitate in using intelligence agencies for their personal political motives. Prime Minister, Zulfikar Ali Bhutto, further expanded the ISI's political role by creating an internal security wing/political cell primarily for monitoring his political opponents. One official of that time confirmed this saying, "[…] even his ministers' phones and offices were bugged and their personal lives monitored since Bhutto trusted no one and relished replaying tapes in front of those who had fallen from grace." Another incident during his regime was recalled by Late B. Raman, a senior RAW Officer of India stated, "ISI's Internal Political Division had Shah Nawaz Bhutto, one of the two brothers of Benazir Bhutto, assassinated through poisoning in the French Riviera in the middle of 1985, in an attempt to intimidate her not returning to Pakistan for directing the movement against General Zia-ul-Haq." The political cell was used for rigging the 1977 election as well as against the Balochi Nationalists. According to author Zahid Hussain, Bhutto also used the ISI to keep surveillance not only on his opponents but also on his party men and cabinet ministers".[15]

Robert B. Oakley and Franz-Stefan Gady (Radicalization by Choice: ISI and the Pakistani Army. Institute for National Strategic Studies, National Defense University, Strategic Forum-No. 247, October 2009) have highlighted the role of the army and the ISI in politics, and their zeal to dismember India. They also described the role of ISI and the army in the future of Pakistan: "For better or worse, the Pakistani army and its intelligence unit, the Inter-Services Intelligence Directorate (ISI), remain the most important elements in determining Pakistan's future. The army establishment is the glue that holds this large multi-ethnic, nuclear-armed Muslim country together. The Pakistani army and the Inter-Services Intelligence Directorate remain essential for the security and stability of Pakistan. Both organizations have deliberately embraced Islamic radicalism as a means to address the conventional military gap between Pakistan and India. The perils of the present situation in Pakistan are enormous not only for that country and Afghanistan but also for the entire region, including India. The danger of another military confrontation between India and Pakistan is very much alive, with the risk that it could develop into a nuclear exchange".[16]

The ISI supported Taliban to disturb the Karzai government and force US and NATO allies to leave Afghanistan. All actions and operations of the Taliban government in Afghanistan were being accomplished and top-off by the Pakistan army. Three to four attacks of Taliban terrorists-managed and administered by Pakistani ISI against the Indian targets in Kabul and Jalalabad. In 2008, the ISI ordered the Taliban to attack the Indian Embassy in Kabul-killing 58 people and wounding 141, and in October 2009, in an attack against Indian targets, they killed 40 and injured more than 100. This time, the US, NATO, India and Afghanistan accused the agency of being behind the attacks. The Indian national security advisor said his country had documentary evidence of the ISI involvement in 2008 attacks. Later on, ISI constituted an attack against the US embassy in Kabul in September of 2011, killing at least seven people and wounding another nineteen. However, in September 2013, the ISI instructed the Taliban to attack the Indian consulate in Jalalabad. The agency shamelessly targeted Indian, American and Afghan military and government installations, and killed women and children, but neither the US army and government, nor international community reacted directly, or indirectly.

In his fathomless and yawning analysis of the US policy towards Pakistan and their polarity and breach on the role Pakistan played in Afghanistan, Daniel Markey (America's Perennial Pakistan Problem: Why Washington Failed to Win Over Islamabad—and Prevent a Taliban Victory, Foreign

Affairs-September 9, 2021) has documented the role of ISI in Taliban government, the war crime, while its relationship with Taliban, the ISIS and al Qaeda, and the designated terrorist Ministers in Taliban cabinet raised several important questions: "These questions are even more urgent following the U.S. exit from Afghanistan. With its client established in Kabul, Pakistan remains deeply entangled in its neighbor's politics. Future solutions to the threats posed by a Taliban-dominated Afghanistan— including the potential resurgence of al Qaeda or similar terrorist groups— will likely run through Islamabad. Recent U.S.-Pakistani dialogues on these issues show signs of friction: Pakistani officials have downplayed the extent of the Taliban's domestic crackdown and have sought public praise for their assistance in evacuating third-country officials, while U.S. diplomats remain less sanguine about Taliban reprisals and more focused on the threat of resurgent al Qaeda and Islamic State (also known as ISIS) affiliates in Afghanistan. The United States has a vital interest in understanding why it failed for two decades to influence Pakistani behavior in Afghanistan— and in developing a new, less militarized strategy for advancing its goals in the region".[17]

The Pentagon and NATO used Pakistani agencies for furthering their agenda and war crimes in Afghanistan. With the re-emergence of Al-Qaeda and other groups in Pakistan, the ISI revived its policy of killing and dumping in Afghanistan. In 2003, the ISI once more relaunched covert proxy war in Afghanistan. From 2001-2003, the US, UK and NATO policy towards Pakistan was enigmatic due Pakistan's bilateral cooperation and engagement in war against so-called terrorism. From 2014-2015, Kunduz fell to the Taliban. In his book (Pakistan's Inter-Services Intelligence Directorate: Covert Action and Internal Operations), Professor Owen Sirrs noted: "A secret cell planted within an intelligence agency that has tight compartmentalization, rigid communication security procedures, and a network of former intelligence officers to aid militant groups and conduct plausibly deniable operations".[18] Research scholar and analyst, Chris Alexander (Ending Pakistan's Proxy War in Afghanistan, the Globe and Mail-21 July 2021) in his research and investigative paper spotlighted terrorist organizations sponsored by Pakistani ISI and the army:

"Although many members of the Quetta Shura and the Haqqani Network appeared on UN and Al-Qaida sanctions lists after 2001, they continued to operate with impunity throughout Pakistan. Their assets were never frozen; their ready access to arms, funds, and munitions never cut. On the contrary, their families lived in relative comfort while ISI minders prevented journalists, investigators, and other officials from pinpointing their whereabouts in Pakistan. For years Pakistan's political and military leaders swore up and down that no Taliban leader had ever set foot in their country. It was a prodigious lie. When the Taliban, with comprehensive support from Pakistan's military, ramped up operations over 2005-06 into a full-blown offensive threatening to overwhelm Afghan government defenses and seize provincial capitals, Pakistan's President Pervez Musharraf, under increasing US pressure, brought his egregious fabrications to Kabul during his second visit to the country. (His first was on April 2, 2002.) In a September 7, 2006 speech to Afghan leaders and parliamentarians, Musharraf again pleaded ignorance: "We have to see where their command structure is, who their commander is, and we must destroy the command structure...When you attack the command structure, the thing falls" (Gall 2006). Musharraf was playing dumb. Pakistan has never, then or later, moved against its Taliban proxies. In this regard Pakistan's policy of proxy war, as managed almost entirely by the ISI, has been utterly consistent: Pakistan's security forces have never sought to reduce the Taliban's capabilities to launch attacks in Afghanistan. On the contrary, from Benazir Bhutto's second term as prime minister, when the Taliban was formed, through Nawaz Sharif's first term; during Musharraf's coup, military rule, and brief stint as a civilian president; right down to the more recent governments of Asif Ali Zardari, Nawaz Sharif's second term, and now Imran Khan, the Taliban and their allies have received unstinting support from Pakistan's military".[19]

Although there are signs of a shift in Pakistan's short-term strategic priorities and recognition that the challenge of home-grown Taliban is not just a U.S. problem, India will remain the focal point of Pakistan's long-term national security. Progress toward reordering Pakistan's strategic priorities and effecting a fundamental change in its strategic culture is bound to be slow and difficult. Furthermore, it cannot be forced by the United States. The history of relations between Pakistan and the United States is complicated and ambiguous, largely due to Pakistani perceptions of past U.S. abandonment. Any new U.S. strategy for Pakistan has to be considered against realistic expectations, which in turn have to take due account of the longstanding, fundamental nature of the factors that have shaped Pakistani strategic priorities and culture. Emigrating to my footpath, I will begin with Prime Minister Zulfiqar Ali Bhutto who came to power (Barrister and politician who served as the 9th Prime Minister of Pakistan from 1973 to

1977), in 1973, reorganized the IB and materialized it as a pure civilian intelligence agency with its deep-rooted networks in civilian population. When the PPP won parliamentary elections in 1977 by a wide margin, the military establishment perturbed and opposed the PPP and Bhutto's personality. On 05 July 1977, Muhammad Zia-ul-Haq deposed Bhutto in a military coup. General Zia-ul Haq had a bitter experience of the IB role in politics, he introduced some reforms within the intelligence infrastructure of the country, and made the Inter-Services Intelligence (ISI) strong and competent. The Afghan war was a good opportunity and iron on the fire to reorganize its infrastructure and emerge as a professional intelligence agency in South Asia.

In 1979, after the Soviet invasion of Afghanistan, the ISI and MI were restrained and encumbered the fun and game to train Afghans and transport them to Afghanistan for fight against the Soviet forces. As per my personal attainment, more than 80 percent of ISI officers and field informers had no access to social media and newspapers in the 1980s. They were honest and stalwart but their communication with headquarters was only by post and main landline telephone, in view of the fact, mobile communication was absent from half of the country. They were unable to visit the houses of Ministers, landlords, industrialists and parliamentarians for investigation purposes on account of their lack of education and culture of inferiority complex. They were non-technical, unschooled, untutored, uninformed and unacquainted to enter into pontification with journalists and politicians.

In 1980s and 1990s the ISI and MI retrieved professional training and obtained best experience of intelligence information collection in war and peace. The intelligence bureau (IB) became weak and dematerialized when its management received 70 percent of posting from the military establishment to further skeletal civilian intelligence infrastructure, and use it against civilian society, politicians, and dissidents. War of strength between the IB and ISI intensified remarkably. The IB was below far weak and incapacitated on account of inattention of military establishment, lack of funds, and intelligence information collection technology. The IB had become fully dematerialized and its operational mechanism was copied from military intelligence. Thus, the culture of civilian intelligence was gradually undermined and murdered, and the ISI became jumbo and yahoo, and became ally of sectarian organizations to destabilize India and Afghanistan. The ISI and IB were already packed with Mujahedeen and Taliban, and their commanders were receiving instructions from sectarian organizations, such as Tablighi Jamaat, Salafi groups and Jamaat Islami. The ISI and RAW have been fighting their war of credibility while creating misunderstandings between political leadership and military establishment. Their law of intelligence and counterintelligence is quite different and complicated. Intelligence analysis and relationship with the policy makers differ fundamentally for counterterrorism.[14] Christian Menkveld, (Understanding the complexity of intelligence problems. Institute of Security and Global Affairs, Leiden University, The Hague, the Netherlands-2021) has elucidated this role in his well-written paper:

"The complexity of an intelligence problem (required intelligence assessment on a certain subject) determines to a great extent the certainty that intelligence and security services can provide on such an assessment. Even though this claim sounds almost obvious, its implications are significant, because it means that the public value of an intelligence service can vary depending on the complexity of an intelligence problem. This ranges from providing 'actionable' intelligence that can lead to interventions (legal, military, interruption operations, etc.) to providing insights that can be used as input for policymakers, and as context for interventions. Therefore, to be effective, intelligence and security services need to take the complexity of an intelligence problem into account when determining the aims of their investigation, the strategy of intelligence collection and its analytic approach. Which also means that intelligence clients and oversight officials and legislators should take the complexity of intelligence problems into account when directing and appraising the performance of services.... All intelligence problems are complex, but some are more complex than others."[21]

The IB experienced underwhelming ball-games under the shade of military establishment. After the butt-end of military government and Soviet occupation of Afghanistan, civilian intelligence infrastructure was near to disintegration and sinking fast. Its well-trained senior officers were superannuated. When Benazir Bhutto assumed responsibilities as a civilian Prime Minister, she was still unable to reinvent the IB against the willpower of the ISI and military establishment. She was helpless and with hands tied. She was designated as an anti-state and India's-RAW agent. Thus, Mian Nawaz Sharif assumed power with the help of ISI, General Hamid Gul and Osama Bin Laden in 1997, and served until his removal in 1999 by military takeover, and was tried in a plane hijacking case.[22] The ISI and military establishment were not happy with Nawaz Sharif and his ISI chief General Javed Nasir-member of Tablighi Jamaat of Pakistan.

12

General Javed Nasir supplied weapons to Muslim fighters in Bosnia. Meltablishment and Musharraf decided to sideline Nawaz Sharif through a military coup in 1999 after they failed to defeat the Indian army in Kargil. In July 2008, the PPP government notified the Interior Ministry to take control of ISI, but had to backtrack within 24 hours when the military establishment expressed its displeasure. Senator Farhatullah Babar of the PPP was the convener of the three-member committee which prepared the report. Every agency in the country was above the law and they were free to detain, kidnap and harass civilians in many ways. General Pervez Musharaf and General Raheel Sharif have committed war crimes in FATA, Baluchistan and Waziristan. They sold their countrymen to the CIA, and killed, tortured and humiliated children and women. General Shahid Aziz once unveiled secrets business of General Musharraf in a TV interview with Hamid Mir, in which he admitted that the army killed thousands of Pashtuns, Afghans and Balochs.[23]

Asif Ali Zardari served as eleventh President of Pakistan from 2008 to 2013, and remained a strong US ally in war in war on terrorism in Afghanistan, notwithstanding public disapproval in the United States following the Raymond Davis incident and the NATO attack in Salala check post in 2011. President Zardari was not in favor of ISI's involvement in politics. He directed the Interior Ministry to bring ISI under democratic control, but faced a disheartening situation. The ISI threatened him with dire consequences. On 07 June 2013, Sharif again sworn in for an unprecedented third term, but faced numerous challenges, including military establishment, the ISI and US drone strikes against civilian population in Pakistan's tribal regions. After he assumed power, Tehreek Insaf and Thahir-ul-Qadri arranged a protest movement with the support of ISI, while civilian intelligence was supporting Nawaz Sharif. The ISI and military establishment arranged a sit-in of 2500 radicalized elements in 2016.[18]On 28 July 2017[24], he was disqualified by the court in a fake case, and Imran Khan Nizai became the Prime Minister of Pakistan in 2018[25]. Mr. Imran Khan was crippled when foreign and security policy was controlled by the military establishment, and appointed more than 400 military experts on various civilian posts. He was also supported by the ISI and GHQ, but he never gave importance to the IB and demonstrated single-mindedness in the dematerialization of civilian agency.

The weak and fragile government of Imran Khan has been unable to introduce intelligence reform as the ISI doesn't allow civilian intelligence to operate independently. The ISI is the dominant actor in Pakistan's political life, despite some improvements in civil-military relations in recent years. The agency supports sectarian groups in Pakistan who had emerged from the conflict in Afghanistan and by the US invasion in the country. The ISI, IB, and FIA all serving the interests of corrupt military establishment and dancing in gangway and lobby of National Accountability Bureau (NAB). The ISI first dematerialized the IB and FIA, then controlled the whole process of terrorist's infiltration into India and Afghanistan, and received billions of dollars from NATO and the United States. The ISI proxies carried out suicide attack in Afghanistan and India from different perspectives. On 13 February 2015, General Musharaf admitted that he had instructed the ISI to recruit suicide bombers and organize attacks against Afghan army and government institutions to force the Karzai administration to close unnecessary diplomatic presence of India in Afghanistan.[21]When the ISI atrocities intensified in Afghanistan after the announcement of Biden administration, and its policy of confrontation failed, Pakistan relinquished supporting Kashmir and allowed India to properly control and oversee it legally. The army also commenced peace efforts in Afghanistan on one hand, and attacked different districts and provinces of the country to save its strategic depth on the other. Blabbermouth, tattler, double-crosser and whistle-blowers within civilian intelligence kicked up one's heel and raised their voices against the total control of ISI and the IB managements.

Most policy makers and analysts viewed domestic politics and intelligence infrastructure as authoritarian and militarized. Intelligence liaison between India and Pakistan, and between Afghanistan and Pakistan was underwhelming. On 31 October 2013, Economic Times reported Nawaz Sharif's consent to allow the ISI covert operation in Kashmir.[22] Prime Minister Nawaz Sharif asked the ISI back in May 1992, to continue its covert operations in Kashmir, despite a stern warning by the US that it could designate Pakistan as a state sponsoring terrorism. "In the letter dated May 10, 1992, Baker threatened that unless Pakistan discontinued its support for terrorism in Kashmir, the US might declare it a state sponsor of terrorism. We have information indicating that ISI and others intend to continue to provide material support to groups that have engaged terrorism". ET reported. Pakistan Institute for Conflict and Security Studies (Intelligence Bureau (IB) in the Limelight: Apparent Tussle between Agencies-October 3, 2017) in its commentary documented turmoil with the IB management and the petition filed in Islamabad High Court by a serving assistant sub-inspector (ASI) of IB, Malik Mukhtar Ahmed Shahzad:

"A serving assistant sub-inspector (ASI) of IB, Malik Mukhtar Ahmed Shahzad, accused his senior officers of not taking action against terrorism suspects and filed a petition before the Islamabad High Court (IHC) requesting it to refer the matter to the Inter-Services Intelligence (ISI) for a thorough probe. In the petition filed through his counsel Masroor Shah, Mr. Shahzad has said he joined the IB in 2007 and that he "reported against various terrorist groups having roots in Uzbekistan, Iran, Afghanistan, Syria and India". "However, to the petitioner's utter dismay, no action was ever been taken by IB despite concrete evidence provided to it in the form of the intelligence reports", the petition says. "Upon thorough intelligence gathering process, it transpired those certain high officials of the IB themselves were directly involved with the terrorist organizations having linkages with hostile enemy intelligence agencies" the petition read. It further said that the matter was even reported to the IB director general, who also did not take any steps. It uncovered some IB officials travelled to Israel and had direct links with Afghan intelligence and a terrorist group from Kazakhstan. The Intelligence Bureau (IB) in its written reply submitted before the Islamabad High Court (IHC) that if the allegations of ASI Malik Mukhtar Ahmad Shahzad were pursued in an open court, it would have adverse effects on Pakistan's relations with numerous countries. It said entering into the controversy, alleged in the writ petition, would amount to exposing the secrecy and confidentiality of the department, which the agency respectfully claims are subject to privilege. Hence, the court may kindly refrain from delving into the details of the writ petition. The IB was on the opinion that the contents of writ-petition and the annexures therewith were in utter violation of the terms and conditions, service rules, and practices of the Intelligence Bureau, as no functionary was permitted to retain any copies of the secret information reports that are submitted by them. Elaborating their point of view in the letter, it said ever since his initial appointment, the petitioner has been incessantly harassing the agency by filing numerous cases with various courts, and has as per our record, filed a total of 14 different cases against the agency till now"[26]

Analyst and expert, F.M. Shakil in his article (The growing 'tug-of-war' between Pakistan's spy agencies: Conflict between the civilian Intelligence Bureau (IB), and the military's Inter-Services Intelligence (ISI) is at boiling point, with the former accused of overstepping constitutional bounds, Asia Times. 04 October, 2017) has highlighted the tug-of-war between the ISI and the Intelligence Bureau (IB) that besmirched credibility of both civilian and military intelligence: "The bubbling rivalry between the IB and ISI boiled over in June this year when a Joint Investigation Team (JIT) probing alleged money laundering by the Sharif family made a written complaint to the Supreme Court that the IB was wiretapping JIT members, including ISI and Military Intelligence (MI) personnel. Other JIT members from the National Accountability Bureau (NAB), the Federal Investigation Agency (FIA), the State Bank of Pakistan (SBP) and the Security & Exchange Commission of Pakistan (SECP) were also alleged to have had their phones bugged. The JIT further reported that the IB was hampering its inquiries, adding that military-led intelligence agencies were not on "good terms" with the IB. It said the IB had collected intelligence on members of the JIT from the National Database and Registration Authority (NADRA) and presented it to Nawaz to use against them. The Supreme Court inquired how the IB came to be working for a "private person" instead of the state, adding that – as it owed its loyalty to the latter – it seemed, prima facie, to have been misused"[27]

The ISI and military intelligence death squads has been making things worse as they target civilian populations particularly Pashtun and Baloch activists with impunity since the 2000s. These squads have killed prominent Pashtun and Baloch leaders but no independent investigation has been allowed to find out the real story behind these killings. Former terrorist leader and member of TTP spokesman Ehsanullah Ehsan disclosed that the Pakistan army asked him to lead its death squad. On 13 August 2020, he babbled that the ISI authorities had given him a hit list of people who they wanted to be killed in Khyber Pakhtunkhwa.[27] In an audio, he claimed that after some time of his surrender he was given the list of prominent voices in order to facilitate Pakistan in eliminating rogue elements. Daily Times reported his confession audio, in which he admitted: "I was asked to lead a death squad and accept killing of the listed people from Khyber Pakhtunkhwa and Pashtuns from all walks of life including journalists. In the audio, he talked about his conversations with ISI and the parleys that took place. Ehsanullah Ehsan (Liaqat Ali) was a former spokesman of Tehreek-e-Taliban Pakistan (TTP) and Jamaat-ul-Ahrar. In April 2017, Inter-Services Public Relations (ISPR) Director-General Asif Ghafoor announced that Ehsan had surrendered himself to Pakistan's security agencies. In early February 2020, Ehsanullah claimed that escaped from the custody of Pakistani Agencies.[29]

The Sunday Guardian (06 September, 2020) also reported Mr. Ehsanullah Ehsan's conversation with Taliban leader Mullah Wali-ur-Rahman of for making an alliance between ISI and TTP: "Maulana Wali-ur-Rehman took a letter out of the envelope and gave it to me and told me to read it. I opened the letter and read it aloud. After doing so, Maulana Wali-ur-Rehman said to me, "You must have known why you were called in an emergency for this meeting." I smiled and said, "Yes, I know." The letter I read was written by the DG ISI, General Shuja Pasha to Maulana Wali-ur-Rehman Mehsud. In it, General Shuja Pasha made an offer to the TTP leadership that if the TTP gave up its armed struggle against Pakistan, the ISI would not only provide them with a safe passage against NATO forces in Afghanistan but also provide financial and military support in every possible way. In this letter, General Shuja Pasha also praised the strength and capabilities of the TTP and called the TTP a necessity for Pakistan. He wrote that we should work together to remove the misunderstandings between the Pakistan army and the TTP and work together to drive the great enemy US (America) and NATO out of Afghanistan. General Pasha also noted in his letter if TTP accepted the demands, the TTP would not just be able to demonstrate its abilities in Waziristan but the whole of Pakistan would be open for the TTP and that the cadre of TTP and their children would be able to work in this country by getting education from educational institutions in Islamabad and Peshawar......In this detailed letter, General Shuja Pasha had repeatedly referred to the Indian "occupation" of and "atrocities" in Kashmir he had written to Maulana Wali-ur-Rehman saying that his forefathers had fought many wars for the independence of Kashmir and had made many sacrifices because they were true and patriotic Pakistanis.[30]

In books and newspapers, there are stories about the failure of intelligence agencies in Pakistan to undermine terrorism and extremism. Recruitment from the business community, wealthy and landlord societies, generals and politicians for intelligence agencies prompted bureaucratic culture. Intelligentsias and political circles have often pointed to the fact that involvement of the agency in political confrontations badly affected its professional credibility. Some circles are trying to radicalize agencies, but the big concern is that all military, civilian and policing agencies have already 'purified' their souls in Tablighi congregations in Raiwind. Sectarian elements within the IB and ISI ranks are purveying secret information about the planning of political parties and military leadership, to their favorite religious and political leaders. Secondly, military intelligence agencies do not cooperate with civilian intelligence agencies on national security issues.

The challenges of democratic consolidation and security sector reform lies in the fact that in Pakistan, there is little public awareness about the function and operation of intelligence agencies. Major political and religious parties have no basic knowledge about the organization of intelligence. For the reason, this book will be the prime source of knowledge for politicians and civil society-containing basic knowledge of the manner of intelligence operation, and its role in politics. Thus, ignorance about intelligence communities is combined with fear, which perpetuates inadequate dissemination of information. In modern states, security and intelligence agencies play a vital role in supporting the government in its domestic, defense and foreign policies by supplying and analyzing relevant intelligence and countering specified threats. Over the past two decades, the role and scale of Pakistan's intelligence agencies has grown over and above their prescribed functions, to the degree that their operations, often undercover and at odds even with each other, have earned them the reputation of being a "State within a State". In most parts of the country, intelligence information collection faced numerous difficulties since the Taliban and other militant groups returned to important strategic locations. Having faced serious difficulties in dealing with insurgent forces in Baluchistan and Waziristan, the agencies started translating their anger into the killing and kidnapping of innocent civilians with impunity. A secret war goes on between the ISI, and the IB which paints a murky picture of concordance and cooperation. It is known that the officials from the military's ISI agency had their phone calls eavesdropped at the height of civil-military tension in 2014.

Musa Khan Jalalzai

October, 2021, London

Summary

Failure of CIA, ISI and NATO Intelligence Agencies to Prognosticate the Collapse of Afghan State and Government

The sojourn of ISI Chief Faiz Hameed in Kabul sparked adhesive and tight criticism. He fragmented and cracked Taliban's alliance by interjecting and squeeze-in wanted terrorists into their cabinet. Afghan politicians enormously condemned the constitution and composition of the Taliban Cabinet on an improvised bases by the ISI Chief to permanently spawn dither and confusion among the Afghan leadership. On 03 September 2021, Faiz Hamid arrived in Kabul-leading a delegation of senior Pakistani officials, to reconstitute the pieces of Afghan national army, redesign the Afghan state, and structure of government. On 04 September, 2021, Pakistani Prime Minister convinced the United Nations Secretary General Antonio Guterres of consecutive support for UN's humanitarian work in Afghanistan. Journalist, scholar and editor of *The Friday Times* Lahore, Mr. Najam Sethi in his editorial page (30 August, 2021) noted differences between the Haqqni and Mullah Brader on inclusive government, which were the signs of mismatched development in Kabul. Mr. Khalilu Rehman Haqqni also demonstrated intransigence by urging Pakistan army and the ISI to negotiate with Tehrik Taliban Pakistan (TTP). Analyst Najam Sethi has painted an interesting picture of bubbling scenario in Afghanistan:

> "Clearly, Khalilur Rehman Haqqani is saying that Pakistan should hold negotiations with the TTP and Baloch separatists and not press the Taliban for kinetic action against them. He is also advising China to look after its religious minorities (Uighurs) and resolve their grievances peacefully. Therefore it is highly doubtful that Mullah Baradar was persuaded by the CIA Director to allow American counter-terrorism experts and intelligence to assist the Taliban in going after Al Qaeda and IS in Afghanistan. The Afghan Taliban's reluctance to launch counter-terrorism operations against these

groups suggests that, given the support-networks and ideological affinities that exist among them not just inside Afghanistan but also in Pakistan – as evidenced by the attack on Chinese engineers in Gilgit , Gwadar, etc., recently–there is little chance of success of military action. Indeed, even when the Americans were in full flow with all their sophisticated armaments, Intel and training, they were unable to wipe out pockets of Al-Qaeda and IS whose attacks were becoming more outrageous and bloody over time. Under the circumstances, short of a significant "foreign" intervention aided by the Taliban government to wipe out these groups – an impossibility when the Taliban are not even ready to allow some extra time for evacuating the tens of thousands of Afghan civilians wanting to flee – there is no possibility of the new Taliban government swiftly addressing regional and international concerns on counter-terrorism."[1]

When the Taliban invaded Afghanistan, India and neighbouring states warned that Pakistani ISI will turn Afghanistan into an epicentre of terrorism and extremism, but the US and UK remained tight-lipped, for the reason that they were sharing criminal syndicate with Taliban, and supported their atrocities against the people of Afghanistan militarily and financially. The United nation also demonstrated scathebrained. Having contemplated and reviewed the Indian reaction, Editor and analyst Shampa Sen (How Pakistan helped Taliban come to power in Afghanistan: Many believe within India's diplomatic and intelligence establishments that the Taliban control over Afghanistan was only possible because of Pakistan, DNA Web Team, 20 Aug, 2021) has noted the real strategy of Pakistan's support to Taliban in Afghanistan, and exhibited reflections of Indian political elite: "Days after the Taliban took over the reins of power in Afghanistan, India's External Affairs Minister S Jaishankar in an address to the United Nations Security Council (UNSC) said that the events in Afghanistan have naturally enhanced global concerns about their implications for both regional and international security. 'Whether in Afghanistan or against India, groups like Lashkar-e Taiba and Jaish-e-Mohammed continue to operate with impunity and encouragement. Heightened activities of the proscribed Haqqani network justify growing anxiety," he said. "What is true of COVID is true of terrorism. No one is safe until all of us are safe. (But) Some countries undermine our collective resolve. S. Jaishankar noted.

Writer and analyst Alexander Cooley (August 23, 2021) criticized the Biden administration for mismanaging the troop withdrawal and damaging Washington's global credibility. Ali Harb, (Afghanistan shows 'limitations' of US military, Al-jazeera--21 Aug 2021) raised important questions about the collapse of Afghan government and state institutions, which he understands it was the limits of Washington's military power: "President Joe Biden's critics, however, said the scenes of desperate Afghans attempting to flee Kabul were a sign of US weakness and proof of the necessity for global American military engagement. As much of the world's focus rightly remained on efforts to get Afghans to safe places outside the country, the Taliban's victory was spurring a heated debate in Washington in August 2021 about the US's role in the world. "A military-led project of state-building and nation-building was always going to be doomed to failure," said Annelle Sheline. Anxiety over abuses under Taliban rule, including the rights of women as well as the safety of Afghans who worked with the US, was on display in the chaos at Hamid Karzai International Airport. "This Trump-Biden withdrawal was a big mistake," a former US official John Bolton, who served under George W Bush and Donald Trump, wrote on Twitter: "Beijing and Moscow, they are laughing. Tehran and Pyongyang have seen that the Administration was credulous when it comes to claims by devoted adversaries of the United States. It makes us look like we're suckers..........Critics of the withdrawal have warned that it may compromise Washington's credibility in the world as well as its commitment to its allies".[2]

When the Biden administration decided to withdraw forces from Afghanistan, it was deeply criticized by intellectual and academic circles in Europe and Asia. There was criticism of the fact (Najmuddin Shaekh-Dawn, 09 September 2021) 'that the Afghan government had not been consulted and yet was required, as part of the US-Taliban agreement, to release 5,000 Taliban prisoners. Many reports asserted that those released included not only the Taliban but also adherents of Al Qaeda and, most significantly, of the Islamic State group's Khorasan chapter.'[3]However, in his *Hindustan Times* article (05 September 2021), analyst and expert, Shashi Shekhar highlighted operational mechanism of extremism across the world and Afghanistan: "Extremism is spreading across the world through phones and computers. Now news, videos, and photos of the Taliban's excesses in Afghanistan will make this mix even more lethal. There are apprehensions that more violent incidents may take place in different places in the days to come".[4] Writer and analyst Rezaul H Laskar (August 27, 2021-*Hundustan Times*) also spotlighted operations of ISIS-K in Kabul. "Six years after its expansion into Khorasan, the historic name for the area encompassing Afghanistan, Pakistan and parts of India, the IS affiliate in Afghanistan has proved it continues to have the ability to carry out devastating terrorist assaults with the suicide attack at Kabul airport."[5]

The US invaded Afghanistan in 2001 in partnership with NATO, killed thousands in so-called war against terrorism. Al Qaeda is still dancing in Afghanistan, while the Taliban and the ISIS-K emerged to help the US army in exploiting the country's mineral resources. The United States army committed war crimes by using criminal militias in night raids. Pakistan's nuclear physicist and activist and a distinguished professor at the Forman Christian College, Pervez Amirali Hoodbhoy (11 September, 2021 *Dawn*) noted some aspects of extremism and the Taliban and ISIS-K in Afghanistan: "The Taliban are puppets of the Americans and the 'Western crusader' because they met CIA and US officials! There can't be a wackier, stupider claim but this one led to the Islamic State Khorasan (IS-K) sending a young heaven-seeker who blew himself up at Kabul airport on Aug 27, killing up to 170 including 13 American soldiers and, according to one Taliban official (later denied), 28 members of the Taliban militia coordinating the evacuation. Extremists targeting extremists; the irony should not be lost. Even if IS-K excels in suicide attacks on large gatherings of Afghan civilians, the Taliban have done their share too. Both have spread fear through beheadings and limb chopping, forced girls into marrying their fighters, and looted ordinary people. One might have expected a close alliance since both have fought America. But, in fact, they are bitter foes. What splits IS-K from the Taliban is ideology; they differ on what a true Islamic state is. To achieve its supreme goal, each considers no sacrifice to be too great. All militant groups strewn across Afghan-is-tan—Al Qaeda, TTP, IMU (Uzbek), and ETIM (Uighur)—dream their respective sectarian dreams".[6]

The Taliban acting like a sustained fencing for Pakistan in Afghanistan," a Pakistani parliamentarian Mufti Abdul Shakoor of Maulana Fazal Rehman group told parliament in his speech on 12 July, 2021. "The Afghan Taliban were making sacrifices to save Pakistan", he said. Comments of major American, British and Pakistani newspapers pointed to the fact that why Afghan army abruptly collapsed and why it failed to secure major cities, the fact of the matter is, the Pentagon, CIA and the Ghani-Abdullah administration had secretly ordered the ANA commanders to leave all military bases and weapons to Taliban and intercept the ANA units from attacking their forces. However, some districts and provinces were secured by Taliban with the help of tribal elders persuading military commanders and provincial administration to surrender. Expert and analyst, P.

Michael McKinley (We All Lost Afghanistan: Two Decades of Mistakes, Misjudgements, and Collective Failure, 16 August, 2021) spotlighted causes of US and UK intelligence failure, and the abrupt collapse of the Afghan state. He also noted failure of the US military policy:

"The seeds for that eroding stalemate were sown early on. The failure to invest in Afghanistan's police and military in the first years after 2001 meant a loss of valuable time to build a capable fighting force when the Taliban were on the defensive. The building of an air force was not prioritized for more than a decade; the training of a new generation of Afghan pilots began only in 2009 and was slower than necessary because of a decision to transition the Afghan fleet from Russian craft to Black Hawks. And while the Afghan air force had more recently come to be seen as relatively effective, any success was undermined by the decision this year to withdraw the thousands of contractors who provided maintenance and support for operations as U.S. advisers began to leave in 2019. Indeed, the failure to transfer the services of the 18,000 contractors who worked with the Afghan military—or to provide the financial guarantees to cover the costs—proved damaging to the government in Kabul, although it is now unclear whether the ANDSF would have fought even with that support. These services may have sustained the logistics flow to the ANDSF in the field and the maintenance of the Afghan air force despite the withdrawal of U.S. forces. Instead, July night-time U.S. departure from Bagram Air Base, a key logistics fulcrum, will become an enduring symbol of our military failure in Afghanistan. (The failure to maintain a logistics capability had another consequence: hampering the evacuation of embassy personnel and tens of thousands of Afghans, beyond just interpreters, who worked with the U.S. military, diplomatic mission, and assistance programs). In light of the Taliban's rapid takeover of Afghan city after Afghan city in recent days, perhaps the most striking American misjudgement is our ongoing overestimation of the capabilities of the Afghan National Defence and Security Forces. Even without tactical American military support, the ANDSF should have been in a position to defend major cities and critical military installations. As numerous observers have pointed out, the ANDSF on paper was significantly larger and far better equipped and organized than the Taliban. The Afghan Special Forces were compared with the best in the region."[7]

The United States never demonstrated truly and sincerely to stabilize Afghanistan and train the Afghan army. We know there is massive corruption in the US military establishment, but why did the Pentagon entrusted 200 to 300 sophisticated weapons to the Taliban against the Afghan army. This was double-dealing of the US army that never exhibited its interest in rebuilding Afghanistan. In the tail-end of withdrawal from Afghan airport, American military experts destroyed all transport and military plans shamelessly. The CIA established terror militias to further discredit Afghan armed forces. The Trump administration gave us the mother of all bombs that killed hundreds of innocent children in Afghanistan in case of biogases. Expert and analyst, Andrew Mumford (Joe Biden and the future of America's foreign policy: By withdrawing from Afghanistan so determinedly, Biden has firmly pressed the 'reset' button-01 September, 2021) has noted some aspects of US negligence, resentment and war crimes in Afghanistan:

"The harrowing pictures after the bombing attack at Kabul Airport were the result of a desire on behalf of President Biden to draw a line under a war he never truly believed in and shift the direction of US foreign policy away from under the long shadow of the "war on terror" as it nears its 20th anniversary. In short, Biden is trying to ensure that an ongoing response to the events of September 11, 2001, is not the major cause of US action abroad. The US president has been rightly criticized for presiding over an ill-thought-through pull-out that took international allies and the Afghan people themselves by surprise. But the logic behind his decision rests on his long-standing belief that the war in Afghanistan was never winnable. As foreign-policy analyst Edward Luce put it, "There is no elegant way to quit a war you have lost." The US has poured $1 trillion into training the Afghan National Army over nearly two decades. Successive US administrations have been frustrated by the levels of incompetence and corruption at the heart of Afghan politics. Mindful of this – and aware of the overwhelming historical record that demonstrates Afghanistan's imperviousness toward the imposition of external military rule – Biden decided that enough was enough. Of course, Biden's predecessor, Donald Trump, originally signed a deal with the Taliban in February 2020 that had agreed to the withdrawal of US forces. Yet in order to understand why Biden went ahead with this deal, we must understand two things. First, his track record opposing many key elements of the war in Afghanistan. And second, the wider foreign-policy overhaul he is trying to engender".[8]

By quoting the SIGAR report, analyst Meghann Myers noted some aspects of weak and unprofessional training of Afghan security forces by US warlords. He also noted allocation of more than $950 billion funds to support rebuilding and retraining of Afghan forces, but, unfortunately they collapsed within a month. In his *Military Times* analysis (August 17, 2021) he suggested: "The U.S. government also clumsily forced Western technocratic models onto Afghan economic institutions; trained security forces in advanced weapon systems they could not understand, much less maintain; imposed formal rule of law on a country that addressed 80 to 90 percent of its disputes through informal means; and often struggled to understand or mitigate the cultural and social barriers to supporting women and girls," according to the SIGAR". The bill totalled $145 billion spent on building military and government organizations, with another $837 billion on fighting insurgencies. "The extraordinary costs were meant to serve a purpose—though the definition of that purpose evolved over time," according to the report. "At various points, the U.S. government hoped to eliminate al-Qaeda, decimate the Taliban movement that hosted it, deny all terrorist groups a safe haven in Afghanistan, build Afghan security forces so they could deny terrorists a safe haven in the future, and help the civilian government become legitimate and capable enough to win the trust of Afghans."[9]

American experts like Lara Seligman (Kabul's collapse followed string of intelligence failures, Politico.com.16 August 2021) raised many questions about the collapse of Afghan army, state and government, and noted the US officials warnings that Afghan army can collapse within weeks: "Military planners sounding the alarm about Afghanistan's imminent collapse failed to predict the speed with which the Taliban would overrun the country, leaving the Biden administration scrambling to evacuate thousands of American citizens, embassy staffers and vulnerable Afghans from Kabul's international airport. Though officials warned repeatedly over the past few weeks that the Afghan government could fall far sooner than previous estimates—weeks or months after the last American troops departed the country—they overestimated the capability and will of the Afghan security forces to fight back as the Taliban seized city after city in recent days……..
That miscalculation reached the very highest levels of the administration, Jake Sullivan, the national security adviser, acknowledged during a TV interview. "The president didn't think it was inevitable the Taliban would take control. He thought the Afghan forces could fight," Sullivan said on ABC's "Good Morning America." "We spent 20 years, tens of billions of dollars training them, giving them equipment, giving them support of U.S. forces for 20 years. When push came to shove, they decided to not fight for their country."[10]

As I noted human rights violation by the Taliban forces in various province of Afghanistan, Associate Asia Director, Human rights watch, Patricia Gossman, (How US-Funded Abuses Led to Failure in Afghanistan-06 July 2021) also raised the same question in her comprehensive analysis on Human Rights Watch website that the US funded abuses led failure in Afghanistan, and also pointed to the fact that during the last 20 years, human right of civilians were sternly violated: "The primary and defining characteristic of the armed conflict in Afghanistan over the last two decades has been harm to civilians caused by massive human rights abuses and war crimes by all sides. These rampant abuses have in turn fuelled the cycle of conflict in numerous ways, including by inspiring recruitment to the insurgency, rendering political dialogue nearly impossible, and undermining efforts to promote stability through better governance. Successive U.S. administrations have largely perceived human rights more as an obstacle than as an essential component of addressing Afghanistan's problems. This approach has been catastrophic. I have spent much of these past 20 years talking to Afghans about the consequences of counterterrorism gone wrong – the civilian deaths and injuries that never made it into the Pentagon's airstrike death count; the night raids that turned into summary executions targeting people who had the bad luck to live in a contested district; the torture of people in custody that destroyed lives and motivated revenge. I have also talked to many Afghans about the unforeseen consequences of these actions – the Taliban resurgence abetted by Afghan government abuses and corruption; the grievances and disillusionment that drove people to lose faith that post-2001 Afghanistan would be better; and the rise of the Islamic State (ISIS) in Afghanistan, an offspring of Pakistan pandering to Islamist extremism and Afghan warlords' mis-governance in Afghanistan's east".[11]

Director Patricia Gossman raised the question of warlords and militia commanders who consecutively abused civilians, looted their houses, and kidnapped their sons and daughters: In Kandahar, Paktia and Khost, warlords and US criminal militias have been killing innocent Afghans in night raids since years: "Throughout, U.S. policy was guided by a number of myths. One was that the Afghan strongmen, warlords, and militia commanders the United States chose as allies in ousting the Taliban could help to provide security and stability, despite their records of abuses. In fact, the opposite proved to be the case. Persistent human rights abuses by warlords were a source of insecurity, and worse, over time, they fuelled widespread resentment, undermined efforts to foster good governance at the local and national levels, and helped the Taliban obtain new support and recruits".[12] Authors Tom Blanton, Claire Harvey, Lauren Harper, and Malcolm Byrne (The US National Security Archive's Briefing book-772, Washington, D.C., August 19, 2021) highlighted the US failure in Afghanistan under four Presidents that misled the American people for nearly two decades about progress the in Afghanistan:

"While hiding the inconvenient facts about ongoing failures inside confidential channels, according to declassified documents published today by the National Security Archive. The documents include highest-level "snowflake" memos written by then Secretary of Defence Donald Rumsfeld during the George W. Bush administration, critical cables written by U.S. ambassadors back to Washington under both Bush and Barack Obama, the deeply flawed Pentagon strategy document behind Obama's "surge" in 2009, and multiple "lessons learned" findings by the Special Inspector General for Afghanistan Reconstruction (SIGAR) – lessons that were never learned. Estimates of Taliban controlled districts in Afghanistan as of mid-July 2021 ranged as high as more than half, according to the Special Inspector General for Afghanistan Reconstruction, Quarterly Report, July 31, 2021, p. 55. The number had increased from 73 in April to 221 in July, a harbinger of the August takeover in Kabul. The recent SIGAR report to Congress, from July 31, 2021, just as multiple provincial centres were falling to the Taliban, quotes repeated assurances from top U.S. generals (David Petraeus in 2011, John Campbell in 2015, John Nicholson in 2017, and Pentagon press secretary John Kirby in 2021) about the "increasingly capable" Afghan security forces. The SIGAR ends that section with the warning: "More than $88 billion has been appropriated to support Afghanistan's security sector".[13]

The United States and the United Kingdom accused Taliban of "war crimes" in Spin Boldak. Taliban massacred dozens of civilians in revenge killings, but US and UK were tight-lipped by demonstrating negligence. The diplomatic lashing comes after Afghanistan's Independent Human Rights Commission warned that the fighters had indulged in revenge killings in Spin Boldak. "After taking over Spin Boldak district, the Taliban chased and identified past and present government officials and killed these people who had no combat role in the conflict," the group said, adding at least 40 people had been killed by the Taliban. Women, and children were being massacred, as provincial cities fell one after another and the Taliban group, which the US and the Afghan government were trying to make peace with, was making more territorial gains as war escalated nationwide. As a whole situation was at worse where thousands of innocent people were killed and injured, many families were fleeing for safety. Those families in Kabul displaced due to unparalleled Taliban onslaughts, urged to take shelter in mosques. The US, UK and Pakistani ISI were all but responsible for their grievances and pain.

On 9 Sep, 2021, an award-winning journalist and filmmaker John Pilger told RT News that 'the US-led invasion of Afghanistan in 2001 should be called what it was – an imperialist war launched under the guise of a fight against terrorism'. He warned against remembering the military misadventure as a sort of "good war" justified by the threat of terrorism. RT reported. However, Gerry Hassan (Afghanistan, "Forever Wars" And the Reality Of Empire State Britain-The National, 31 August 2021) also spotlighted some aspects of the UK state, and its involvement in conflicts; "Above all, the Afghan operation and 20 years of "forever war" illustrate profound home truths about the British state. Permanent war and military interventions come at a cost to the society waging them as well as the countries being invaded. Professor Colin Crouch has stated that the UK post-9/11 shifted from "a welfare stare to a warfare state"–one centred on solidarity and social responsibility to one defined by the brute power of the neo-liberal economy, market forces, and the military. The elite version of the UK will not change without some kind of rupture or radical shift. Thirty-three years of Labour Government have not managed to dramatically alter how the UK sees and projects itself on the world stage. In the past twenty years, the UK has grown even more captivated by the illusion that Empire and imperialism were good things."[14]

If we read stories of all these war crimes of the US, and Pakistan in newspapers and books, we can find clues of US, and ISI collaboration with the Taliban. The CIA Chief met with the Taliban, Britain met with the Taliban, and finally allowed the Pakistan army and the ISI to form a controversial government of their choice. The British army chief Gen Nick Carter described his concocted story about the Taliban/ISI takeover of Kabul, while his forces remained empty-headedness, half-knowledge and unawareness: "It was the pace of it that surprised us and I don't think we realised quite what the Taliban were up to." BBC asked whether military intelligence was wrong, he said the government received intelligence from a variety of sources. There has been criticism of the way the West withdrew from Afghanistan, with questions over how the Taliban was able to seize control of the country at such speed. Speaking to the BBC's Andrew Marr show, Nick was asked how the predictions had been wrong. "I think everybody got it wrong is the straight answer," he said. "Even the Taliban didn't expect things to change as quickly as they did." General Nick told the BBC.

Former Afghan intelligence Chief, Rahmatullah Nabil authenticated the Taliban Cabinet as the Madrasa of Haqqania convention and the ISI trained terrorists. The Taliban cabinet consisted of two known terrorists who killed, tortured and sexually abused innocent Afghan women and children-wanted by the FBI, but the Taliban cabinet didn't sheepishly focus on their colleagues' war crimes, and stony-hearted acts that deeply impact civilians' society. During the first half of 2021, Taliban and ISI forces killed 900 civilians. *The Hindustan Times* (08 September 2021) published an analysis of expert Joydeep Bose, in which he highlighted the disbelieving cabinet of Taliban. The male-dominated cabinet, mostly Durranis, included a top official who was on the Federal Bureau of Investigation (FBI)'s 'most wanted' list, with a bounty of up to $10 million on his head. Hindustan Times reported. Hindustan Times news analysis also noted:

"Sirajuddin Haqqani, who has been named the Interior Minister of the new interim government, has reportedly been a senior leader of the Taliban since 2016. The United States termed him as a "specially designated global terrorist" with close ties to al Qaeda, and with the man now being named to one of the senior most posts in the Afghan state machinery, experts believe that the United States has cause to worry." According to the FBI page for Haqqani, the man is known by several aliases – including Siraj, Khalifa, Mohammad Siraj, Sarajadin, Cirodjiddin, Seraj, Arkani, and Khalifa Sahib. The 'rewards for justice' programme under the United States department of state was offering a reward of up to $10 million for information leading directly to the arrest of Sirajuddin Haqqani". *Hindustan Times* reported. Mullah Hassan Akhund was credited with the destruction of the giant 6th century Buddha statues of Bamiyan in 2001. The side-lining of Baradar is to be attributed to the political tension between him and the Haqqani Network, but ISI interfered and threatened Mullah Brader of dire consequences. Baradar's conciliatory politics with former Afghan President Hamid Karzai earlier cost him eight years' incarceration in an ISI jail–until former US president Donald Trump wanted him in Doha. The ISI never trusted him".[15] On July 25, 2021, *Asia News International and ToloNews* reported the killing of 33 people in Kandahar province......The Taliban reportedly killed some detainees, including relatives of provincial government officials and members of the police and army. "There were grave concerns that Taliban forces in Kandahar committed war crimes and further attacks to retaliate against the government and security forces,"

Patricia Gossman, Associate Asia director at HRW noted. The United States, and Britain allowed ISI to control Afghanistan, and then shamelessly close-lipped on Pakistan war crimes in Kandahar and Helmand. Their withdrawal from Afghanistan was badly planned and chaotic–it was more like an escape. Washington did not even inform their NATO allies that assisted them for almost two decades.

On 03 September, 2021, *Tehran Times* noted a leaked UK Foreign Office report seen by British media warned government Ministers on July 22, 2021 that the withdrawal of U.S.-led foreign forces from Afghanistan would lead to "rapid Taliban advances". The department's own intelligence suggested that Afghanistan's cities were in danger of being taken over in the aftermath of the departure of foreign military personnel at the end of August 2021. During a two-hour grilling, former British Foreign Secretary, Dominic Raab, was asked by the Foreign Affairs Committee as to why he didn't act on the assessment warning by his own Ministry. Raab did admit the UK had been "caught out and surprised by the scale and speed of the fall of Kabul", accepting lessons would have to be learned from how the intelligence assessment was made.[16]The British Foreign Minister accepted criminal negligence, his intelligence (MI6) failure and his inability to provide latest information to parliamentarians. The British Foreign Secretary, Dominic Raab was later on demoted by Prime Minister Johnson due to his incompetency low quality disinformation.

Chairman of the Foreign Affairs Committee, Tom Tugendhat, dismissed Raab's assessment saying "the [leaked] document clearly indicates "the fall of cities", the "collapse of security forces" and that the embassy "may need to close"… a warning like this... was made on 22 July 2021". He also said there has been an "intelligence failure" on the part of the British Government. *Tehran Times* reported. US intelligence had failed before the collapse of the Afghan government and the state in August 2021. If we look at the US military and civilian strategic demonstration, the US never established a strong cultural, political and military intelligence infrastructures in Afghanistan to keep the war machine intact. The British and US armies and their intelligence agencies were cognizant of their inflicted calamity. Analyst and expert, David Priess (Afghanistan, Policy Choices, and Claims of Intelligence Failure-August 26, 2021) explained the failure of US intelligence before the Taliban takeover Kabul and raised important about the abrupt failure:

"Without knowing the details of intelligence that had reached President Biden, observers have nevertheless been deploying the phrase regarding the situation in Afghanistan. "This is an intelligence failure," Rep. Jackie Speier, D-Calif., told *NBC News* on Aug. 15—just after the network's chief foreign correspondent, Richard Engel, tweeted about it as "a huge US intelligence failure." The next day, Bill Roggio, a senior fellow at the Foundation for Defence of Democracies, called it not only "an intelligence failure of the highest order" but also the "biggest intelligence failure" since the missed Tet Offensive in the Vietnam War. At each fundamental stage of the intelligence cycle—collection, analysis and dissemination—errors occur. When wrong intelligence data or assessments factor into major national security decisions, you've got a no-kidding intelligence failure.......... What did intelligence community assessments back to the start of the year say about developments in Afghanistan—including the likelihood of Taliban advances, the ability and willingness of Afghan government forces to fight, the Taliban timetable for seizing territory, the credibility of any Taliban assurances to the U.S. about Kabul in particular, and so on? There have been to date only anonymous leaks of selected phrases from supposed intelligence documents, not enough to speak with any certainty on these questions".[17]

From 2016-2020, more than 16, 000 Afghan children were killed by the NATO, US and Afghan sponsored militias. Now, Children live in constant fear of dying, or seeing loved ones killed. The European Union delegation in Afghanistan condemned what it said was a "despicable act of terrorism". *Afghanistan Times* reported the killing of students in a girls' school: "The United Nations Assistance Mission in Afghanistan (UNAMA) expressed its "deep revulsion" at the blast. Iranian Foreign Minister Mohammad Javad Zarif condemned the bombing close to a girl's school in Kabul city and called on all Afghans to end the violence. According to Iran's Fars news, Zarif said: "We mourn the innocent and fasting girls who have become the oppressed victims of the ISIL Takfiris; the Takfiris who showed that they know nothing of Islam and humanity." "It is time for all those who like Islam and Afghanistan to put an end to fratricide" and integrate to make the situation hard for Daesh terrorists, he said. China's Foreign Ministry Spokesperson Hua Chunying said: "We are shocked by the attacks and strongly condemn such violent acts. China opposes violent extremism in all its manifestations. We will continue our firm support for the Afghan government and people in their efforts to combat terrorism and safeguard national security and stability. We also stand ready to work with the international community to help Afghanistan realize peace at an early date."

Bomb attack near a school in west Kabul caused the death of 85 students. However, fighting also erupted in Afghanistan after the US pull-out deadline. Afghan President Ashraf Ghani condemned the attack. "The Taliban, by escalating their illegitimate war and violence, shown that they were not only reluctant to resolve the current crisis peacefully and fundamentally, but by complicating the situation," Ghani said. The Taliban condemned the attack, apparently aimed at civilians, and denied any responsibility. Al Jazeera reported. Looking backward, on 13 April 2017, US army dropped Mother of Bombs in Nangarhar's Achin District. The US army used the largest non-nuclear bomb in its arsenal, the GBU-43/B Massive Ordnance Air Blast (MOAB), with the goal of destroying tunnel complexes used by the Islamic State of Iraq and the Levant – Khorasan Province (ISIL-KP or ISIS-K), a branch of the Islamic State of Iraq and the Levant. Former Afghan General, Atiqullah Akmarkhail, said such bombs have a long-lasting impact. "They have three-stage effects: They impact the eyes; people will feel irritation in their eyes. Second, they impact the inner organs of those who breathe the air where it was used. He said. The Mother of Bomb destroyed Jalalabad province and caused many incurable diseases. *The TOLOnews* Reporter, Abdulhaq Omeri (01 December 2019) interviewed residents and reported their grievances in his report:

> "In April 2017 the US Air Force dropped its most powerful non-nuclear bomb onto a Daesh stronghold in Nangarhar. Almost two and a half years after the United States dropped the "mother of all bombs" onto a Daesh hideout in eastern Afghanistan, locals say they have been afflicted by "many diseases" and agricultural lands are not yielding crops". Journalist Omeri witnessed many children and teenagers suffering from skin problems and listened to many residents speak of the bomb's lasting effects. Omeri reported. "In April 2017, US Forces dropped a bomb on a Daesh stronghold of caves and tunnels in eastern Nangarhar province. The bomb, nicknamed the "mother of all bombs "was one of the most powerful conventional (non-nuclear) weapons in the US arsenal. Anyone within 300 meters was vaporized, experts said, while those in a one kilometre radius outside ground zero were left deaf. Nangarhar residents said the bomb has had a lasting effect on the area. Omeri noted.

The US and NATO committed war crimes by killing members of civil society, journalists, doctors, prosecutors and villagers. The type of killings, Afghanistan Times noted "reminiscent of the killings during the chaos period several years ago that Afghanistan cascaded into a civil war, silencing the voice of high-profile figures for their narrow interests". Business of killing continues to inflict fatalities on Afghan society, while foreign war criminals are on the run. Afghanistan Times authenticated intelligence reports that Taliban had established a network of ISI backed criminals to carry out assassination attacks, In Kabul University, the US and NATO sponsored militias killed 100 high school students. Such agents of darkness, Afghanistan Times called devil forces. "We are worried about our children who are facing daily risk with no guarantees of returning home from education facilities. The utter wickedness of the enemies is to play a business of fear with the peaceful and educated Afghan lovers, to stop their children from going to education centres. But such evils will never fade away the quest of our young boys and girls from pursuing education. Nevertheless, the attack on the education centre was obviously a horrendous attack, underscoring the burning plan for dismantling this inhumane and un-Islamic group". Afghanistan Times noted. However, the newspaper in its editorial page also noted the story of 16 years old boy who escaped the Taliban prison where children were being abused:

"A 16-year-old boy who has recently escaped the Taliban tells the tale. He substantiates the fact that children are used for guerrilla attacks and roadside mines. The boy revealed that there were even foreign terrorists recruiting teenagers and training them for suicide attacks. There were earlier claims that such innocent children were brainwashed into thinking that war was necessary in Afghanistan and were thus killed. Meanwhile, the United Nations in its annual report verified that around 3,410 grave violations against 3,245 Afghan children were committed by the militants, Afghan and international security forces in 2019. Of the total 3,149 children, including 2,226 boys, 910 girls and 13 at least 874 were killed and 2,275 maimed. These are horrendous figures and shouldn't be ignored. It's very unfortunate to see our children being victimized and used as a fuel for a war they never want. In the meantime, the sad reality is that the alleged crimes against the children are not only noticed in the militants' ranks; there are accounts of such exploitation and mistreatment of the children by the government as well while the foreign forces pay no heed to their lives....Sadly, Afghanistan is still the second-largest drug-producing country in the world since 1994 as the value of narcotics produced in Afghanistan surpassed the country's exports between 2017 and 2018, according to a report of the Special Inspector General for Afghanistan Reconstruction (SIGAR). Meanwhile, a recent study launched by the Afghanistan Research and Evaluation Unit (AREU) titled "The Helmand Food Zone: The Illusion of Success", identified the issue of drugs as a key challenge that the new Afghan government, whose formation seems to be around the corner, will have to tackle". *Afghanistan Times* reported".

Sanctimonious, pietism and phoniness of the Biden administration towards the people of Afghanistan and commiseration for Taliban was clearly understandable from the fact that Taliban have been receiving modern military technology from the United States since 2004 to exploit mineral resources in the country. Accordingly, Taliban have also been receiving salaries in dollar, and their war crimes were considered jihad by Pakistani ISI and Haqqani and Durrani Mullahs. Pentagon killed hundreds in Kabul Airport, then killed innocent children in a house of a poor family, and now secretly engaged in face-to-face conversation with the Taliban, and all terrorist groups that receive weapons and funds from the US army. *Daily Dawn* newspaper on 09, 09 2021 reported US Secretary of State Antony Blinken's determination to work with terrorist Taliban and authenticated that war on terrorism was sharp practice, double-dealing and skulduggery. US Secretary told Afghan ToloNews TV: "My hope and, beyond hope, expectation is that the future government of Afghanistan will uphold those basic (human) rights. And if it does, then that's a government that we can work with. If it doesn't, we won't. Asked if the US would recognise the Taliban government, he said: "That will depend entirely on what it does, not just on what it says. And the trajectory of its relationship with us and with the rest of the world will depend on its actions."[18] On 25 August 2021, before the US abrupt approach to Taliban, China's ambassador to the United Nations Human Rights Council said; "foreign forces should be held accountable for human rights violations in Afghanistan". Chen Xu was speaking at the council's special meeting on Afghanistan. He said China was ready to cooperate with Afghanistan and help with its reconstruction.

On 08 September 2021, Human Rights Watch reported Taliban authorities in Afghanistan detaining and assaulting journalists and imposing new restrictions on media work, Human Rights Watch noted. The Taliban needed to drop the restrictions, and ensure that Taliban members who were responsible for abuses against protesters and journalists needed to be appropriately punished. Since early September 2021, Human Rights Watch reported Afghan women and girls in several cities held protests against Taliban's violations of women and girls' rights, including denial of their right to education and access to employment. HRW reported.[19]The Express Tribune reported war crimes of Taliban terrorists in Afghanistan:

"The Taliban has been continuing its mayhem in Afghanistan after the US drawdown, killing civilians and has no regard for human rights violations. As per the Afghanistan Independent Human Rights Commission (AIHRC), which were issued last month, 33 assassination incidents were reported in the southern Afghan province of Kandahar after the Taliban overtook a crossing point with Pakistan, the newspaper reported. The attacks targeted religious scholars, tribal elders, civil society activists, journalists, and human rights defenders. The United Nations Security Council condemned what is called deliberate attacks on civilians in Afghanistan. It also declared its opposition to the restoration of Taliban rule in Afghanistan. The Express Tribune noted.[20]

Professor of Philosophy, Public Policy and Governance, University of Washington, Michael Blake (17, August 2021) in his recent analysis deeply criticized the Biden administration for its immature withdrawal from Afghanistan. "The Taliban has proved itself willing to engage in widespread violation of basic human rights - in particular, the human rights of women. The decision to withdraw is likely to lead to enormous suffering in the years to come. A hypothetical decision to remain in Afghanistan, however, would also have led to significant moral costs - that decision would continue to put American soldiers in harm's way. As a political philosopher whose work focuses on international affairs, I have tried to understand how ethical reasoning might be applied to such cases."[21] John Walsh (Biden exits Afghanistan, heads in the wrong direction: The US has learned nothing from 20 years of war, Asia Times, 08 September 20201) has noted political mistakes of the Biden Administration, and his love for the killed US soldiers in Afghanistan but failed to exhibit sympathy with hundreds of thousands of Afghans killed as a direct result of the war, hundreds of thousands more as a result of disease and malnutrition. "Instead of apologies from Biden and an offer of reparations, there came news that the US was freezing more than $9 billion in Afghan foreign assets needed by this starving nation lying in ruins. The United States has apparently learned nothing either in terms of the limits of its power or the morality of its foreign policy if we are to take Biden's speech and actions as any indication. To say the least, it will not be easy to change this, but we have no choice. A calamity beyond imagination awaits us if we fail".[22] However, in June 2021, in a NATO Summit, President of the Czech Republic, Milos Zeman, called the decision to pull troops out of Afghanistan a betrayal.

Chapter 1

The ISI Atrocities and the Murder of Civilian Intelligence Culture in Pakistan

My tangible pontification and debate opening in this chapter on war of strength between civilian and military intelligence in Pakistan. War on interests, between the IB and ISI now reached dangerous position as Miltablishment has been stipulating to manage a democratic government, the state and resources since 2018. Communication and interconnection, and knit-togetherness between military and civilian intelligence agencies in Pakistan have never been companionable since 1977, when General Zia dethroned Prime Minister Zulfiqar Ali Bhutto in a coup d'état. The military government immediately set a motion to reorganize the weak, poor and unprofessional military intelligence agencies while dematerializing civilian agencies in order to incapacitate and murder the culture of civilian intelligence in Pakistan. The IB and FIA became part of the ISI war against politicians and opponents.

They were now the ears and eyes of the military government. In 1979, after the Soviet invasion of Afghanistan, the ISI and MI were restrained and encumbered the fun and game to train Afghans and transport them to Afghanistan for fight against the Soviet forces. As per my personal attainment, more than 80 percent of ISI officers and field informers had no access to social media and newspapers in the 1980s. They were honest and stalwart but their communication with headquarters was only by post and main landline-telephone. In view of the fact, mobile communication was of limited access in the country. They were unable to visit the houses of Ministers, landlords, business lords, industrialists and parliamentarians for investigation purposes on account of their lack of education and culture of inferiority complex. They were non-technical, unschooled, untutored, uninformed and unacquainted to enter into pontification with journalists and politicians.[1]

In the 1980s and 1990s, the ISI and MI retrieved professional training from the CIA and Pentagon and obtained the best experience of intelligence information collection in war and peace. The intelligence bureau (IB) became weak and dematerialized when its management received 70 percent of posting from the military establishment to further skeletal the civilian intelligence infrastructure, and use it against civilian society, politicians, and dissidents. The IB was below far weak and incapacitated on account of inattention of military establishment, lack of funds, and intelligence information collection equipment. The IB had become fully militarized and its civilian operational mechanism was copied from military intelligence. Thus, the culture of civilian intelligence demonstration was undermined. The ISI and IB were packed with Mujahideen and Taliban, and their commanders were receiving instructions from sectarian organizations such as Tablighi Jamaat and Jamaat Islami.[2]

Pakistan's Intelligence Bureau was established by Major General Sir Charles MacGregor in 1885 in order to make military forces professional and competent by purveying them with fresh intelligence information. After the partition, the IB was fully independent together with its huge network in civil society in Pakistan. The IB had to play a crucial role in protecting the state and security, and tried to strengthen its civilian culture of intelligence information collection. It also played a professional role in 1965 and 1971 wars by keeping the army, government and politicians updated about the activities of Indian forces. The IB was initially Pakistan's main and bigger intelligence agency with the responsibility for strategic and foreign intelligence. Between 1950 and 1980, the IB was monitoring politicians, dissidents, terrorists and emerging developments in Bangladesh and India. The agency also secretly informed Prime Minister Zulfiqar Ali Bhutto of the coup organized by General Gul Hassan Khan, Marshal Abdul Rahim, and preparations of General Zia-ul-Haq to dethrone Prime Minister Bhutto. The Zia military government deeply concentrated on strengthening the ISI to monitor IB and politicians, but enfeebled the agency and divided its infrastructure between military and civilian units. In the 1990s, democratic governments helped the IB in gaining international reputation. In 1996, the IB started monitoring and controlling information dissemination via mail, wire, or electronic medium.[3]

Within the ISI offices the IB was under pressure, powerless to have a say in security meetings. The European Asylum Support Office (16 October 2018) in its report noted that 'civilian candidates for the posts of Directorate General of ISI had to pass through a transparent and systematic process comprising written tests, interviews, medical examinations and, in some cases, intelligence and psychological tests as well. Security clearance of the selected candidates is carried out by the vetting agency of the ISI, keeping in view the standards and peculiar requirements in accordance with the mandate of the Directorate. A panel of highly qualified senior officers select the candidates keeping in view the sensitive nature of jobs to be assigned/performed, and the candidates are tested/interviewed with particular emphasis on their potential, trends, zeal, devotion, dedication and psychological suitability required for the job. It is, therefore, in the larger interest of the country to make the recruitment of the posts of Directorate General ISI by the department itself instead of FPSC.[4]

Civilian Intelligence (IB) experienced under whelming ball-games under the shade of military establishment. After the butt-end of military government and Soviet occupation of Afghanistan, civilian intelligence infrastructure was nearly disintegrated and sinking fast. Its well-trained senior police officers had superannuated. When Benazir Bhutto assumed responsibilities as a civilian Prime Minister, she was still unable to reinvent the IB against the willpower of the ISI and military establishment. She was helpless to remove military officers from the infrastructure of civilian intelligence. Mian Nawaz Sharif was upraised by the military establishment as a future Prime Minister. She was designated as an anti-state and India's-RAW agent. Mian Nawaz Sharif assumed power with the help of ISI, General Hamid Gul and Osama Bin Laden in 1997, and served until his removal in 1999 by military takeover and was tried in a plane hijacking case. The ISI and military establishment were not happy with Nawaz Sharif and his ISI chief General Javed Nasir (member of Tablighi Jamaat of Pakistan). General Javed Nasir supplied weapons to Muslim fighters in Bosnia. Meltablishment and Musharraf decided to sideline Nawaz Sharif through a military coup in 1999 after they failed to defeat the Indian army in Kargil. Thus, Nawaz Sharif was dethroned and forced to take refuge in Saudi Arabia.[5]

However, Asif Ali Zardari served as the 11th President of Pakistan from 2008 to 2013, and remained a strong US ally in war on terrorism in Afghanistan, notwithstanding public disapproval in the United States following the Raymond Davis affairs and the NATO attack in Salala check post in 2011. President Zardari never supported ISI's involvement in politics and terrorist attacks in India and Afghanistan. He directed the Interior Ministry to bring ISI under democratic control, but faced a disheartening situation. The ISI threatened President Zardari with dire consequences.

On 07 June 2013, Sharif was sworn in again for an unprecedented third term, but faced numerous challenges, including military establishment sarcastic attitude, the ISI vandalism, and US drone strikes against civilian population in Pakistan's tribal regions.

After he assumed power, Tehrik Insaf and Thahir-ul-Qadri arranged a protest movement with the support of ISI, while civilian intelligence was watching ISI from different angles. The ISI and military establishment arranged a sit-in of 2500 radicalized elements in 2016, while the IB documented participating leaders one-by-one. On 28 July 2017, Prime Minister Nawaz Sharif was disqualified in a fake Aqama case by the court. The war of strength between civilian and military intelligence agencies intensified. Thus, Imran Khan Nizai became the Prime Minister of Pakistan with the support of ISI in 2018. But he was crippled when foreign and security policy was controlled by the military establishment, and he was forced to appoint more than 400 military experts on various civilian posts. The IB became hopeless due to this new alliance of Bajwa-Imran and the ISI.[6]

The weak and fragile government of Imran Khan has been unable to introduce intelligence and security sector reforms to bring the ISI and other agencies under democratic control. The ISI is the dominant actor in Pakistan's political life, despite some improvements in civil-military relations in recent years. Most of the agency officers used secret Afghan funds for their personal and family expenditures. The ISI supports sectarian groups in Pakistan who had emerged from the conflict in Afghanistan and by the US invasion in the country. The ISI first dematerialized the IB and FIA, then controlled the whole process of terrorist's infiltration into India and Afghanistan, and received billions of dollars from NATO and the United States, but never shared the cake with both IB and FIA, while their experts were implicated in different scandals. The ISI proxies carrying out suicide attack in Afghanistan and India. On 13 February 2015, General Musharraf admitted that he had instructed the ISI to recruit suicide bomber and organize attacks against Afghan army and government institutions to force the Karzai administration to close the unnecessary diplomatic presence of India in Afghanistan. When the ISI atrocities intensified in Afghanistan after the announcement of the Biden administration, and its policy of confrontation failed, Pakistan relinquished supporting Kashmir and allowed India to properly control and oversee it. The army also commenced peace efforts in Afghanistan but attacked the country after the US withdrawal. Blabbermouth, tattler, double-crosser and whistleblowers within civilian intelligence kicked up one's heel and raised their voices against the total control of ISI and its war crimes in Afghanistan.[7]

The complex reciprocation among the internal and external forces fashioning Pakistan today called on to an in-depth evaluation of their influence on the country's future-in the context of both continued state stability and Pakistan's potential to jump-start broader security priorities in the region. Established in 1948, the ISI was tasked with acquiring intelligence of strategic interests and assessing the intensity of foreign threats, but political and military stakeholders used the agency adversely and painted a consternating picture of its working environment. The civilian intelligence agency (IB) has been gradually neglected, humiliated and enfeebled due to the consecutive military rule and weak democratic governments. Serving and retired military officers were being appointed in increasing numbers to senior posts in the IB, including to the post of DG. In the 1990s, the IB remained actively involved to curb sectarianism and fundamentalism in the country. Many of its operations were directed towards infiltration, conducting espionage, counterespionage, and providing key information on terrorist organisations.[8]

War of strength between the ISI and Intelligence Bureau (IB) has been reported time and again by Pakistani newspapers to manifest that a decade long fight of state intelligence agencies might jeopardize national security of the state that hitherto affianced with neighbours in geographical altercations. The IB headquarters in Punjab has customarily been looted and plundered by the ISI commando groups in 1980s, 1990s and 2000s, and all secret records of domestic and international intelligence information was despoiled. The rough and tumble of intelligence information technology between the two secret agencies brought shame to the country when ISI refused to share intelligence technology with the IB management. Once, a former DG of Intelligence Bureau chronicled the real story of controversial intelligence technology in an hour-long meeting with me in his Lahore headquarter. By reading that draft, I realized the sensitivity of the war of power between the ISI, IM, IB and FIA. The FIA was under the control of the Nawaz Sharif family for a decade, when General Musharraf came to Power in 1999, Choudhry Bradaran full controlled the agency to further their interests in Spain and UK. My best friend Khawar Zaman (DG FIA-IB) told me a single time that he was forced by Choudhry Shujaat to cancel the transfer of four Directors of FIA, but he refused. The reason that Khawar Zaman was appointed as Ambassador to Australia. However, a former Joint Director (My close friend) evinced a critical document about the ISI's political demonstrations and its illegal interference in civilian institutions and government. He told me that ISI and military establishment bribe judges and media owners in cases of their own interests.[9]

The ISI in 2017, recruited a serving Assistant Sub-Inspector (ASI) of IB, Malik Mukhtar Ahmed Shahzad, who filed a petition before the Islamabad High Court (IHC) requesting it to refer the matter to the Inter-Services Intelligence (ISI) for a thorough probe. The purpose of that petition was to further dematerialize the IB. Mr. Shahzad said he purveyed intelligence report to the management against terrorist groups of Uzbekistan, Iran, Afghanistan, Syria and India. Malik noted that upon thorough intelligence gathering process, it transpired that certain high officials of the IB themselves were directly involved with the terrorist organizations having linkages with hostile enemy intelligence agencies. However, the IB circulated a list of 37 Lawmakers who had established secret interconnection with ISI to update the agency about the intentions of Prime Minister Nawaz Sharif and his close colleagues. Mian Nawaz Sharif, later on, directed Law Minister Hamid to take action against the channel through the Pakistan Electronic Media Regulatory Authority. Moreover, DG IB Aftab Sultan openly declared war against the illegal interference of ISI in government's decision-making process, and visited Nawaz Sharif in London.[10]

Dawn newspaper reported Islamabad High Court Registrar's Office fixation of the petition before Justice Aamer Farooq who referred the case to IHC Chief Justice Mohammad Anwar Khan Kasi, with a note that the matter should be transferred to Justice Shaukat Aziz Siddiqui since an identical matter was pending in his court. In the petition filed through his counsel Masroor Shah, Mr. Shahzad said he joined the IB in 2007, and that he "reported against various terrorist groups having roots in Uzbekistan, Iran, Afghanistan, Syria and India". The ASI told the court he had reported against terrorist groups from various countries but no action was taken: "However, to the petitioner's utter dismay, no action has never been taken by IB in this respect despite concrete evidence provided to it in the form of the intelligence reports", the petition says. "Upon thorough intelligence gathering process, it transpired that certain high officials of the IB themselves are directly involved with the terrorist organizations having linkages with hostile enemy intelligence agencies", the petition reads. It goes on to say that the matter was even reported to the IB director-general, who also did not take any steps. It says some IB officials travelled to Israel and had direct links with Afghan intelligence which, it was later found, had links with another terrorist group from Kazakhstan. "These terrorists used to disguise themselves as citrus dealers in Kot-Momin and Bhalwal, Sargodha. The business was a mere camouflage," the petition said.[11]

Moreover, the petition revealed that the son of Joint Director IB (Punjab) had established links with these terror groups. The petition uncovered that some officials of Afghan and Iranian intelligence used to take refuge in the places of the citrus dealers. The petition named certain IB's officials who were on the payroll of foreign intelligence agencies which included a Joint Director General, Directors and Deputy Directors. The petitioner said: "Senior IB officials also facilitate Afghan nationals in getting Pakistani nationality. Mr. Shahzad said he "has been running from pillar to post including approaching the Prime Minister of Pakistan to raise this issue of national security and protection of lives of the citizens of this country but in vain." The petitioner requested the court that the issue of connivance, complacency and involvement of officials of IB and other senior bureaucrats raised in the petition may graciously be entrusted to ISI for investigation. Dawn also reported that the Intelligence Bureau (IB) also came under attack by a Joint Investigation Team (JIT) consisting of officials from ISI, Military Intelligence and officials from other departments for 'hampering the investigation' into the assets of former Prime Minister Nawaz Sharif's family. The Intelligence Bureau (IB) was accused by one of its own spies of "protecting" terrorists. That petition prompted misunderstandings between the ISI and the Intelligence Bureau (IB).[12]

The unending resultant tussle between civilian and military intelligence agencies forced former Prime Minister Nawaz Sharif to restructure the IB and make it more effective to counter ISI's influence in political institutions. The Prime Minister allocated huge funds to the IB to recruit and employ more agents to meet the country's internal and external challenges. The greatest challenge Nawaz Sharif faced was on the national security front, where he failed to take control of the security policy of Kashmir and Afghanistan. The miltablishment was not happy with his democratic intentions. The Intelligence Bureau is the country's main civilian intelligence agency that functions under the direct control of the Prime Minister, tackling terrorism, insurgency and extremism. Over the last four decades, the ISI operated in changing security environment, but the agency mostly targeted democracy and political parties, strengthened miltablishment and its illegal business of land grabbing, nuclear smuggling and drug trafficking. The intelligence community of Pakistan was once described by the Daily Frontier Post (May 18, 1994) as an invisible government, and by the Daily Dawn (April 25, 1994)[16] as secret godfathers consisting of the Intelligence Bureau (IB) and the ISI. While the IB comes under the Interior Minister, the ISI is part of the Ministry of Defence (MOD). Each wing of the Armed Forces maintains its own intelligence directorate. After the PTI Chief Imran Khan became Prime Minister, the IB started dancing to his tango. Analyst Azaz Syed (28 September 2018) noted some developments within the intelligence infrastructure as Prime Minister Imran Khan restructured the agency and fitted it to the recurrent nature of his Charleston:

"Amid a major reshuffle within the premier civilian intelligence outfit, the Intelligence Bureau (IB) has been directed to concentrate on fighting corruption instead of countering terrorism. The Friday Times noted that the IB Chief Dr. Suleman Khan denied this development. Sources within the agency insist that they had been tasked to bring forward corruption cases against prominent political figures and pay attention to these areas. "There are other agencies and organizations which were trained for anti-corruption efforts. IB should not do this. Its expertise is in countering terrorism and its focus should not be redirected towards corruption," said Ehsan Ghani, a recently retired former chief of the IB while talking to TFT. Dr. Suleman, who also served the agency in Khyber Pakhtunkhwa, was counted among those who played a vital role in countering terrorism in the province with the help of the police and the Counter-Terrorism Department (CTD). Now, he has agreed to shelve counter-terrorism as a subject of the agency, as another agency has been tasked to deal with it. Dr. Suleman was appointed chief of the agency by former Prime Minister Shahid Khaqan Abbasi on the recommendation of Aftab Sultan, the then IB chief. But Dr Suleman denied this. "I come from a background of counter-terrorism, how I can abandon something I have worked on for years"[13]

The third most important agency-having something on the ball during the Musharraf, Zardari and Nawaz Sharif government is Federal Investigation Agency (FIA). My best friend-Chief of the FIA and IB (Khawar Zaman) once told me the agency had also been playing a political role for different governments since the 1970s. The FIA's main objective is to protect the nation's interests and defend Pakistan, to uphold and enforce law in the country. The Federal Investigation Agency (FIA) was established on 13 January 1975, after being codified in the Constitution with the passing of the FIA Act in 1974. The FIA is headed by the Director-General who is appointed by the Prime Minister, and confirmed by the President. Appointment for the Director of FIA either comes from the high-ranking officials of police or the civil bureaucracy. The DG FIA reports to the Interior Secretary of Pakistan.

The FIA is the biggest intelligence agency in Pakistan. During the last four decades, FIA has been used against alliance making and punishing political opponents. On 07 October 2020, *Newsweek Pakistan* reported former Director General of Pakistan's Federal Investigation Agency (FIA), Bashir Memon, summoned by military establishment and ISI, pushed to register a case against Maryam Nawaz and her husband Muhammad Safdar over a picture of the first lady that was circulated on social media. He told Matiullah Khan that he asked under what law he could register the case. "It was a picture of the first lady on social media. How is this terrorism? There is a definition of terrorism in law. It was a normal picture; how was that terrorism?" he said, adding that this had happened shortly after the 2018 general elections. While refusing to name anyone directly, he stressed that the demand had come from the "highest office" of Pakistan, in a seeming reference to Prime Minister Imran Khan. He However said; "[I was told] to take action on this against [Maryam Nawaz's] social media cell. I didn't say this couldn't be done. I just asked under what law? Because we have to work according to the law," he said, adding that the government's expectations of the FIA had since been "fulfilled" by the National Accountability Bureau (NAB). Memon said. When Mr. Memon was asked to register cases of corruption against them, he replied: "I told them that all of this is the mandate of the provincial anti-corruption [unit]. They can do this, we cannot because the FIA is a law enforcement agency. A law enforcement agency will [handle] law. We will remain within our mandate. We can't go and jump around," he said, adding that he had been criticized for not pursuing such cases against the PMLN. "[P.M. Khan said] 'you didn't do this, you didn't do that, you released that person' and all I said was 'sir NAB is there' [to pursue such cases]," Memon added.

However, *Express Tribune* reported former Federal Investigation Agency (FIA) Chief Bashir Memon retracted his allegations that Prime Minister Imran Khan had instructed him to initiate a probe against Supreme Court's judge Justice Qazi Faez Isa. In his interview with a private television channel, DG FIA said his meeting with the Prime Minister lasted only for two to three minutes and the premier did not discuss any specific case with him. "The Prime Minister just appreciated my professionalism and told me that being a courageous person, I can do it," he said. Allegations levelled in a TV interview by Bashir Memon were painful. He was, later on called to the Prime Minister's Office for a meeting where the premier told him that he was "a very good officer" who has been registering "good cases" in the past and that he should "take courage" and register a good case this time as well. He said, "At that time, I was not aware of the nature of the case and whom I was supposed to proceed against". Memon claimed that it was at Akbar's office that it was revealed to him that he is to proceed against Justice Qazi Faez Isa.

On 24 June 2021, the ISI directed FIA to summon journalist Muhammad Bilal Ghauri for his critical reporting. Thus, Federal Investigation Agency's Cyber Crime Reporting Centre in Islamabad summoned journalist Muhammad Bilal Ghauri for questioning for alleged defamatory remarks made through his YouTube channel. The International Federation of Journalists (IFJ) urged authorities to cease the intimidation of journalists who have a right to freedom of expression and questioning attacks on their profession, but the military establishment refused to clear Mr. Ghauri. The summon notice was issued on June 22 under the Pakistan Electronic Crime Act (PECA) and ordered Ghauri to appear before the Cyber Crime Reporting Centre of the Federal Investigation Agency (FIA) in Islamabad. According to a letter from M. Waseem Sikandar, a sub-inspector at the FIA, the summons was in response to a complaint filed by Syed Abbas Mohiuddin, a politician from Attock district and member of the provincial assembly. The letter warned that failing to adhere the notice's order would result in further legal action under section 174 of Pakistan Penal Code.[14]

As I acknowledged earlier, the Federal Investigation Agency was politicized by successive Pakistani governments. Mr. Khawar Zaman, Chief of the FIA once told this author that Prime Minister Choudhry Shujaat Hussain forced him for illegal appointments. FIA has been the source of human trafficking in Europe and South Asia since 1980s. On 28 April, 2021, Pakistan's Supreme Court ordered the FIA to remove the 53-illegally appointed officers. A three-member bench of the apex court headed by Chief Justice of Pakistan Justice Gulzar Ahmed conducted hearing of a contempt petition against FIA for making unlawful recruitments in the agency and not complying with the Supreme Court order dated 21-02-2001. The FIA counsel informed that four employees have died, while three have passed the competitive exam. He said that after the SC judgment, the FIA employees approached the high courts. Justice Ijaz said that the Supreme Court judgment cannot be overruled by the high courts. Civilian control over intelligence agencies and oversight in Pakistan is a challenging issue. Intelligence agencies in Pakistan operating without oversight became sarcastic. On 04 November 2013, Dawn reported recommendations of the Senate Standing Committee on Human Rights which "recommended an effective role of parliament in monitoring the Inter-Services Intelligence (ISI) agency and putting it under civilian control. The report was unanimously adopted by the committee and presented in the house. The committee unanimously approved recommendations on 05 September 2013, and voiced for setting up a bicameral intelligence and security committee to suggest ways of addressing the issue of enforced disappearance of citizens".[15]

Chapter 2

President Zardari Never Danced to the ISI's Jitterbug

In July 2008, when the PPP government notified the Interior Ministry to take action against the ISI political bargaining, the military establishment expressed displeasure. Analyst and Senator Farhatullah Babar of the PPP was the convener of the three-member committee which prepared the report. Every agency in Pakistan is operating illegally by detaining, kidnapping and harassing civilians in many ways. They are kidnapping businessmen, journalists and writers for ransom. There are many cases of kidnapping, in which Naval intelligence, and Field Intelligence units in Punjab have been deeply involved since the 1990s. General Pervez Musharraf and General Raheel Sharif committed war crimes in FATA, Balochistan and Waziristan. They sold their countrymen to the CIA, and killed, tortured and humiliated children and women in Waziristan. General Shahid Aziz once unveiled the secret business of General Musharraf in a TV interview with Hamid Mir, in which he admitted that the army killed thousands of Pashtuns, Afghans and Balochs.

The way military intelligence operated over the past decades was shameless. Instead of tackling national security challenges, the ISI, along with Military Intelligence (MI) and the IB, unnecessarily concentrated on making political alliances and countering democratic forces within the country. When the intelligence war among military and civilian agencies intensified, the blame-game became the main focus of literary debates in newspapers and electronic media. Democratic forces stood behind civilian intelligence agencies, while pro-establishment forces supported the ISI and its undemocratic business. Turmoil and conflagration within the ISI infrastructure triggered debates in social media and newspapers. In 2014, officials from the ISI had their phone calls eavesdropped at the height of civil-military tension. On 13 September 2013, Dawn newspaper reported allegations of the Directorate General of Inter-Services Intelligence (ISI) against the 34 civilian inspectors who filed petitions with the Islamabad High Court (IHC) that they were compromising national security and hampered the smooth functioning of the organization as well.[1]

In August that year, the ISI inspector Abdul Rahim filed a petition with the Islamabad High Court saying that contrary to the court restraining orders the Directorate of ISI had posted him to Sui in Baluchistan and also evicted him from the official residence in Islamabad. However, Mr. Justice Shaukat Aziz Siddiqui suspended the posting orders of Mr. Rahim also restrained the ISI from evicting him from the official residence as well. Moreover, before this petition, on 01 July 2013, Dawn newspaper reported a petition of the promotion case of civilian officers against the ISI Directorate. The litigation related to the service matter of a number of civilian officials working within offices of Inter-Services Intelligence (ISI) indicated that it was difficult for them to reach even BPS-21-grade in their entire service. Because of this, the names of civilian officials cannot even be considered for the post of Director General which is a BPS-22 position. However, that year, three more petitions were also filed with the Islamabad High Court (IHC) by the civilian officials of the Inter-Services Intelligence (ISI). All but 30 civilian officials of the ISI Directorates filed their petition against the agency Directorate-stating that a civilian official working in ISI offices hardly gets only one-time promotion during his entire 25 years of service. Reports indicated more than 325 officers were working in BPS-17 to 21 in the five different cadres of the ISI. Out of the 325, only one officer enjoyed BPS-21. Seven others were in BPS-20 and were working as Deputy Directors. Lt-General (retired) Talat Masood said despite being a civilian organization, there was hardly any oversight of the civilian governments over the ISI.[2]

The ISI management has been treating civilian employees like slaves and look at them with scorn. They have no voice, no promotion, and no housing rights. One of my close friends-Assistant Director of ISI's Lahore directorate, received a single promotion in the past two decades. He was a highly educated officer. Military officers within the agency offices are managing intelligence operations but don't share information with civilian officers. There are countless civilian officers who live hand to mouth as they cannot manage monthly expenditures of their families with a trivial salary they receive, while military officers receive huge salaries. Several disparate civilian friends of this author within the ISI management bawled and yelled before me of their hardship and poverty inflicted by the military management. One of my friends (M) got only one promotion after 25 years, another two left the agency with tears, disposition and protestation. With this culture of militarization and intransigence within the management, it means things are not going on right direction. *The Dawn* newspaper on 07 March, 2013, reported contempt petition of civilian employees against the ISI management and its Director-General:

"In what may be the first such case in Pakistan's history, four civilian employees of the Inter-Services Intelligence (ISI) have approached the Islamabad High Court (IHC) with complaints about their own chief, ISI Director-General Lt-Gen Zaheerul Islam. They claim that he, along with other senior government officers, should be charged with contempt of court, regarding an IHC ruling on regularization of employees. The four men, Grade-18 officers, claim to have been working for the past seven years as junior analysts in the ISI, on a contract basis. They claim that their contractual appointments were limited to five years, after which they were to be made permanent employees. Along with other federal government employees, the four officers came to the Islamabad High Court late last year, and on December 31, the IHC directed the government to "regularize the services of contract employees". A cabinet subcommittee supervised the process at various ministries and departments, but these ISI employees were not regularized. The ISI employees have asked the IHC to initiate contempt of court proceedings against Lt-Gen Zaheerul Islam; Lt-Gen (retired) Asif Yasin Malik, Secretary of Defense; Taimur Azmat Usman, Secretary of the Establishment; and Syed Khursheed Ahmed Shah, chairman of the cabinet subcommittee on regularization of contractual employees. They claim that the respondents did not comply with the IHC's December 31 ruling. An ISI official, however, told Dawn that contract appointments in the ISI are different from those in other departments. "Regular appointments can only be made after candidates complete competitive exams and undergo psychological and intelligence tests," he said. The four petitioners, he claimed, "cannot get permanent positions in the ISI without going through these steps".[3]

The perspicacity that ISI is a No-one intelligence agency in South Asia is not accurate; the agency is weak, militarized and its national security approach is controversial. It collects intelligence based on ethnicity, sectarian, and discriminatory manner. Nepotism, race and ethnic cards have been using against Pashtun and Balochs since years. Thousands of cases of mutual dispute, such as land grabbing, and money extortion are being settled by the involvement of intelligence agencies. The ISI intelligence officers are not so greatly educated and unable to use modern intelligence technology properly. There are thousands of volunteer informers who work for the agency in different environments but don't even know the basic knowledge of intelligence information techniques. Their purveyed low-quality intelligence information lead policy makers in the wrong direction. As they receive trivial salaries, sometimes they implicate an innocent civilian in fake cases to win a reward. The second underwhelming thing is that military and civilian officers working within the agency have adopted two intelligence collection and analysis cultures that created confusion within the management. In view of the fact that for civilian officers, working in a militarized agency with a militarized way of operation and administration, is an exasperating task. The ISI collects intelligence information in a militarized manner, analyzes it in a militarized way, and disseminates it inaccurately[4]for the reason that its operational technique has become militarized, and its civilian approach remained controversial as the agency arrested and disappear/kidnap those listed by the establishment. Consequently, civilian don't cooperate with the agency in intelligence information collection and counter espionage operations.

The agency consecutively purveyed sophisticated weapons to the Taliban group to harm national critical infrastructure, undermine Afghan security forces and kill innocent civilians. Alexandra Gilliard noted: (Pakistan's Inter-Services Intelligence Contributes to Regional Instability. Global Security Review, Jun 7, 2019) "Pakistan's primary goal was to prevent India from gaining ground and obtaining too much influence. As the Taliban vies for more control, the ISI has provided it with military aid to ensure Afghanistan remains in a state of perpetual instability. Should the Taliban gain power, Pakistan will have bought itself a staunch ally in the region, with the potential to form a strategic partnership against India. The ISI arrests journalists and political activists in Pakistan.[5]John. R. Schmidt (ISI Wrongfully Accused of Killing Journalist?) has highlighted operational mechanism of the ISI:

> "But now there are accusations, publicly embraced by U.S. officials (including Joint Chiefs chairman Admiral Mike Mullen), that ISI ordered the murder of Pakistani journalist Saleem Shahzad, whose tortured and severely beaten body was found outside Islamabad on May 31. Shahzad had recently written a piece for the Asia Times alleging that the Pakistani Navy had arrested several naval personnel for helping al-Qaeda attack the Pakistani naval base in Karachi on May 22. Suspicion that ISI may have been responsible for his death surfaced after it was revealed he had earlier told colleagues he had

received death threats from the intelligence agency. These threats had allegedly come in the wake of a previous article he had written accusing Pakistani authorities of releasing Afghan Taliban deputy leader Mullah Baradar in October 2010 after eight months in custody. According to Shahzad, senior flag rank ISI officials had pressed him to reveal the source of his information and, when he refused, had made a point of telling him they had recently gotten a hold of an Islamic terrorist hit list and would let him know if his name was on it. Shahzad interpreted this as a threat. The speculation following his death was that the Karachi-naval-base story was the last straw and that ISI had ordered his murder, not just in retaliation, but as a warning to the entire Pakistani journalist community, whose criticisms it believed had gotten out of hand. If ISI was responsible for murdering Shahzad, it may well have been a first...None of the fifteen fit a plausible ISI scenario. But why would ISI choose Shahzad as its first victim? He was not a big-name journalist, nor was he among those who raised embarrassing questions about ISI and the army over the Abbottabad raid on bin Laden. His Karachi-naval-base story did not accuse ISI of improper conduct, and it is not clear why it would have killed him over a story that, if it embarrassed anyone, would have embarrassed the Pakistani Navy, a relatively minor player in the nation's military firmament. ISI was well aware that some of its senior officers had recently "had a word" with Shahzad and should have realized that if he suddenly turned up murdered ISI might be blamed for it, further sullying its already battered reputation. And that, of course, is exactly what happened"[6]

Digital Desk of Sentinel (19 September, 2020) has documented multirole stories of the ISI in Pakistan, and quoted journalist's Declan Walsh book to uncover misgivings of the agency approach to national security and neighboring states: "Inter-Services Intelligence, Pakistan's spy agency is afflicted by the same bungling and corruption as the rest of the Pakistani state, according to a new book. The book titled, "*The Nine Lives of Pakistan*" has been authored by Declan Walsh, the Cairo bureau chief of the New York Times. He covered Pakistan for nine years as an international correspondent for The Guardian first and then the Times, before he was expelled from the country. The book points to the fact that ISI uses fear as a weapon but its abilities are often overestimated. "The ISI does little to dispute its reputation as an omnipotent force. Fear is a powerful weapon. But talk of a 'rogue agency' is misplaced, and its abilities are frequently overestimated. While it is effective on street level, and seen by Western spy agencies as superior to its Indian rival, the Research and Analysis Wing (RAW), the ISI is not a professional service in the mold of the CIA or Britain's MI6," according to the book excerpts. "The organization is afflicted by the same bungling and corruption as the rest of the Pakistani state. It has frequently lost control of its most dangerous assets–Puppet masters who can't control their puppets,' as Robert Grenier, a former CIA station chief in Islamabad, put it," the book says. "And when it comes to analysis, the ISI has a poor record. 'They saw everything through pre-determined ideological prisms, rather like the KBG during the Cold War, a senior British official who worked with the ISI for decades told me. 'Frankly,' he added. 'None of their analysis was worth the paper it was written on,'" it adds.[7]

Rivalry between the IB and ISI boiled over in June 2017, when a Joint Investigation Team (JIT) probing alleged money laundering of the Sharif family made a written complaint to the Supreme Court that the IB was wiretapping JIT members, including the ISI and military intelligence personnel. The JIT further reported that the IB was hampering its inquiries, adding that military-led intelligence agencies were not on "good terms" with the IB. More worrisome was that IB was collecting intelligence information on members of the JIT from the National Database and Registration Authority (NADRA) and presented it to Prime Minister Nawaz Sharif to use it against them. The shortcomings of the civilian security apparatus were numerous[8] *Dawn* newspaper published an article by journalist Almeida, which said that some in Pakistan's civilian government confronted military officials at a top-secret national security Committee meeting. They said that they were being asked to do more to crack down on armed groups, yet, whenever law-enforcement agencies took action, "the security establishment...worked behind the scenes to set the arrested free". He also reported that the civilians warned that Pakistan risked international isolation if the security establishment didn't crack down on terrorist groups operating from Pakistan. After these leaks, the National Security Council and its committee became controversial. Pakistan's Chief Executive General Pervez Musharraf formally established the National Security Council on 21 August 2002. Under Article 152A of the Pakistan Constitution, the President of Pakistan and the Prime Minister of Pakistan serves as Chairman and Vice Chairman respectively.[9]

The Council remained unpopular and resented by leading political parties and liberal politicians pointing to the fact that the NSC primarily takes on the oligarchic structure of high-ranking military retirees and elite civilian officials close to the military. The Dawn leak's story uncovered fractured relationship between military establishment and democratic government in Pakistan where the two stakeholders have been trying to push ISI and IB to the brink.[10] In a meeting between the army and civilian administration on security issue, Chief Minister warned that the army support to militant organization may possibly exacerbate Pakistan's political and economic challenges in international community. Relations between the army and the Nawaz government were deteriorating by the day, while the ISI and Imran Khan's associates were anxious that clandestine relationship of Indian RAW and the Sharif family might damage the country's image abroad. Prime Minister Nawaz Sharif was hopeful that friendly relations between India and Pakistan will bring prosperity to the region, but the armed forces didn't support his line of argument.[11] *Express Tribune* newspaper (26 April, 2017) in its report noted some important points of the leaked argument:

"One member each from the ISI, Military Intelligence and Intelligence Bureau were included in the panel. Establishment Secretary Tahir Shahbaz, Punjab's Ombudsman Najam Saeed and the Federal Investigation Agency Director Usman Anwar were also part of the committee.[12] The committee was assigned the job to establish the identity of those who allegedly planted the story. Former information minister Pervez Rashid has already lost his portfolio on grounds that he failed to play his role effectively to restrain the journalist from running the controversial story". Journalist Cyril Almeida (Act against militants or face international isolation, civilians tell military-DAWN 06 October, 2016) in his story noted stunning inside fight between the democratic government and military establishment:

"In a blunt, orchestrated and unprecedented warning, the civilian government has informed the military leadership of a growing international isolation of Pakistan and sought consensus on several key actions by the state. As a result of the most recent meeting, an undisclosed one on the day of the All Parties' Conference on Monday, at least two sets of actions have been agreed. First, ISI DG Gen Rizwan Akhtar, accompanied by National Security Adviser Nasser Janjua, is to travel to each of the four provinces with a message for provincial apex committees and ISI sector commanders. The message: military-led intelligence agencies are not to interfere if law enforcement acts against militant groups that are banned or until now considered off-limits for civilian action. Gen Akhtar's inter-provincial tour began with a visit to Lahore. Second, Prime Minister Nawaz Sharif has directed that fresh attempts be made to conclude the Pathankot investigation and restart the stalled Mumbai attacks-related trials in a Rawalpindi anti-terrorism court. Those decisions, taken after an extraordinary verbal confrontation between Punjab Chief Minister Shahbaz Sharif and the ISI DG, appear to indicate a high-stakes new approach by the PML-N government.........The foreign secretary's unexpectedly blunt conclusions triggered an astonishing and potentially ground-shifting exchange between the ISI DG and several civilian officials. In response to Foreign Secretary Chaudhry's conclusions, Gen Akhtar asked what steps could be taken to prevent the drift towards isolation. Mr Chaudhry's reply was direct and emphatic: the principal international demands are for action against Masood Azhar and the Jaish-e-Mohammad; Hafiz Saeed and the Lashkar-e-Taiba; and the Haqqani network. To that, Gen Akhtar offered that the government should arrest whomever it deems necessary, though it is unclear whether he was referring to particular individuals or members of banned groups generally. At that point came the stunning and unexpectedly bold intervention by Punjab Chief Minister Shahbaz Sharif....Earlier in the meeting, ISI DG Gen Akhtar stated that not only is it the military's policy to not distinguish between militant groups, but that the military is committed to that policy prevailing. The ISI chief did mention concerns about the timing of action against several groups, citing the need to not be seen as buckling to Indian pressure or abandoning the Kashmiri people"[13]

Moreover, *Daily Dawn* reported on military establishment's standpoint of leaks on 14 October 2016. Participants of a Corps Commanders meeting at General Headquarters in Rawalpindi expressed serious concern over what they said was a leak from a security meeting which was reported by Dawn. In a statement issued by Inter-Services Public Relations (ISPR), participants of the meeting expressed serious concern over "feeding of a false and fabricated story of an important security meeting held at PM House and viewed it as breach of national security." Chief of Army Staff (COAS) General Raheel Sharif presided over the meeting which was attended by all corps commanders and principal staff officers. Almeida's name was added to the Exit Control List–preventing his travel abroad after he wrote the news report "Act against militants or face international isolation, civilians tell military".

The Prime Minister Office rejected the story thrice since it was published on October 6 2017.[14] In an Editor's note, *Dawn* clarified its position and stated on the record that the story "was verified, cross-checked and fact-checked." The note further stated: "Many at the helm of affairs were aware of the senior officials, and participants of the meeting who were contacted by the newspaper for collecting information. Therefore, the elected government and state institutions should refrain from targeting the messenger, and scapegoating the country's most respected newspaper in a malicious campaign." In the wake of the travel ban on Almeida, human rights and journalists' organizations including the HRCP, PFUJ and CPNE protested and rallied in his support. Most TV news channels also ran reports and conducted programmes criticizing the government's decision. The newspaper reported. Moreover, on 12 October 2016, *Dawn* newspaper reported the fallout of the story:

"The fallout of the story has been intense, and on Tuesday evening, the government placed Dawn's senior writer, Cyril Almeida, on the Exit Control List. While any media organization can commit an error of judgement and Dawn is no exception, the paper believes it handled the story in a professional manner and carried it only after verification from multiple sources. Moreover, in accordance with the principles of fair and balanced journalism, for which Dawn is respected not only in Pakistan but also internationally, it twice carried the denials issued by the Prime Minister's Office. Journalism has a long and glorious tradition of keeping its promise to its audience even in the face of enormous pressure brought to bear upon it from the corridors of power. Dawn reported. "Time has proved this to be the correct stance. Some of the most contentious yet historically significant stories have been told by news organizations while resisting the state's narrow, self-serving and ever-shifting definition of 'national interest'. One could include in this list, among others, the Pentagon Papers detailing US government duplicity in its conduct of the Vietnam War; the Abu Ghraib pictures that exposed torture of prisoners at the hands of US soldiers in Iraq; the WikiLeaks release in 2010 of US State Department diplomatic communications; and Edward Snowden's disclosure of the National Security Agency's global surveillance system. Even more so in Pakistan, where decades of a militarized security environment have undermined the importance of holding the state to account—something that certain sections of the media have become complicit in despite their long, hard-won struggle for freedom—such a furor as generated by the Dawn report was not unexpected." Dawn noted.[15]

The Almeida report found Prime Minister guilty, On 20 April, 2017, Press Trust of India reported proxy war between the government and armed forces, and noted removal of Tariq Fatemi, advisor to the Prime Minister after an inquiry found him guilty of "leaking" to a prominent newspaper vital information from a high-level National Security meeting. In October 2016, the columnist for *Dawn* newspaper, Cyril Almeida, wrote a front-page story about a rift between Pakistan's civilian and military leaderships over militant groups that operate from Pakistan but engage in proxy war against India and Afghanistan. The government had set up the inquiry committee to probe the controversy surrounding a controversial report by Dawn newspaper about a key meeting on national security. According to the inquiry committee report, it was Fatemi who was primarily responsible for leaking a report of the key meeting to the newspaper without due permission. *Press Trust of India* noted.[16] On 10 June 2017, *The Wire* reported the explosive news story with anonymous sources about a confrontation between Pakistan's Prime Minister and the country's top intelligence chief resulted in several government officials losing their jobs and a newspaper being intimidated, revealing Pakistani state and military officials' limited regard for press freedom......Pakistan's interior ministry first denied the story and put Almeida on the Exit Control List (ECL), an extraordinary measure usually reserved for hardened criminals or people involved in mass fraud and corruption. When Almeida's publication stood by him and refused to reveal their source, the government was forced to remove Almeida from the ECL and launched its own investigation into the source of the leak.[17]

On April 29, General Asif Ghafoor, the spokesman for the Inter-Services Public Relations (ISPR) expressed his institution's dissatisfaction over the government's probe into the leak that put the military and the civilian government on a collision course. "Notification on *Dawn* Leak is incomplete and not in line with recommendations by the Inquiry Board. "Notification is rejected," Ghafoor said on Twitter. When Ghafoor was writing that tweet, he probably had no idea it would anger a large number of people in Pakistan. Journalist Almeida's story came out at a particularly sensitive time for Islamabad, as its ties with New Delhi deteriorated following tensions on the Kashmir border. Indian Prime Minister Narendra Modi vowed in a speech that he would work to isolate Pakistan internationally due to its alleged support to Islamic militants in Kashmir. Pakistani establishment never allowed controlling the hydra of intelligence agencies to introduce security sector reforms, and fit it to the fight against radicalization, terrorism and jihadism. Consequently, the ISI strategies became militarized and became a tool of miltablishment to harass politicians and those who write against the corruption of military Generals. Scholar Frederic Grare (18 December 2015) noted some aspects of the business of military establishment in his well-written paper:

"Despite more than eight years of continued civilian power, Pakistan can be labeled as a transitional democracy at best. True, the country has experienced two successive and relatively democratic elections in February 2008 and May 2013, and the mainstream political parties--essentially the Pakistan Muslim League Nawaz faction (PML-N) and the Pakistan People's Party (PPP)--are no longer willing to let themselves be played off the other by the military, thereby limiting the margin of manoeuvre of the security establishment...........Today, as much as in the past, "operations against dissenting politicians, objective intellectuals, and other activists, are still carried out through systematic harassment, disinformation campaigns, fictitious trials, kidnap, torture, and assassinations", as demonstrated by the de facto genocide in Baluchistan."[18]

The continuous militarization and Talibanisation of society, and instability led to the catastrophe of disintegration and failure of the state, which was further inflamed by the US so-called war on terrorism, and involvement of NATO forces in Afghanistan. Pakistan's weak and unprofessional diplomatic approach towards Afghanistan prompted a deep crisis, including the closure of trade routes and a diplomatic impasse. According to the Constitution of Pakistan, every democratic government is answerable to the people of Pakistan. But in reality, they are actually answerable to the Army headquarters in Rawalpindi. Every single Prime Minister in Pakistan can only do his or her job smoothly if they completely surrender defense, interior, strategic decisions and foreign policy to the Army. It means the rules for civilian governments are pre-decided and they have been told to go by the book and not cross the red-lines defined by the defense establishment. This makes it a "State within a State '' that, instead of ruling the country from the front, prefers that the politicians and civilian governments implement their decisions and exercise power. On 22 September 2015, I put in writing that radicalized elements within the army can facilitate the access of Taliban, ISIS and Lashkar-e-Toiba to steal material for dirty bombs. My predictions became a reality when military intelligence and ISI arrested Dr. Wasim Akram and Brigadier Raja Rizwan (retd), who the ISPR described as an employee of a "sensitive organization. Dr. Wasm was working as a nuclear scientist at the Kahuta Nuclear Research Labs, Pakistan's main uranium enrichment facility.[19]

Over the last two decades, the role and scale of Pakistan's intelligence agencies grown over and above their prescribed functions, to the degree that their operations, often undercover and at odds even with each other, have earned them the repute of being a "State within a State". In most parts of the country, intelligence information collection faced numerous difficulties since the Taliban and other militant groups returned to important strategic locations. Having faced serious difficulties in dealing with insurgent forces in Baluchistan and Waziristan, the agencies started translating their anger into the killing and kidnapping of innocent civilians with impunity. They needed to adopt a professional mechanism in countering insurgency in Waziristan. The way intelligence operated over the past decades was not based on traditional or cultural patterns. Instead of tackling national security challenges, the ISI, along with Military Intelligence (MI) and other units, mostly concentrated on countering democratic forces within the country[20]

On 06 October 2016, Dawn newspaper reported an unprecedented warning of the civilian government to the military leadership of a growing international isolation of Pakistan and sought consensus on several key actions by the state. "First, DG of ISI Gen Rizwan Akhtar, accompanied by National Security Adviser General Nasser Janjua, was instructed to travel the four provinces with a message for provincial apex committees and ISI sector commanders. The message warned that military-led intelligence agencies must not interfere when law enforcement acts against militant groups that were banned or until now considered off-limits for civilian action. Second, former Prime Minister Nawaz Sharif directed that fresh attempts be made to conclude the Pathankot investigation and restart the stalled Mumbai attacks-related trials in a Rawalpindi anti-terrorism court. Those decisions, taken after an extraordinary verbal confrontation between Punjab Chief Minister Shahbaz Sharif and the DG ISI, appeared to indicate a high-stakes new approach by the PML-N government". Dawn reported. However, during the meeting, Gen Akhtar offered that the government should arrest whomever it deems necessary, but Shahbaz Sharif told Gen Akhtar that when action is taken against certain groups by civilian authorities, military intelligence worked behind the scene to set the arrested free. Dawn reported[21]

In July 2019, Prime Minister Imran Khan on his official visit to the United States admitted the presence of 30000-40000 armed terrorists in his country. The agencies established links with fundamentalist parties such as the Jamaat-i-Islami and its offshoots, the Tablighi Jamaat and Markaz Dawa-al Irshad. This interaction also allowed the Islamic fundamentalist parties in Pakistan to extend influence over armed forces personnel. The U.S. Country Reports on Terrorism described Pakistan as a "Terrorist safe haven" where terrorists are able to organize, plan, raise funds, communicate, and recruit fighters, while the ISI, has often been accused of playing a role in major terrorist attacks across India including terrorism in Kashmir. President Hamid Karzai was regularly reiterating allegations that militants operating training camps in Pakistan used it as a launch platform to attack targets in Afghanistan. Pakistan's relations with Afghanistan have been in strain due to the former Chief Executive General Musharaf's short-sighted policies. The General shamelessly genuflected to the United States demands of it's so called war on terrorism, and accepted all terms and conditions of allowing US and NATO forces to bomb Afghanistan from their bases inside Pakistan. By virtue of Musharraf's short-sighted policies, Pakistan was pushed into the Afghan quagmire. Pervez Musharraf came under instant U.S. and NATO pressure to act against Al-Qaeda leader Osama bin Laden, who was hiding in Pakistan. In an interview aired by a private channel in 2018, Mr. Musharaf acknowledged that terrorists were trained in Pakistan. "We trained the Taliban and sent them to fight against Russia. Taliban, Haqqani, Osama bin Laden and Zawahiri were our heroes then," he said.

The arrest of Afghan Ambassador Mullah Abdul Salam Zaeef by the ISI military units further caused misunderstanding between the people of Afghanistan and Pakistan. The ISI committed war crimes in Afghanistan and Waziristan. Former Afghan Ambassador Mullah Zaeef was arrested and handed over to US agencies by Pakistani ISI. He was humiliated by the CIA in the presence of ISI in Islamabad. John F. Burns 04 January 2002) published a detailed story of his humiliation and torture in New York Times. Pakistani analyst Ayaz Amir (Daily Dawn. 22 September 2006) also noted some aspects of his painful instant:

"We know, to our lasting shame, how our overlords, dazzled by American power, and afraid of God knows what, handed over the ex-Taliban ambassador, Mullah Abdus Salam Zaeef, to the Americans in January 2002—in violation of every last comma of international law. But until now we have not been privy to the details: how exactly did the handing-over take place? Now to satisfy our curiosity, and perhaps outrage our feelings, comes Mullah Zaeef's own account, published in Pashto and parts of which have been translated into Urdu by the Express newspaper. To say that the account is eye-opening would be an understatement. It is harrowing and mind-blowing. Can anyone bend so low as our government did? And can behavior be as wretched as that displayed by American military personnel into whose custody Zaeef was given? On the morning of 02 January, 2002, three officials of a secret agency arrived at Zaeef's house in Islamabad with this message: "Your Excellency, you are no more excellency." One of them said no one can resist American power or words to that effect. "America wants to question you. We are going to hand you over to the Americans so that their purpose is served and Pakistan is saved from a big danger." Zaeef could have been forgiven for feeling stunned. From the "guardians of Islam" this was the last thing that he expected, that for the sake of a few "coins" (his words) he would be delivered as a "gift" to the Americans. Under heavy escort he was taken to Peshawar, kept there for a few days and then pushed into his nightmare. Blindfolded and handcuffed, he was driven to a place where a helicopter was waiting, its engines running. Someone said, "Khuda hafiz" (God preserve you).[22]

Ayaz Amir also reported his painful journey, and noted Pakistan's constraints as well. This was Pakistan's bigger mistake that changed the attitude of every Afghan about the country. Mullah Abdul Salam Zaeef, the Taliban Government's Ambassador to Pakistan in his book "My Life with the Taliban" has described his heartbreaking story: "When we arrived in Peshawar, I was taken to a lavishly-fitted office. A Pakistani flag stood on the desk, and a picture of Mohammad Ali Jinnah hung at the back of the room. A Pashtun man was sitting behind the desk. He got up, introduced himself and welcomed me. His head was shaved — seemingly his only feature of note — and he was of an average size and weight. He walked over to me and said that he was the head of the bureau. I was in the devil's workshop, the regional head office of the ISI. He told me I was a close friend —a guest —and one that they cared about a great deal. I wasn't really sure what he meant, since it was pretty clear that I was dear to them only because they could get a good sum of money for me when they sold me. Their trade was people; just as with goats, the higher the price for the goat, the happier the owner. In the twenty-first century there aren't many places left where you can still buy and sell people, but Pakistan remains a hub for this trade. I prayed after dinner with the ISI officer, and then was brought to a holding-cell for detainees.........Finally, after days in my cell; a man came, tears flowing down his cheeks. He fainted as his grief and shame overcame him. He was the last person I saw in that room. I never learnt his name, but soon after—perhaps four hours after he left — I was handed over to the Americans. Even before I reached the helicopter, I was suddenly attacked from all sides. People kicked me, shouted at me, and my clothes were cut with knives. They ripped the black cloth from my face and for the first time I could see where I was. Pakistani and American soldiers stood around me. The Pakistani soldiers were all staring as the Americans hit me and tore the remaining clothes off from my body. Eventually I was completely naked, and the Pakistani soldiers—the defenders of the Holy Qur'an—shamelessly watched me with smiles on their faces, saluting this disgraceful action of the Americans".[23]

The ISI established relationships with numerous groups and political organizations in Afghanistan, but its persisting policy inside the country caused distrust. The agency wants Indian intelligence to curtail its presence in Afghanistan but doesn't want to undermine its own networks. The ISI never tolerated the Indian RAW presence in Afghanistan, the reason that its role in managing several anti-India proxy networks was also unmistakable. On 07 May 2018, Javid Ahmad in his article revealed so many new things about the ISI role in Afghanistan:

"In Afghanistan, ISI's Afghan operations are undertaken by at least three units. The first is Directorate S, the principal covert action arm that directs and oversees the Afghan policy, including militant and terrorist outfits and their operations. The second unit is the Special Service Group (SSG), also known as the Pakistani SS, and is the army's Special Forces element that was established in the 1950s as a hedge against the communists. Today, some SSG units effectively operate as ISI's paramilitary wing and have fought alongside the Taliban until 2001. In other instances, SSG advisors have allegedly been embedded with Taliban fighters to provide tactical military advice, including on special operations, surveillance, and reconnaissance. In fact, encountering ISI operatives fighting alongside the Taliban in Afghanistan has become a common occurrence that no longer surprises Afghan and American forces. The third ISI unit is the Afghan Logistics Cell, a transport network inside Pakistan facilitated by members of Pakistan's Frontier Corps that provide logistical support to the Taliban and their families. This includes space, weapons, vehicles, protection, money, identity cards and safe passage. Such ISI support networks have been designed to break Afghanistan into pieces and then remold it into a pliant state. The objective is to complicate Afghanistan's security landscape and drive its political climate into an uncharted constitutional territory to create a vacuum, which inevitably places the Taliban in the driving seat. These support actions have visibly made the group more effective. However, the Pakistani mantra is that they maintain contacts with the Taliban but exercise no control over them".[24]

Chapter 3

The Director Generals of Inter Services Intelligence (ISI)

Pakistan's army has committed war crimes in Afghanistan in August 2021. The army has been killing every tribal and political leader in Afghanistan and Pakistan who criticize the racist approach of generals toward Pashtuns, Baloch and Sindhis since 2001. Why the Taliban and ISI military units killed 900 innocent Afghans, and why their wives and young girls were sexually abused by sex hungry generals' and officers? Why Amnesty International and Human Rights Watch demonstrated criminal negligence, and why they were not condemned openly? The United States has finally destroyed the Afghan Airforce shamelessly by ransacking helicopters, transport and military plans, and all military and intelligence centres. Amit Chaturvedi, of *Hindustan Times* in 31, 2021 quoted the daily Mail letter narrating the presence of those in the court who committed crimes: 'The Taliban used this tactic of issuing threats using the letters in villages when they were in power in Afghanistan more than 20 years ago. But this time, they are now being widely circulated in cities. This shows that the governing style of the insurgent group has hardly changed from its last rule, despite Taliban leaders portraying the group as moderate.'[1]

However, a Research Fellow of the Institute for Conflict Management, Ajit Kumar Singh noted 'fear among masses across Afghanistan, forcing thousands to run towards the Hamid Karzai International Airport in Kabul, to escape a dreaded future. Unsurprisingly, the Kabul Airport and its surroundings have since become the epicenter of violence'. When the ISI military Units were dragging 900 Afghans from their houses, blindfolded, and killed one by one with impunity, why Amnesty International and Human Rights Watch didn't yell about their pain. When the ISI units killed all 900 Afghans in Kandahar, Chaman and Helmand, and put their wives under lock and key for sexual exploitation, at what place were Amnesty International, and the British so-called human rights organizations to ask the ISI sex hungry units about the where-about of kidnapped young Afghan girls and children. Why they didn't yell for the lives of 900 innocent Afghans, why the US army and the NATO co-conspirators and atrocious forces remained uncommunicative, close-mouthed and unresponsive. Who will ask Pakistani army generals where and at what place they dumped bodies of 900 Afghans and where they have put under lock and key the wives and young girls. The army and its military units committed war crimes in Kandahar, Helmand, Chaman and Ghazni provinces.[2] Analyst and research scholar, Shaun Gregory (ISI and the War on Terrorism. Studies in Conflict & Terrorism Volume: 30 Issue-12, December 2007) in his paper highlighted the role of Pakistani ISI in the war against terrorism in Afghanistan and Pakistan:

"Pakistan's Directorate of Inter-Service Intelligence ISI plays an ambiguous role in the War on Terrorism. An important ally for Western intelligence with whom it has very close links, the ISI also has a long history of involvement in supporting and promoting terrorism in the name of Pakistan's geostrategic interests. However, the ISI's strategy deeply conflicts with that of the West, a point underlined by the resurgence of Al Qaeda and the Taliban almost six years after the War on Terrorism began. With grave new trends evident in Pakistan, reliance on the ISI is failing and a Western rethink of its intelligence strategy toward Pakistan is now imperative........ Notwithstanding these complexities, there is no question that the ISI was essential to the United States and the West in the early phase of the War on Terrorism. The ISI helped the United States to arrest many hundreds of suspected Al Qaeda and Taliban members, among them many leading Al Qaeda figures. These included Abu Zubaydah (captured 28 March 2002 in Faisalabad), Khalid Sheikh Mohammed (captured 1 March 2003 in Rawalpindi), Ahmed Ghailani (captured 26 May 2004 in Gujerat), Amjad Farooqi (killed 26 September 2004 in Nawabshah), and Abu Faraj Al-Libbi (captured 2 May 2005 at Mardan near Peshawar).63 The case of Khalid Sheikh Mohammed, the alleged mastermind of the 9/11 attacks, is particularly instructive. Sheikh Mohammed was tipped off and narrowly escaped arrest in Karachi in September 2002 and was finally captured in Rawalpindi."[3]

On 12 March, 2021 (ToloNews) journalist Haseeba Atakpal once more defined the role of ISI in the Afghan conflict and noted that Gulbuddin Hekmatyar travelled to Pakistan on the invitation of senator Siraj ul Haq, the leader of Jamaat-e-Islami where he had day-long meeting with the ISI officers. "He addressed a grand meeting of Pakistani religious scholars in the city of Lahore on 13 March," Humayoun Jarir authenticated. At least five Afghan politicians have travelled to Pakistan in less than five months with some of them arguing that Pakistan's approach towards Afghanistan has changed. "In our perspective, Pakistan will have an important role in peace for two reasons: First, Pakistan is an important neighbour to Afghanistan like Iran. Second, Pakistan has close ties with the Taliban," Jarir said. "We will soon achieve peace if Pakistan wants, but the fact is that the Taliban does not want peace, they act contradictory in their words and actions," said Abdul Rashid Ayoubi, a presidential adviser". The ISI has never been a friend of the United States and Afghanistan. Its friendship with all states is based on its own interests. Haseeba Atalpak noted[4]

In 2016, leaked documents exhibited Inter-Services Intelligence (ISI) officer in 2009 paid $200,000 USD to a terrorist group to pave the ground for a suicide attack on the America Central Intelligence Agency (CIA) base in Afghanistan. Documents obtained by a research institute at George Washington University in the United States reportedly showed the ISI funding to Haqqani Network's suicide attack on the CIA base in Khost province in Afghanistan. The documents indicated that the attack was conducted by a suicide bomber driving a vehicle laden with explosives in which seven CIA employees were killed and six others wounded. "During discussions at an unknown date between Haqqani, Salar, and an unidentified facilitator or facilitators, Haqqani and Salar were provided $200,000.00 to enable the attack," the cable noted.

The Pakistan army and its death squads were making things worse as they targeted civilian populations, particularly Pashtun and Baloch activists with impunity. These squads have killed prominent Pashtun and Baloch leaders but no independent investigation has been allowed to find out the real story behind these killings. Former terrorist leader and member of TTP spokesman Ehsanullah Ehsan revealed that the Pakistan army asked him to lead a squad. On 13 August 2020, he revealed that Pakistani authorities had given him a hit list of people who they would like to be killed in Khyber Pakhtunkhwa. In an audio, he claimed that after some time of his surrender he was given the list of prominent voices in order to facilitate Pakistan in eliminating rogue elements. Daily Times reported his confession audio, in which he admitted: "I was asked to lead a death squad and accept killing of the listed people from Khyber Pakhtunkhwa and Pashtuns from all walks of life including journalists. In the audio, he talked about his conversations with ISI and the parleys that took place. Ehsanullah Ehsan (Liaqat Ali) was a former spokesman of Tehreek-e-Taliban Pakistan (TTP) and Jamaat-ul-Ahrar. In April 2017, Inter-Services Public Relations (ISPR) Director-General Asif Ghafoor announced that Ehsan had surrendered himself to Pakistan's security agencies. In early February 2020, Ehsanullah claimed that escaped from the custody of Pakistani Agencies.[5] Journalist and Analyst, Kunwar Khuldune Shahid (The diplomat--April 20, 2020) documented important aspects of Ehsanullah Ehsan's mission:

"Military officials have claimed that Ehsan was an important counterterror asset who had been helping the military take down TTP hideouts across the country, especially in the former tribal areas along the Afghanistan border. The military and government officials have refused to comment on Ehsan, only confirming his escape initially, while claiming that "a lot" is being done in its aftermath. The Army aired Ehsan's confessional statement in April 2017, which was followed by an interview with Pakistan's top media house. However, the Geo TV interview was blocked from being aired by the Pakistan Electronic Media Regulatory Authority (PEMRA) over the "glorification of a terrorist." The aired trailer of the interview was deemed insensitive by many, given that the interviewee had taken responsibility for the killings of thousands of Pakistanis. The attacks Ehsan owned on behalf of the TTP and JA included bombings targeting religious minorities and marginalized Islamic sects. Among the most high-profile attacks claimed by Ehsan on behalf of the Taliban was the one aimed at now Nobel Laureate and education activist Malala Yousafzai in October 2012.......Ehsan recalls that many in the TTP and JA had left to join IS when the group first began to expand from the Middle East to South Asia. That resulted in multiple attacks across Pakistan being simultaneously claimed by the Taliban and the Islamic State. The former Taliban spokesman, however, believes that following the February deal with the United States, it is the Afghan Taliban who holds the most clout in the region as far as the militant outfits are concerned".[6]

The Sunday Guardian (06 September, 2020) also reported Mr. Ehsanullah Ehsan conversation with Taliban leader Mullah Wali-ur-Rahman about the secret mission of their fighters and suicide bombers. He mentioned of ISI Chief Shuja Pasha letter, in which he had invited TTP for a joint work: "Maulana Wali-ur-Rehman took a letter out of the envelope and gave it to me and told me to read it. I opened the letter and read it aloud. After doing so, Maulana Wali-ur-Rehman said to me, "You must have known why you were called in an emergency for this meeting." I smiled and said, "Yes, I know." The letter I read was written by the DG ISI, General Shuja Pasha to Maulana Wali-ur-Rehman Mehsud. In it, General Shuja Pasha made an offer to the TTP leadership that if the TTP gave up its armed struggle against Pakistan, the ISI would not only provide them with a safe passage against NATO forces in Afghanistan but also provide financial and military support in every possible way. In this letter, General Shuja Pasha also praised the strength and capabilities of the TTP and called the TTP a necessity for Pakistan.[7]

He wrote that we should work together to remove the misunderstandings between the Pakistan army and the TTP and work together to drive the great enemy US (America) and NATO out of Afghanistan. General Pasha had also written that if TTP accepted the demands, the TTP would not just be able to demonstrate its abilities in Waziristan but the whole of Pakistan would be open for the TTP and that the cadre of TTP and their children would be able to work in this country by getting education from educational institutions in Islamabad and Peshawar......In this detailed letter, General Shuja Pasha had repeatedly referred to the Indian "occupation" of and "atrocities" in Kashmir. He had written to Maulana Wali-ur-Rehman Sahib saying that his forefathers had fought many wars for the independence of Kashmir and had made many sacrifices because they were true and patriotic Pakistanis. He, in the letter, had added that he should also join the Pakistan army in the "Ghazwa-e-Hind" war against India, because the war against India is a true and just jihad against the real infidels and polytheists. He also mentioned some Pakistan-backed organizations (Lashker-e-Tayyaba and Jaish-e-Mohammad) who were fighting against India in Kashmir and said that despite all the international pressure, Pakistan army was helping them because they were fighting for Pakistan.[8]

Professor of American University, Stephen Tankel, (Domestic Barriers to Dismantling the Militant Infrastructure in Pakistan, September 2013) in his research paper documented Pakistan's sponsorship of Taliban and Sectarian terrorists groups, and noted how the ISI used these groups against India and Afghanistan. He also noted that by supporting the US war on terrorism in Afghanistan, the ISI established links with Al Qaeda and Taliban to destabilize the Karzai government. General Musharraf admitted in his interview with the Guardian newspaper (February 2015) that due to Karzai's close relationship with India, he had ordered the ISI to target his government institutions. Pakistan's sponsorship of terrorism in Afghanistan and India is not a new thing, its sponsorship of sectarian groups inside Afghanistan received worldwide criticism. Stephen Tankel noted:

"Pakistan played host to numerous militant groups during the 1990s. One way to understand the militant milieu at that time is to consider sectarian affiliation. Most groups belong to the Deobandi sect, which follows the Hanafi School of Islamic jurisprudence. The major groups emerged from or were tied to the Deobandi Jamiat Ulema-e-Islam (Assembly of Islamic Clergy, or JUI) as well as the robust madrassa (religious school) system associated with it. The largest and most notable of them included: Harkat-ul-Jihad-al-Islami (HuJI); Harkat-ul-Mujahideen (HuM), which splintered from HuJI, Jaish-e-Mohammed (JeM), which broke from HuM, Sipah-e-Sahaba Pakistan (SSP), and Lashkar-e-Jhangvi (LeJ), which initially formed as the militant wing of SSP before nominally splitting from it. Separately, Lashkar-e-Taiba (LeT) was the biggest and most significant group to emerge from the Ahl-e-Hadith movement, which is Salafi st in orientation. Strong divisions existed between LeT and the Deobandi outfit. Collectively, these entities are known as Punjabi militant groups, a moniker that derives from their being headquartered, and having their strongest support base, in Punjab, Pakistan's most populated and powerful province. Elsewhere, Tehreek-e-Nafaz-e-Shariat-e-Mohammadi (TNSM), formed by a dissident member of Jamaat-e-Islami named Sufi Muhammad in 1989, was based in Malakand and had a blend of Deobandi and Wahhabi leanings. Domestic Barriers to Dismantling the Militant Infrastructure in Pakistan Another way of understanding the militant milieu at the time is to consider activities by location. In addition to indigenous Kashmiri groups, during the 1990s the Pakistani security apparatus also backed a welter of Pakistani groups against Indian security forces in Indian-administered Kashmir. These included the Deobandi HuM, HuJI, and JeM, as well as the Ahl-e-Hadith LeT".[9]

M. Ilyas Khan (Uncovering Pakistan's secret human rights abuses, BBC News, Dera Ismail Khan, 02 June 2019), in his commentary on BBC website documented atrocities of Pakistan army in North Waziristan: "In May 2016, for example, an attack on a military post in the Teti Madakhel area of North Waziristan triggered a manhunt by troops who rounded up the entire population of a village. An eyewitness who watched the operation from a wheat field nearby and whose brother was among those detained told the BBC that the soldiers beat everyone with batons and threw mud in children's mouths when they cried. A pregnant woman was one of two people who died during torture, her son said in video testimony. At least one man remains missing. Local activists say more than 8,000 people picked up by the army since 2002 remain unaccounted for".[10]

General Hamid Gul was a defence analyst and Chief of ISI during the Zia regime (1987-1989). He was the architect of Afghan jihad and father of the Afghan Taliban. He was a supporter of Kashmiri Mujahideen, Chechen, Uighurs and Bosnian Mujahideen. In 1988, with the support of Osama Bin Laden, he formed Islamic Jamhoori Attehad against the Pakistan People Party. On 15 August 2015, he died of brain haemorrhage in Murry. On 12 March 2007, Gul marched alongside activists from the liberal democratic parties and retired former senior military officers against General Pervez Musharraf. In 2007, Benazir Bhutto wrote to General Musharraf about the involvement of General Hamid Gul, Chief of Intelligence Bureau (IB) Brigadier Ijaz Shah, the then Chief Minister of Punjab Chaudhry Pervaiz Elahi, then Chief Minister of Sindh Arbab Ghulam Rahim, in the terrorist attacks in Karachi. However, he was placed on US Global Terrorism list in 2008.

On 16 August 2015, DW news quoted a Pakistan's news channel indication that Hamid Gul was not dead; he was alive in the form of numerous jihadist organizations, including the Taliban, and in the Islamist narratives of the Pakistani state that have persisted since the 1980s Afghan War. Gul's role in spearheading an Islamist insurgency in Indian-administered Kashmir is also well-documented. New Delhi holds him responsible for diverting militants and arms from the Afghan war to Srinagar toward the end of his job as spy chief in 1989. India and Pakistan have fought two wars over Kashmir since their independence from Britain in 1947. Following his retirement, Gul became a security expert and could be seen on television defending both the Taliban and Kashmiri militants. He was frequently invited by the Islamist parties to their anti-West rallies. DW news reported.[11] Moreover, on 15 August 2015, BBC reported critics describing him as a delusional conspiracy theorist who had little regard for democratic politics, hard-liner supporters considered him a patriotic Pakistani:

"A self-styled master strategist, Gen Gul spent much of his time since retiring as a pundit propounding various conspiracy theories. Once a close ally of the American CIA, he became passionately anti-US. After the 11 September attacks, he was seen as a prominent apologist for Osama Bin Laden and the jihadi groups. He was seen as a hero by pro-army, right-wing clerics and politicians. His critics say he reflected an aggressive and often delusional military mindset. Gen Gul derived much of his significance from his brief two-year stint as director-general of the ISI. The late eighties were a crucial time in the region. The Afghan war against the Soviets was coming to an end and the Kashmiri insurgency against India was starting.

In Pakistan, Gen Gul's mentor President General Zia ul-Haq died in a mysterious plane crash in August 1988, paving the way for the first party-based national polls in eleven years. As Pakistan's chief spymaster, Gen Gul played a key role in influencing and shaping those events. His supporters credit him with diverting fighters, funds and guns from the Afghan Jihad to the Kashmir front. At home, he was accused of rigging the 1988 election by propping up a hardline Islamist alliance to prevent Benazir Bhutto from coming into power". BBC reported.[12]

Analyst Shekhar Gupta (25 May 2018) noted his love for anti-India elements in 1987 when Zia-ul-Haq named him as Chief of ISI. After Zia's death, Bhutto detested him as much as he hated her. The previous year, he had masterminded the raising of Islamic Jamhoori Ittehad (IJI) to keep her out of power. But even now, he was too powerful for her to remove as ISI chief. That opportunity came the following year. With Zia gone, and the new chief of the army staff (Mirza Aslam Beg) way more reckless and stupid, Gul had a free run. For the first time, he threw the might of Pakistani army regulars to fight alongside the Mujahideen and defeat the army of Najibullah after the Soviet withdrawal. This was a disaster. Mr. Shekhar noted. One more personality of the same valour and resilience was General Javed Nasir, Director General of the Inter-Services Intelligence (ISI), and an active member of Tablighi Jamaat in Raiwind Lahore, where he had established different intelligence unites for intelligence information collection from different parts of Pakistan. He used Tablighi Jamaat as an international spy campaign across the world. In the military circles, Maj-Gen. Nasir was described as a "moderate person" who rediscovered the Islam in 1986 during the midst of the Russian war in neighbouring Afghanistan. In 1989, he was appointed as Director-General of Frontier Works Organization (FWO).[13]

On 14 March 1992, Prime Minister Nawaz Sharif appointed Lt-Gen Nasir as the Director-General of the Inter-Services Intelligence (ISI) against the recommendations and wishes of General Asif Nawaz, then-Chief of Army Staff. In April 1992, Lt-Gen. Nasir became an international figure when he played a major role in amalgamating the scattered Afghan mujahedeen groups when the power-sharing formula was drafted. He also trained Afghan and Pakistani Mujahideen and sent them for fights against the Serbian army in Bosnia. From Jalalabad Airport, the Pakistan army and the ISI were transporting Afghans to Bosnia. In 1992–93, Nasir defied the UN arms embargo placed on Bosnia and Herzegovina when he successfully airlifted the POF's sophisticated anti-tank guided missiles, which ultimately turned the tide in favor of Bosnian Muslims and forced the Serbs to life the siege much to the annoyance of the U.S. government. In 2011, the International Criminal Tribunal for the former Yugoslavia demanded the custody of the former ISI director for his alleged support of the Inter-Services Intelligence activities in Bosnia and Herzegovina to Muslim fighters of Bosnia against the Serbian army in the 1990s, the Government of Pakistan refused to hand Nasir to the UN tribunal, citing poor health. The ISI role in Bosnia, Afghanistan and India is seen by military and intelligence experts a destructive and shameful.[14]

Pakistan Press International on 15 May 2005, reported the PPP reference against the DG ISI Lieutenant General Javed Nasir for financial bungling and compromising national secrets, with the National Accountability Bureau (NAB). Through its counsel Shah Khawar, the PPP asked Chairman of the NAB to investigate press reports Javed Nasir' involvement in defalcation of bank loans, committed financial irregularities and compromised national secrets. PPI noted. However, Pakistan Press International noted his involvement in loan default and other cases. The PPP contended that the ex-ISI chief was investigated for unpaid loans and alleged involvement in drugs by the NAB, but the investigations were halted by the government. PPI noted.[15]

The Kargil crisis was initiated by the ISI and General Musharraf in 1999. G Parthasarathy (Rogue army runs the show-11 January, 2003, The Pioneer) noted some aspects of the ISI role in conflicts in South Asia: "Despite protestations of innocence by General Musharraf, the ISI still deals with these parties more or less as natural allies. After ousting Ms. In 1991, the army funded the opposition alliance that brought Mr. Nawaz Sharif to power. Mr Sharif himself entered politics as a protégé of General Zia.....
The role of the ISI in spreading Islamist terror across the globe has come into sharper focus since the commencement of America's war on terrorism. Despite denials, it is now established that the ISI sent senior officers, soldiers and ex-servicemen to sustain and fight alongside the Taliban regime. The ISI also actively connived with the Taliban in supporting terrorist groups ranging from the Chechens to the Islamic Movement of Uzbekistan in Central Asia and Abu Sayyaf in the Philippines. Former ISI Chief General Javed Nasir has now revealed that the Americans had sought his ouster in 1993 because he secretly arranged for the airlift of anti-tank missiles and other weaponry to Bosnian Muslims in violation of United Nations sanctions".[16] Director-General of the Inter-Services Intelligence (ISI), Lt Gen Zaheerul Islam, was involved in politics by supporting Imran Khan

against Nawaz Sharif. "I was told to step down and go home. I said whatever you want to do, do it I will not resign from the office of the prime minister," Nawaz Sharif said. Later on, he constituted a coup against Nawaz Sharif. In a detailed commentary on the involvement of ISI in the PTI Dharna, The Herald Magazine on 06 October 2015 highlighted the real game and the role of General Zaheer:

"There were rumours in the air. During the 126-day-long dharna by Pakistan Tehreek-e-Insaf (PTI) against the ruling Pakistan Muslim League–Nawaz (PMLN), there were murmurs of a coup d'état. Other than General Shuja Pasha, the former intelligence officer who is known to be a close friend and supporter of PTI Chairman Imran Khan, the other name that was repeatedly brought up was that of Zaheerul Islam, the then director-general of the Inter-Services Intelligence (ISI). Allegedly, the two were conspiring to create a rift between Prime Minister Nawaz Sharif and Chief of Army Staff General Raheel Sharif. In the past, the premier had acted against generals whom he had differences with. It was expected that he would again act in a similar manner, under the presumption that the dharna had the general's backing. But the events did not play out as expected. Not exactly...Not everyone took from his experience. In an interview with the BBC in August 2015, Senator Mushahidullah Khan claimed that an audiotape obtained by the Intelligence Bureau was played during a meeting between Prime Minister Nawaz Sharif and Raheel Sharif in 2017, in which Islam could be heard giving instructions to raid the prime minister's office. According to the senator, when questioned by General Raheel Sharif, Islam confirmed that the voice was his own. Khan later clarified that he himself had not heard the tape. Never mind the fact that he kept referring to the ex-ISI Chief as Zahirul Islam Abbasi – the major general who had plotted to overthrow the Benazir Bhutto government in 1995, and who died six years ago – the damage had been done".[17]

General Javed Nasir and General Zaheerul Islam have been dancing from darkness since 1990s. Journalist Saleem Shahzad (Cracking open Pakistan's jihadi core Posted in Broader Middle East, 19-Aug-04, Asia Times) in his article uncovered suspicious activities of the jihadist core of Pakistan army, and its affiliation with jihadist terrorist organizations. He also unmasked the jihadist core support to Lashkar-e-Toiba and other extremist groups that fought jihad in Kashmir and Afghanistan:

"The recent arrest of two top Pakistani jihadis, Maulana Fazalur Rehman Khalil and Qari Saifullah Akhtar, marks the beginning of the end of an era that started in the mid-1980s when the dream of an International

Muslim Brigade was first conceived by a group of top Pakistan leaders. The dream subsequently materialized in the shape of the International Islamic Front, an umbrella organization for militant groups formed by Osama bin Laden in 1998 and loosely coordinated by the Lashkar-e-Toiba (LET) of Pakistan. The arrests in Pakistan, made under relentless pressure from the United States, are aimed at tracing all jihadi links to their roots, which are mostly grounded in Pakistan's strategic core. As a former Pakistan Inter-Services Intelligence (ISI) operator and air force official, Khalid Khawaja, commented in the Pakistani press on the arrests of the two jihadis, "Every link of the arrested jihadi leaders goes straight to top army officials of different times. To keep the Arab movements under control, an al-Badr facility was organized in Khost province in Afghanistan. A dynamic law and master of arts graduate from Karachi University, Bakhat Zameen Khan, a member of the Jamaat-i-Islami (JI), a powerful religious party (who originally hailed from Dir in North West Frontier Province), was chosen as commander. He brought together all Arab jihadis at the facility, and linked senior ones to the ISI. Out of this camp, the Palestinian Hamas emerged, as well as the Arab-sponsored Moro liberation movement led by Abu Sayyaf. Khan was gradually weaned from the JI, and he exclusively allied al-Badr with the Hezb-i-Islami (HIA) led by Gulbuddin Hekmatyar, who today plays a key role in the Afghan resistance. As a result, the JI announced its separation with al-Badr when it launched the Hizbul Mujahideen militant movement in Kashmir in 1989. Al-Badr was kicked out of Afghanistan after the emergence of the Taliban in the mid-1990s because of its affiliation with the HIA. The ISI then set up new camps for al-Badr in Pakistani Azad Kashmir - that portion of Kashmir administered by Pakistan. In the Kargil operation of 1999, which almost brought Pakistan and India to all-out war, al-Badr fighters were initially sent by the Pakistan army to occupy Indian bunkers. Later, another ISI connection, the recently arrested Khalil, and his fighters battled side-by-side with Khan and the Pakistan army against Indian forces"[18]

On 30 September 2020, Express Tribune reported former Prime Minister Nawaz Sharif's warning to PMLN members that parliament had been turned into a "rubber stamp" as he had been told that somebody else was running it instead of the legislators. "How independent is the parliament you are a member of?" the PML-N supreme leader asked while virtually addressing a meeting of the party's Central Executive Committee from London. "We have come out of the slavery of the colonialism only to be enslaved by our own," he claimed. "We are not free citizens... ask yourself if you are a free citizen. The time is not far away when all these things will have to be accounted for. "The convicted former premier said he had decided not to live a life of "humiliation". "If the nation also decides that it has to take a stand against tyrants and oppressors, then the real change will come in a few months and weeks, not years."..."I received a message in the middle of the night," he added. The PML-N supreme leader said he was warned that there would be consequences if he did not step down and martial law could also be imposed. "I said go ahead with whatever you want to do but I won't resign." The newspaper reported.[19]

Daily Express Tribune's News Desk (November 13, 2020) reported Nawaz Sharif's attack against the miltablishment and ISI for their alleged plot to remove him from power. "I cannot blame the entire army for the lawlessness of a few individuals," he said while addressing via video link his Pakistan Muslim League-Nawaz's (PML-N) latest power show in Swat. The Newspaper reported. However, Express Tribune also reported Nawaz had for the first time named the army chief and DG ISI, saying that there was "a state above the state" in the country. "My only crime is to talk about the rights of common man, constitution and democratic principles," Nawaz said in today's address. He reiterated that his fight was not against Prime Minister Imran Khan but those "who brought him to power". Meanwhile, his daughter Maryam continued her rhetoric against the incumbent government and said it was a "wall of sand that needs one final push". The Newspaper reported.[20]

The ISI and military establishment's involvement in manipulating cases in High-courts and Supreme Court against political leaders. Islamabad High Court Judge (India.com News Desk, July 22, 2018) warned that the ISI had been attempting to control the country's judiciary to get favourable verdicts in different cases including that of Nawaz Sharif. He alleged that ISI has asked the Chief Justice of Pakistan to not let former Chief Minister Nawaz Sharif and his daughter Maryam Nawaz out of jail till the elections. While speaking at the Rawalpindi Bar Association, Islamabad High Court judge Justice Shaukat Siddiqui, said that ISI has been trying to control the judiciary. "Today the judiciary and media have come under the control of 'Bandookwala' (army). Judiciary is not independent. Even the media is getting directions from the military. The media is not speaking the truth because it is under pressure and has its interests," he said. "In different cases, the ISI forms benches of its choice to get desired results. The ISI had asked the chief justice to make sure that Nawaz Sharif and his daughter Maryam Nawaz should not come out of jail before the July 25 election. It also had asked him not to include me in the bench hearing the appeal of

Nawaz Sharif and his daughter in the Avenfield case. The CJ told ISI that he would make a bench of its choice," he said.[21]

The Mumbai attacks introduced the ISI Chief General Pasha as a controversial personality within the intelligence community of South Asia. In 2008, President Asif Ali Zardari had instructed Pasha to go to India to share intelligence after a request from Indian Prime Minister Manmohan Singh, but under pressure from the Pakistan military, the decision was, however, procrastinated within a few hours. Lt. General Pasha was involved in the memo gate controversy of 2011–2012, in which an American businessman, Mansoor Ijaz alleged that a senior Pakistani diplomat, former Ambassador Husain Haqqani, had asked him to deliver an unsigned memorandum to Admiral Michael Mullen, Chairman of the US Joint Chiefs of Staff at the time. After his retirement, General Pasha took a foreign job, which war criticized by politicians and parliamentarians.[22]

On 02 August 2018, Dawn Newspaper reported anxiousness of the three-member bench, headed by Chief Justice of Pakistan Mian Saqib Nisar, asked Defence Secretary retired Lt Gen Zamirul Hassan to furnish before the court no-objection certificates issued by the government to former army chief Gen Raheel Sharif and ISI Director General Ahmad Shuja Pasha for joining foreign jobs. "The apex court wondered how the top officers of the armed forces, who were at the helm of affairs and privy to sensitive information related to Pakistan's security, could accept jobs in other countries without completing the mandatory two-year period after retirement. The Dawn newspaper notes a senior government official on condition of anonymity revealed that Federal Government rules, as well as army rules, disallowed officers from accepting any employment without a minimum gap of two years after retirement or unless an NOC was issued by the federal government granting permission to join such services. The defence secretary, however, explained before the court that no officer in the armed forces held foreign nationality. Dawn reported court asked him whether or not Lt Gen Pasha accepted a job in the United Arab Emirates (UAE) just a few days after his retirement whereas Gen Sharif also accepted the post of Commander of Islamic Military Counterterrorism Coalition in the Kingdom of Saudi Arabia. CJP Nisar asked whether or not the ban on job without completing the two-year gap was also applicable to the two officers of the armed forces. The newspaper reported.[23]

The TTP commander Ehsanullah Ehsan (ISI chief begged for Taliban's help in Kashmir, September 6, 2020) who escaped from a safe house operated by the Pakistan army reveals how the Pakistan army and the ISI demanded help of various terror groups to target Indian and US forces. Ehsan wrote in The Sunday Guardian from an undisclosed location.[25] Former ISI Chief, General Asim Munir has also been playing the role of vandals and DAKO mafia group by using the ISI officer to terrify business communities in Pakistan. The News intervention in its heart-touching report about the corruption and vandalism of former Chief of Inter-Services Intelligence (ISI) exposed the real face of Pakistan army and the ISI's sarcastic Director Generals. The news Intervention reported a blatant bribery case of Gujranwala's District senior commander and former ISI Chief General Asim Munir who immediately demanded Rs. 90 crore in extortion money from the CEO of Master Tiles. Former ISI Chief Lieutenant-General Asim Munir had previously held the privileged positions of DG ISI and DG Military Intelligence (MI):

"In February 2017 during the Faizabad sit-in Lieutenant General Asim Munir was the ISI Director-General. Ironically, Major General Faiz Hameed, who was Deputy Lieutenant General at the time Asim Munir was responsible for the ISI's internal security wing, also faced this judgment, but was promoted lieutenant general and took over the reins of the ISI from Asim Munir. Lt. Gen. Asim Munir was unceremoniously removed from the prime post of ISI Director General and had to pass as the Gujranwala Corps Commander, thus earning the dubious distinction of being the ISI Chief for the shortest period. Asim Munir was now approaching his retirement and in order to earn quick money like other officers in the Pak Army, he contacted Sheikh Mahmood Iqbal, the managing director of Master Tiles, and demanded ninety crores of rupees. Dismayed by this blatant extortion request from Gujranwala Corps Commander Sheikh Mahmood Iqbal, CEO Master Tiles wrote a letter to Prime Minister Imran Khan Niazi, dated June 05, 2021, outlining all the details of his meeting with the lieutenant General Asim Munir and his subsequent request for Rs 90 crore in extortion money".[26] In his letter to Prime Minister Imran Khan Sheikh Mahmood Iqbal, CEO Master Tiles (News Intervention-June 5, 2021) described all the details of what the ISI Chief had told him and his subsequent request for Rs 90 crore in extortion money:

"Lieutenant-General Asim Munir sent me a message from a staff member, Colonel Ehtesham, last Thursday morning, saying he wanted to have lunch with me. I started from a meeting with Japanese importers and went to the cantonment to meet him (Asim Munir). I was offered good food, salmon fish cooked with broccoli and olive oil, among other delicacies. As we sipped black coffee with luxurious Cuban cigars, Lt. Gen. Asim Munir said he discovered that the executive range of our bathroom tiles was being smuggled to the Central Asian countries of Tajikistan and Uzbekistan via the Wakhan corridor in Afghanistan. He then said billions of rupees were being lost in taxes to the national treasury. Of course, this was all a plot to trap me, "New Intervention reported. Sheikh Iqbal complained: "... they seized two of our company's trucks in Peshawar on the Afghan border ... this seizure was carried out in the same way that the anti-narcotics force seized 20 kg fake heroin from the car of Rana Sanaullah, who is a leader of the Pakistan Muslim League. (Midday). Asim Munir told me that in political, commercial and espionage operations, perception is more important than reality, and if a perception is imprinted in people's minds that Master Tiles is involved in smuggling, then our share price would fall on the stock markets. I asked Lieutenant-General Asim Munir in a trembling voice what he wanted from me. "Lieutenant General Asim Munir said he wanted five million seven hundred thousand dollars, which equals ninety crore rupees in Pakistani currency. Asim said that if I transferred the money to his bank account in Macau, he would help me smuggle tiles to Central Asia, because Senior Commander Peshawar was his roommate and roommate... ", explained the Sheikh. Mahmood Iqbal in his letter. "... if necessary, in order to save my business, I agree to give this kind of money to Lt. Gen. Munir, but how long can we feed these little Fauji Asim snakes." They trample on the constitution every time. Sometimes they torture journalists Asad Ali and Matiullah Jan, other times, through Papa Jones, they set up a smuggled-funded business empire on the Pakistan-Iran border. I ask you to help me with this problem, otherwise I will move my whole business setup to Dhaka. But then you will have to handle a five thousand crore jobless people in Pakistan. After this incident, I understood that a man loves his self-esteem more than his homeland. The dastardly Satanism and the arrogance of power in those ugly eyes is unbearable. Sometimes when I sleep, this anger wakes me up at night and I have to take some water with aspirin, "said Sheikh Mahmood Iqbal, CEO of Master Tiles in his letter to Imran Khan Niazi". News Intervention reported.[27]

The flagrant and barefaced abrupt retirement of former ISI Chief General Rizwan raised many questions including his brother's illegal business and corruption. General Rizwan abruptly requested for early retirement. In his letter to the army quarters, he asked for "premature release". General Akhtar, replaced by Lt Gen Naveed Mukhtar as Director General (DG) ISI, was posted as President of the National Defence University. The JUI-F's Senator Hafiz Hamdullah said was there any political party which could ask why a seasoned senior general opted for early retirement and what the reasons behind this move were. On 07 October, 2017, in his Tweet, Hashim Azam called Lt Gen Rizwan Akhtar as a "butcher of hundreds of Mohajirs & a corrupt General. He should be arrested & trial on Mohajirs killings & corruption". Prominent journalist and writer, Rauf Klasra claimed that "his brother Air Commodore Imran Akhtar who was appointed as Director Procurement and Logistics Department in PIA was also involved in the deal of a PIA aircraft A-310 which resulted in a loss of Rs 500 million". Similarly there are rumors that as DG Rangers Sindh General Rizwan Akhtar was also involved in corruption amounting to billions, though no evidences have been brought so far but his early retirement has raised concerns. Daily Dawn (Military rejects speculation about ISI chief, Baqir Sajjad Syed, 23 February, 2021) reported military spokesman General Iftikhar Babar's clarification that Director General of Inter-Services Intelligence (ISI) Lt General Faiz Hameed will not be changed in near future.[28]

Chapter 4

The ISI, Military Establishment and an Inefficacious Intelligence Infrastructure

There is no paucity of foreign spies within the ranks and column of Pakistan army but newspapers are afraid of reporting such stories. From Brigadier Ali Khan to General Musharraf and General Raheel Sharif, dozens of high ranking officers and Generals of the army have been on payroll of foreign states to further their agendas since 1980s. General Musharraf not only sold his country's nuclear secrets, but sold Afghan and Pakistani citizens to the United States in low-price. General Raheel Sharif killed innocent children and women in Waziristan to delight his American masters, while now kills children and women in Yemen shamelessly to delight Saudi Masters. In 2019, BBC reported prosecution of a Pakistani General to life for spying for foreign intelligence, and also gave life sentences to a brigadier and a civilian official who spied for the United States. "The trio were charged with espionage and leaking "sensitive information to foreign agencies". However, most observers would naturally point to the CIA. Lieutenant General Javed Iqbal (retired) will serve 14 years of "rigorous imprisonment"a life term in Pakistan. Lt Gen Iqbal held key positions in the military during his active service, including the Director-General of Military Operations, which is responsible for planning and executing all operations inside and outside of Pakistan. Brigadier Raja Rizwan (retired) was given a death sentence, as was Wasim Akram, an official who worked for a "sensitive" organization which has not been named". BBC reported.[1]

On 19 March 2012, the News International reported the relationship of ISI with the military dictatorship in Pakistan and mentioned it as a state within state. However, the newspaper portrayed Intelligence Bureau and FIA as hunting agencies against political opponents. The ISI is supporting terrorist organizations in Afghanistan and South Asia. Lt Gen Rizwan Akhtar was appointed as as DG ISI at a time of great opposition to ISI for its illegal interference in politics.[2] Daily the Nation Pakistan in its report noted accusations against the agency for supporting the PTI-PAT long march on Islamabad to pressurize or oust Prime Minister Nawaz Sharif, and made controversial its operational mechanism. Due to the fear and hopelessness surrounding most quarters, very few sincere and meaningful calls for reform in the ISI were ever made. The Nation reported.[3] Masud Ahmad Khan, (Targeting state institutions, the nation April 05, 2021) in his analysis of the ISI wrong-doing and its terror networks in Afghanistan, noted ISI as unsophisticated intelligence agency. Operating for the GHQ as a proxy group, the ISI never developed professional approach to national security. The News International also noted human rights violations and power abuse of these agencies:

"Pakistan, undoubtedly, needs an efficient intelligence infrastructure and efficiency in intelligence means secrecy. The issue, therefore, really boils down to determining the ideal blend of secrecy and at the same time managing to keep the ISI, the IB and the FIA from becoming a 'state within a state'. How can democracy impose appropriate checks and balances on Pakistan's intelligence outfits? The very first step is enabling legislation. The very first principle to be adopted is the separation of intelligence agencies on the basis of geographical responsibilities-military intelligence for all external intelligence and strictly civilian intelligence agencies for the internal sector. After a formal separation of intelligence agencies on the basis of geography, the three agency-related issues are: their budgets, their operations and their assessment/accountability. Then come checks and balances. There are three possible types of checks: parliamentary, administrative and judicial. In a system of parliamentary checks there are two models: the UK has a unilateral model which was established by the Intelligence Services Act 1994 whereby the Intelligence and Security Committee of parliamentarians monitors "the expenditure, administration and policies" of all intelligence agencies. The US has a multilateral model in which the Executive Branch, the US Senate and the US House of Representatives each have its own mechanism that oversees each and every aspect of intelligence work. Checks and balances have to be at two different levels-an internal mechanism of the agency and then one or more external oversight committees. There are generally two types of parliamentary control: the US practices 'functional oversight' whereby there is usually an adversarial relationship between the agency and the parliamentary oversight committee. The UK, on the other hand, has 'institutional oversight' where there is more of a cooperative relationship between the agency and the parliamentary oversight committee. Parliamentary oversight committees, once formed based on legislation, then exercise control through tasking of the agency, the agency's financial matters, and it's staffing and finally assessing effectiveness."[4]

Senator Farhatullah Babar once said "three years ago, there were internment centres only in ex tribal areas. Many who disappeared ended up in these centres. After the merger these Guantanamo bay prisons are all over the province. Why? Despite merger ex-tribal areas under military control and closed to visitors, outsiders. Why? Disappearance and torture are part of the design to curb dissenting voices particularly those critical of state security polices and the military's intervention in politics. Change policies, change realities, change misplaced notions about yourself to change perceptions of dissenters. Condemn state brutality against peaceful Janikhel Peace March Islamabad. All they demand is peace and implementation of an agreement with them. Neither demanding resignations nor expulsion of foreign envoys. Demanding only peace & end to militants sanctuaries. What's wrong with that? Khushal son of outspoken senator Usman Kakar tells Radio Mashal "It seemed (his father) was grabbed by one person and hit on the head by another."

Prominent analyst and writer, Farhatullah Babar in 10 July 2012 moved a bill to control ISI or bring it under democratic control.[5] President Zardari also wanted to control ISI and its terrorist and extremist networks in South Asia that destabilized Afghanistan and India. No sooner as the bill was tabled, the ISI threatened President Zardari of consequence. On 10 July 2012, the News International reported ignorance of former Chiefs of ISI of the tabled bill. The PPP Chief of Intelligence Bureau, Dr. Shoaib Suddle exercised his power being a Director-General of the IB volunteered parliamentary oversight by drafting a law after examining the legislation in other democracies. No sooner than he was removed from the IB, the draft law prepared under his watch went missing:

"Among the salient features of IB draft law were included the method of appointment of DG IB, his tenure and powers, disciplinary proceedings against the rogue elements within the agency, preventive detention of the wanted persons and its length as well as notification to the detainees family, their legal rights, and the office of the ombudsman for dealing complaints against the agency officials. As far as the appointment of DG IB is concerned, the IB draft law proposed it to be "done by the President on the recommendation of the Prime Minister on such terms and conditions as the President may determine: Provided that the Prime Minister shall consult the Leader of the Opposition in the National Assembly before making a recommendation." And that the DG shall have fixed five-year tenure (not renewable) and be fully empowered in terms of recruitment, training, promotions, transfer, discipline and financial matters. On the question of performance, the IB draft law said the DG shall prepare and submit an annual report on the functioning of the Bureau to the prime minister by March 31 each year, also laying it before the both houses of the Parliament. The draft law also proposed an Ombudsman who shall be appointed for a fixed (and non-renewable period of five years) whose selection will be made in the manner done of DG IB. The Ombudsman office will investigate and resolve complaints from any person involving misuse of authority by the IB officials; resolve the service complaints of the IB officials; suggest changes in the administrative and operational practices of the Bureau; and prepare and submit an annual report on the functioning of the IB to prime minister."[6]

On 16 May 2014, the News International reported Intelligence Bureau's (IB) proposal of oversight law to watch performance of intelligence agencies. Pakistan's premier agencies, the ISI and IB, were formed through executive orders soon after the creation of Pakistan but were left without any laws to govern their actions.[7] However, on February 28, 2014, issue of national security policy was taken under consideration by the government and policy makers. Besides the capacity building of Criminal Justice System, police, civil armed forces and other law enforcing agencies for border management, a key institution to be called the Directorate of Internal Security (DIS), established under the NACTA to coordinate the intelligence and operational work of all civilian and military agencies to effectively counter-terrorism. "Thirty three civil and military operational and intelligence agencies needed to contribute centralized intelligence sharing and dissemination to the NISA," the policy paper said, adding that all the intelligence agencies would be bound to provide any intelligence solicited by the NACTA. One of the tasks of the DIS would be to provide early warnings to law enforcing agencies and other specific recipients with regard to violent-terrorist groups and organizations. The DIS would be led by a DG while its officers and personnel would come from the ISI, IB, MI, interior ministry, FIA, civilian armed forces and provincial police. The DIS is a specialized wings like Intelligence and Analysis Centre, National Internal Security Operational Centre, Operation Planning Centre, Centre Intelligence Team, Air Wing and Rapid Response Force for different operational and analytical functions of NACTA".[8]

On 25 July 2015, the News noted the realization of Mian Nawaz Sharif about the involvement of the former ISI chief in protests against the government. General Zaherul Islam was playing dirty game on behalf of ISI and military establishment to overthrow the Muslim League-N government on the pretext that it has clandestine relationship with India agency RAW. Although, much was speculated by the media including a report saying that the army chief had sought Prime Minister Nawaz Sharif's resignation, in reality, General Raheel was fully behind the secret game of Gen,. Zaheerul Islam. "Defence Minister Khawaja Asif named the former DG ISI for his alleged role in destabilizing the Nawaz Sharif government through the PAT-PTI sit-ins. Khawaja Asif said that General Zaheer had pushed up the 'London Plan' conspiracy against the government. In a TV interview, the minister said that the 2014 London Plan against the Nawaz Sharif government was the work of two former ISI chiefs — Lt General (retd) Shuja Pasha and Lt Gen (retd) Zaheerul Islam. According to the Defence Minister, Gen Zaheer had a grudge against the government for its stance on the Geo issue". Cold war, or tug of war between ISI, IB and FIA become institutionalized when the ISI and IB decided to probe financial corruption of FIA.[9]

On 28 February 2018, Umar Cheema of the News reported the decision of the establishment division to promote officers of the IB and ISI. Tariq Mahmood, Abu Nasr Shuja Akram and Shahid Hussain were IB officers whose promotion had been notified. Hasan Jamal, Sheikh Sheeraz Ahmed, Asghar Ali Awan, Shaukat Ali, Muhammad Siddique Khurram, Abid Imtiaz and Iftikhar Farrukh were from the ISI. They were from civilian cadre of the agency. Civilian officials of the ISI had moved Islamabad High Court in 2013 against slow promotions. On 01 May 2015, the News International reported a high-powered inquiry committee of the Ministry of Interior comprising, of officials from Inter-Services Intelligence (ISI) and Intelligence Bureau (IB) to probe the allegations of financial corruption and misuse of power against a number of officers of Federal Investigation Agency (FIA).[10] On 21 December 2014, Arshad Bhatti in his report argued that "the three leading intelligence agencies (Military Intelligence (MI), the Inter-Services Intelligence (ISI) and Intelligence Bureau (IB), were formed in 1947, 1948 and 1949........When months before the December 16, 2014 carnage, the National Intelligence Directorate was formed with over 30 agencies of various kinds, including MI, ISI, FIA and the IB, its outlook, approach and strategy were dominated and influenced by the ISI and MI". The News reported.[11]

The ISI launched two religious parties for the 2018 elections: Tehrik-e-Labyk Pakistan (TLP) and Allah-o-Akbar Party (AAP). Although neither

82

party won any seats in the National Assembly (NA), they made a significant dent in the baralevi-sunni and Wahabi (religious sects) vote bank of the PML-N in many electoral constituencies of Punjab as well as in other provinces. The IB was supporting differently but certainly had no choice but to support the Nawaz government against the army's engineered election. However, Rai Mansoor Imtiaz Khan noted disqualification of Nawaz Sharif on 28 July 2017 under the judicial dictatorship over the corruption charges against him and sentenced to prison along with his daughter, yet millions of people voted for him during the general election of 2018. On 16 October 2020, Vinary Kaura (Pakistani politics at a crossroads: The new opposition to Imran Khan and to the military establishment, Middle East Institute November 3, 2020) noted former PM's accusations against Chief of Army Staff, General Qamar Bajwa, and the Director of Inter-Services Intelligence (ISI), General Faiz Hameed, of stealing the PML-N's popular mandate:

"The military's interference in domestic politics is nothing new for Pakistan. What is new, however, in this country where the military has traditionally been treated as sacrosanct, is the denunciation of such interference by a mass movement and by figures as prominent as Sharif. Certainly, in the past, the opposition would not have thought to criticize the military in such direct terms in order to gain popularity and power, but anger and frustration have risen to a point where attacks on the shadow government that is the armed forces resonate with the feelings of many Pakistanis. From episodes like Sharif's speech, it is clear that battle lines are emerging in Pakistan. On one side stand Imran Khan, his government, and the armed forces that helped bring him to power. On the other, stands the opposition crystallized by the PMD and increasingly vocal in its condemnation of both Khan and military brass. Pakistan, it seems, is moving toward political deadlock...Even the apparently democratic regimes of the Pakistan Peoples' Party (2008-2013) and the Pakistan Muslim League-Nawaz (2013-2018) were vulnerable to the military's pressures. This was particularly reflected in the dismissal of Prime Minister Yousaf Raza Gilani on the flimsy charge of contempt of court and the disqualification of Prime Minister Nawaz Sharif on even flimsier charges. Gilani fell out of favour with the military following scandalous allegations that civilian leadership had requested American intervention to thwart a coup in the aftermath of the 2011 US raid in Abbottabad that killed Osama bin Laden (and embarrassed the Pakistani military). The generals publicly warned Gilani of "grievous consequences" for his criticism of them...and consequences there were".[12]

On 11 July 2013, the News International reported criticism of former Chief of the ISI against Musharraf, and intelligence infrastructure of Pakistan. He blasted General Pervez Musharraf for caving in before Americans, the political leadership for ignorance, indifference and its lack of a reading culture, all security and intelligence agencies for not performing diligently and journalists as being 'heavily bribed with money, women and alcohol' for launching campaigns against the ISI. General Pasha admitted before the commission that the ISI had brutalized many, even 'decent people' but explained there were now 'changes to its (ISI) mind-set, culture and methodology'. He told the commission that former PM Yusuf Raza Gilani's statement about a 'state within state' and asking who had given a visa to Osama bin Laden angered the army beyond imagination. The news reported.[13]The News International also reported the statement of Prime Minister Gilani in the National Assembly asking who had given a six-year visa to Osama bin Laden and his reference to 'a state within a state. 'The anger in the military over such unfair statements could not be described'. Harassment by ISI, media's suspicious activities and missing persons: Pasha accepted that agency's record was not without blemish, saying many 'decent people' had been harmed by some of its errors.[14] General Pasha said all the intelligence agencies must be held to account for their failure including Military Intelligence, Air Force Intelligence, Naval Intelligence, Intelligence Bureau, Criminal Investigation Department and the Special Branch.[15] None of the said agencies re-aligned their task in the aftermath of 9/11. Very little coordination exists for terrorism-related information sharing with military intelligence services, he disclosed. The police should have a comparative advantage with respect to internal security since it has tentacles down to the district level. The CID, Special Branch and the police have advantage over the ISI because of their spread, area coverage and local knowledge but nothing was done by them, he noted.[16]

Chapter 5

The ISI Atrocities, Military and Political Stakeholders, Crisis of Confidence and lack of Modern Intelligence Technique

Writing on Pakistani ISI is no longer a wearisome and laborious piece of work as great deal of information is available in newspaper, journals, and books. Any author, or journalist who wants to find out secret information in libraries, or archives, he must be aware of the fact that there is no intelligence operations files existed in archives in Pakistan. However, discussion about the military operations in FATA and Waziristan is also forbidden. Discussing the army and ISI illegal war in Waziristan is a crime. If we look at the process of election in 2018, the way intelligence agencies and the army with all speed managed the results reflected the influence of the army and agencies in politics. Scholar Rai Mansoor Imtiaz (14 November 2019) in his recent analysis elucidated the role of military and intelligence in the election process: "The military launched two far-right religious parties for the 2018 elections: Tehrik e Labyk Pakistan (TLP) and Allah-o-Akbar Party (AAP). Although neither party won any seats in the National Assembly (NA), they made a significant dent in the baralevi-sunni and Wahabi (religious sects) vote bank of the PML-N in many electoral constituencies of Punjab as well as in other provinces. It can be seen that TLP caused the defeat of the PML-N in many NA seats in Punjab since the margin of defeat was less than the votes polled by the TLP candidates". Pakistani intelligence agencies have been playing various political and sectarian roles instead of safeguarding security interests of the country since 1980s".[1] The key point that cannot be denied is the agencies have often supported the sectarian organization in elections.[2] There are multifarious agencies operating under the command of the military, political and bureaucratic stakeholders who scamper and whisk their horses on different missions to bring Gallus-Gallus[3.]

As the key providers of information relevant to national security threats, agencies are essential components of every state security system. The need for intelligence (Florina Cristiana Matei and Carolyn Halladay-2019) is a fact of life for modern governments. Few states take the view that they can dispense with a foreign intelligence service and none is sufficiently immune from terrorism or the inquisitiveness of its neighbours' to forgo an internal security service.[4] The fact is; intelligence is crucial to the survival of the state and the mandate of a security intelligence service defines the tasks that the service has to perform, and provides the guiding principles by which the service conducts its operations and measures effectiveness. In the wake of recent series of sectarian and terrorist attacks on civilian and military installations, and growing security concerns has been a wave of new security regulation and unlimited power aimed at expanding intelligence powers across the country.[5] The underwhelming development has been the authorization of preventive investigation powers in protecting domestic security. Dr. Julian Richards, an author of four books and a number of papers and book chapters on a range of security and intelligence issues have contributed a chapter on Pakistan's intelligence agencies in the book (The Image of the Enemy: Intelligence Analysis of Adversaries Since 1945), in which he reviewed some weak aspects of Pakistan's intelligence infrastructure that operates in different directions.[6] He also highlighted successful intelligence operations of ISI and IB in 1965 and 1971 wars, which have been warranted by Indian army generals, but he still believes that the ISI's operational mechanism needs more refinement:

"There is some evidence that a growing preoccupation with domestic affairs led to a damaging lack of resources allocated to military intelligence during the 1965 war with India. Over the ensuing years, the ISI continued to flourish under both civilian and military regimes and became very much the predominant intelligence actor in Pakistan. It involved itself increasingly in gathering intelligence on internal insurrections in Baluchistan, and the North West Frontier Province (now Khyber Pakhtunkhwa province), in orchestrating military and logistical assistance to proxy forces in Afghanistan and Kashmir, in helping to nurture the Taliban as a strategic force in Afghanistan, in establishing a network of spies and intelligence activities throughout India, and in interfering a domestic election within Pakistan, notably in 1990 when the situation was looking unfavourable to the military-bureaucratic centre of power. By the turn of the twenty-first century, the ISI had again become a strategic partner of the United States in the so-called war on terrorism, resuming its role of the 1980s, albeit on built on sometimes shaky level of trust".[7] Any civilian or military government that wants to professionalize its intelligence infrastructure, and prevent it from decaying, needs statecraft, which is comprised of economic power, and a strong military force and mature diplomacy. The case is quite different in India and Pakistan, where emerging contradictions in the state system, ethnic and sectarian divide, and failure of intelligence and internal security strategies generated a countrywide debate, in which experts deeply criticized the waste of financial resources by their intelligence agencies in an unnecessary proxy war in South Asia. The biggest Indian intelligence failure occurred in 1999 in the Kargil war between India and Pakistan, in which RAW failed to report infiltration of Pakistan army intelligence units into the region.

Indian analyst Prem Mahadevan in his research paper (2011) spotlighted important aspects of intelligence failures in Kargil war. He is on the opinion that Pakistani forces crossed Indian border while Indian intelligence was unable to spotlight their locations: "During the summer of 1999, India and Pakistan fought a 10-week limited war in Kargil, a remote area of Kashmir. Fighting broke out in May, when Indian troops discovered that a number of armed men had crossed the Line of Control (LOC) and entrenched themselves on the Indian side. Over the following weeks, the Indian army learned that these gunmen were not Islamist guerrillas, as it had first assumed, but Pakistani soldiers in Mufti. A security crisis erupted, with allegation of 'failure' being thrown at the Indian intelligence agencies."[8] The Mumbai attacks (2008) unveiled a number of terrorist tactics that prevailed in Pakistan. Those tactics and the way terrorists targeted civilians and the police were new to RAW and the IB. Once again, in Delhi, intellectual circles and policymakers began debating with the assumption that counterterrorism operations had been influenced by weak intelligence analyses in the country. They also raised the question of check and balance, while the bureaucratic and political involvement further added to their pain. The exponentially growing politicization, radicalization and sectarian divides within ranks of all Indian intelligence agencies, including RAW and the IB, and violence across the country painted a negative picture of the unprofessional intelligence approach to the national security of India.

The Kargil Review Committee found that human intelligence aspect of Indian intelligence agencies was weak. During the Kargil war, RAW succeeded in intercepting the telephone conversation between General Musharraf and his then Chief of General Staff Lt Gen Aziz, which provided crucial evidence to international media that the operation was being controlled from military headquarters in Rawalpindi. Experts perceived it as a major intelligence success. Moreover, the Kargil Review Committee also criticized military intelligence for its failure related to the absence of updated and accurate intelligence information on the induction and DE induction of military battalions, and the lack of expertise to spotlight military battalions in the Kargil area in 1998. After the 1965 and 1971 wars between Pakistan and India, the ISI succeeded in establishing intelligence networks across India to better understand the intention of a traditional enemy.

The perception that the agencies decide whatever they want without restricting themselves to the advisory role causing misunderstanding between the citizens and the state. Political rivalries of the ISI and IB, their poor coordination, sectarian and political affiliations, uncorroborated reports, and lack of motivation are issues that need the immediate attention of policy makers. Moreover, numerous intelligence committees like the Henderson-Brook Committee on the Indo-China war and India's defeat in 1962; B S Raghavan IAS Committee on the failure of intelligence during the 1965 Indo-Pak war; L P Singh Committee; K.S Nair Committee; the 1999 Kargil Review Committee; and the Ram Pradham Committee on the intelligence failure during the 2008 terrorist attacks in Mumbai have taken place after every big perceived intelligence failure. Notwithstanding the establishment of several investigation committees into the failure of intelligence in yesteryears, and the reform packages passed by parliament, the RAW, IB and military intelligence are still dancing to different tangos, and never been able to respond to a series of terrorist attacks (14 February 2019) in Kashmir. Janani Krishnaswamy (2013) in her research paper on the causes of Indian intelligence failure diverted public attention to the starting point of failures:

"Why do our secret intelligence agencies fail repeatedly? It is because of (a) lack of adequate intelligence, (b) dearth of trained manpower in the intelligence sector, (c) lack of proper intelligence sharing between the centre and the state, (d) lack of action on available intelligence, (e) the current state of political instability or (f) the lack of sensible intelligence reforms? In the aftermath of the terrorist attack at Dilsukhnagar in Hyderabad, India's secret intelligence agencies were subjected to an intense inspection. Heated political debates over the construction of the National Counterterrorism Centre (NCTC), a controversial anti-terror hub that was proposed in the aftermath of 26/11 attacks, was stirred up after five years. Are such organisational reforms sufficient to fix the problems of the intelligence community? Intelligence reviews committees and politicians constantly assess the performance of intelligence agencies and underline numerous failures within the intelligence system."[9]

Pakistan army and its intelligence agencies are facing the same challenges on domestic and international fronts. It spends huge budget on military buildup, and luxurious enjoyment of generals. The fund the military receives from the state budget is in addition to the revenue it gets from its large business operations. Notwithstanding being rich itself, the army continues to be a burden on the country's weak economy. Political instability is endemic to Pakistan with governments alternating between legitimacy and illegitimacy and political leadership propped by the Army, does not have a free hand. That kind of government has never been able to handle an economic crisis. Pakistani Writer and analyst Muhammad Taqi (13 March 2019) has painted an underwhelming picture the army role in politics in a nutshell: "The problem with the army's obsession with becoming the sole arbiter of national interest and security is that it has arrogated itself the right to dictate domestic and foreign policies to suit that rather nebulous creed in which Pakistan and Islam are somehow in perpetual danger and the army is the only saviour they have. These twin delusions of paranoia and grandeur are actually feigned and self-serving to justify the outfit's chokehold on the country and its resources"[10] Civilian intelligence agency (Intelligence Bureau) has been gradually neglected, and phased-down during the consecutive military rule. Military analysts Sanjeeb Kumar Mohanty and Jinendra Nath Mahanty (04 October 2011) in their research paper on the nexus of sectarian takfiri organizations and Pakistan army highlighted the evolution of ISI during the Zia military regime:

"The 1980s were the years when the CIA-ISI relationship blossomed, and during this period the ISI grew in strength and reach. Further, the realization the nuclear neighbors cannot fight a war without the possibility of its slipping out of control led General Zia to tap the mullahs and madrassas to wage a new covert war in India and Afghanistan". Religious movements, such as Jammat-e-Islami and Tablighi Jammat were allowed by Zia to operate inside army barracks. In fact, the imposition of martial law in Pakistan for the first time in 1958 under General Ayub Khan brought the ISI into political realm. Moreover, Ayub gave the ISI primacy amongst the other intelligence agencies in Pakistan, like the MI (Military Intelligence) and the IB (Intelligence Bureau) because it combined in the one agency the dual roles of internal and external intelligence. The ISI, however, concentrated more on internal rather than external intelligence for the first three decades.....Under Zia the ISI grew in size and strength in the power structure due to the dependence of the regime on intelligence and the Afghan operation. From being an implementer of policy, the ISI became the policymaker. In fact, the imposition of martial law in Pakistan for the first time in 1958 under General Ayub Khan brought the ISI into the political realm. Moreover, Ayub gave the ISI primacy amongst the other intelligence agencies in Pakistan, like the MI (Military Intelligence) and the IB (Intelligence Bureau) because it combined in the one agency the dual roles of internal and external intelligence. The ISI, however, concentrated more on internal rather than external intelligence for the first three decades. Till the seventies, the organization had a limited external agenda which was largely India-centric. This was because Pakistan had fought three wars with India and remained preoccupied with an Indian military threat to her national security"[11]

The military rulers acted like warlords and never thought about security sector reforms to make law enforcement agencies fit to the fight against anti-state elements, extremism and radicalization. They acted for the interests of the United States-criminalized trade and agriculture, supported Talibanization in society, and introduced culture of soldiers for sale in Middle East. The state fostering of surrogate militants to serve Pakistan's strategic interests in Kashmir and Afghanistan played a crucial role in the rise of transnational jihadism. Sanjeeb Kumar Mohanty and Jinendra Nath Mahanty in their paper also noted all weather relationship between the ISI and extremist organizations in South Asia, Afghanistan and Central Asia: "During the 1990s, several Kashmir-specific militant outfits were sponsored by Pakistan. The ISI helped create, mentor, finance and train outfits like Jaish-e-Muhammed (JeM), Harkat-ul-Mujahideen (HuM), Lashkar-e-Tayyeba (LeT) and several other shadowy extremist groups to fight a proxy war against Indian forces in Jammu and Kashmir, admittedly part of the larger Pakistani strategy to bleed India with thousand cuts....... At the end of 1995, it was reported that the ISI in collaboration with the Jammat-e-Islami (Pakistan's oldest religious-political party), was raising a Taliban type force consisting of young students from Pakistan with the sole purpose of fighting Indian forces in Jammu and Kashmir. From the 1990s, the LeT became the ISI's favourite terrorist outfit operating in Kashmir and in the rest of India.........During Musharraf's time, the infamous mullah-military alliance was strengthened even in the face of his growing unpopularity after joining the US-led war on terror. Since 9/11, the Pakistani military has tried to distance itself from militancy in Jammu and Kashmir under the intense US and international pressure. The militant groups that had long depended on ISI support described Musharraf's U-turn on Kashmir as a betrayal of their struggle for independence."[12]

Under Muhammad Zia-ul-Haq's leadership, the Inter-Services Intelligence (ISI) grew in strength and resources. The agency received further training from the United States in intelligence collection and technology use to effectively counter Russian intelligence in Pakistan. The agency concentrated more on internal rather than external intelligence for the first three decades-discouraged political forces and fostered sectarian mafia groups to protect its own interests abroad. In 1980s, during the Soviet presence in Afghanistan, the ISI's strength became more important for both Pakistan and the United States. The fact is they were on great mission to disintegrate union of the Soviet. Pakistan's army encouraged jihad to throw Russian forces out of Afghanistan, and promoted the interests of the United States and its NATO allies. The ISI got a chance to support its favourite guerrilla groups and co-ordinate the flow of foreign aid, including the recruitment of volunteers and graduates of local madrassas. Researchers and analysts Grant Holt and David H. Gray in their paper (Winter-2011) highlighted the role of ISI during the Zia regime:

"The Afghan war created a leviathan and powerful intelligence agency in the ISI while Zia mandated Islamic fundamentalism and Deobandism (a strict interpretation of the Hanafi school of Sunni Islam) into their shadowy ranks. With aid from the U.S. and a pivotal and violent struggle against the Soviets in Afghanistan, the ISI cultivated a relationship with extremists from across the globe, including al-Qaeda. While being forced to adhere to fundamental Islam from the Pakistani state, the ISI itself became recognized in the international system and feared within domestic society. Throughout the 1990s, the ISI maintained its relationship with extremist networks and militants that it had established during the Afghan war to utilize in its campaign against Indian forces in Kashmir. ...Many high-profile terrorist incidents, ranging from the September 11, 2001 attacks on New York and Washington to the July 7, 2004 subway bombings in London to the November 2008 assault on Mumbai, have had direct connections to individuals and groups operating in Pakistan (Ganguly and Kapur 47). The sponsorship and recruitment of terrorist and guerilla movements against the Soviets in Afghanistan is paramount when examining historic ties between terrorism and the ISI. However, the agency also took part in, and was responsible for, numerous international operations and violent acts across the globe."[13] The involvement of the military in operational mechanism and function of ISI adversely affected the agency's civilian reach. The agency later on was unable to assess the importance of civilian stratification and intelligence strength of neighbouring states. Normally, civilian intelligence is stronger than the military agency as its civilian roots enable it to manage its operational capabilities. Pakistan corrupt political culture forced the agencies to look at civilian population and government with scorn. They were inculcated that the job of national security is beyond the reach of civilian governments. Rajesh Bhushan (12 January 2019) has assessed the strength of ISI in his well-written analysis. He also estimated the strength of ISI and its annual budget, but management of the agency refused to diaclose the actual amount:

"Until 2018, Pakistan's Inter Service Intelligence (ISI) had around 6,000 people, which includes its handlers, agents and sources. According to German scholar Hein Kiessling, who represented the Hanns-Seidel-Foundation (Munich) in Pakistan from 1989 to 2002 said, "The (real) ISI budget is top secret, only a few people know the figure". "In fact officially the ISI budget today is between $300 and 400 million." According to Kiessling, the personnel strength of ISI is also considered as top secret. "During Zia-ul Haq's tenure it was estimated to be 20,000 men. In the 1990s and in the new millennium there were drastic reductions in personnel. "Therefore, it is now assumed that ISI's base strength is approximately 4,000. Higher estimates often encountered in literature and the press is grossly exaggerated." Hein Kiessling said changes in personnel policies came out in 2009 under the command of Pakistan Army chief General Ashfaq Parvez Kayani. "Today with the exception of six-seven two-star generals, the military personnel in ISI come from the Intelligence Corps of the army —a move that serves towards the professionalism of the service".[14]

Miltablishment used agencies against politicians and its critics to punish them for criticizing corruption of Generals and their cronies. They punished those who wrote stories of forced disappearances, and torture of innocent writers. The ISI professional approach of intelligence mechanism never improved due to its prolixity of involvement in politics. Dr Bidanda M Chengappa noted some aspects of ISI relationship with Afghan Mujahedeen: "Thereafter from the early 1980s the ISI provided strong support to the Afghan mujahedeen against Soviet occupation forces there and ultimately proved successful due to the material resources provided by the US. It is aptly stated that the victory was possible on account of "American weaponry and Afghan bravery".[15]The import of the ISI involvement in Afghanistan is that the ISI developed close working relations with the CIA and Saudi intelligence organizations. More significantly the

ISI developed enormous hands-on expertise to wage a proxy war in terms of handling logistics on an international scale, training Afghan guerillas in low intensity conflict operations (LICO) and intelligence-gathering activities under hostile conditions. The ISI has developed close linkages with various Islamic fundamentalist organizations like the Lashkar-e-Toiba and Harkat-ul-Mujahideen. The ISI funds their activities like para-military training and procurement of arms to wage are against the Indian State. This ISI nexus with fundamentalist parties provides the agency with manpower which can be mobilized as 'street power' to agitate against or support a political party which has taken a decision with national, regional, political, social or economic ramifications. To that extent, the ISI has some leverage to influence decision making owing to its ability to operate through fundamentalist parties"[16]

The ISI is no doubt an incompetent intelligence agency, and is a shame of the nation, but military and political leadership used it against political opponents. This policy of both political and military establishments destroyed the professional capabilities of the agency. The agency was often used against IB and used against journalists and human rights activists, and then used against politicians and FIA. In his research paper, Dr Bidanda M Chengappa has argued that ISI was mainly controlled and used by military against democratic government in Pakistan. There are articles and research papers in international press about the business of ISI and its darling organizations in Afghanistan, Iran and India: "Apparently the ISI is controlled either by the military or the political leadership depending on whichever is in power. The DG-I, as the head of the ISI is known, is an appointment made by the Prime Minister in consultation with the Chief of Army Staff (COAS). The DG-I reports to the Prime Minister considering the ISI has a political section to handle internal intelligence duties. However the army appears to dictate the policy towards India even when the country has an elected leader. To that extent it would be appropriate to state that the PM has a degree of control over the ISI's involvement in internal affairs which the Chief of Army Staff oversees the external role of the agency. The rationale for the evolution of the intelligence service into an extra-constitutional power center is multi-faceted and encompasses military strategy, martial law, involvement in the clandestine nuclear programme, covert support to para-military operations in the Afghan jihad and linkages with fundamental parties. While some of these causes have internal dimensions some are completely external".[17]

In books and newspapers, there are stories about the failure of intelligence agencies in Pakistan to undermine terrorism and extremism. Recruitment from business community, wealthy and landlord societies, generals and politicians for intelligence agencies prompted bureaucratic culture that direct policy maker on wrong direction. Intelligentsias and political circles have often pointed to the fact that involvement of the agency in political confrontations badly affected its professional credibility. Some circles are trying to radicalize agencies, but the big concern is that all military, civilian and policing agencies have already 'purified' their souls in Tablighi congregations in Raiwand. Sectarian elements within the IB and ISI ranks are purveying secret information about the planning of political parties and military leadership, to their favorite religious and political leaders. Secondly, military intelligence agencies do not cooperate with civilian intelligence agencies on national security issues. The ISI never extended a hand of cooperation to civilian intelligence agencies, or even considered IB as an older civilian brother, over the past five decades. Analyst Taha Siddiqui (06 May 2019) noted some aspect of the ISI involvement in politics:

"Domestically, he is known to have manipulated Pakistani politics both covertly and overtly, and was instrumental in doing so in his last stint during the era of General Pervez Musharraf who ruled Pakistan from 1999 to 2008. Internationally, he is known to have linkages with jihadist organizations, including al-Qaeda, the Afghan Taliban as well as Kashmir and India-focused groups.......When Musharraf imposed martial law on October 12, 1999, Brigadier Shah was the director of the Inter-Services Intelligence (ISI) in Punjab, Pakistan's largest and politically dominant province. Thus he became an important ally in the general's attempt at reshaping the politics of the region. Under Shah, the Intelligence Bureau became Musharraf's eyes and ears. It reported directly to the military dictator and helped him continue a countrywide 'political engineering' project."[18]The CIA influence on the ISI operational mechanism and domestic policy making causing misunderstanding between civilian and military stakeholders. The agency's reluctant cooperation with law enforcement agencies, and its grudging intelligence sharing with naval and air agencies, also caused disappointment among different stakeholders. On 01 August 2001, Indian analyst B. Raman in his research paper (No-287) noted some aspects of the evolution of ISI during the Zia-ul-Haq regime:

"Zia-ul-Haq expanded the internal intelligence responsibilities of the ISI by making it responsible not only for the collection of intelligence about the activities of the Sindhi nationalist elements in Sindh and for monitoring the activities of Shia organizations all over the country after the success of the Iranian Revolution in 1979, but also for keeping surveillance on the leaders of the Pakistan People's Party (PPP) of Mrs. Benazir Bhutto and its allies which had started the Movement for the Restoration of Democracy (MRD) in the early 1980s. The ISI's Internal Political Division had Shah Nawaz Bhutto, one of the two brothers of Mrs. Benazir Bhutto, assassinated through poisoning in the French Riviera in the middle of 1985, in an attempt to intimidate her into not returning to Pakistan for directing the movement against Zia, but she refused to be intimidated and returned to Pakistan. The Afghan war of the 1980s saw the enhancement of the covert action capabilities of the ISI by the CIA. A number of officers from the ISI's Covert Action Division received training in the US and many covert action experts of the CIA were attached to the ISI to guide it in its operations against the Soviet troops by using the Afghan Mujahideen, Islamic fundamentalists of Pakistan and Arab volunteers".[19]

Since the departure of Pervez Musharraf in 2008, the military pledged its commitment to protecting democracy. Yet it has consistently undermined civilian governments to maintain military prerogatives and, if not establish direct control of the state, but the ISI is still controlled by the army, and never allowed it to help democratic governments in the process of economic and political stabilization. The ISI kept IB under resources, while its leadership has retrieved policing training, and acts like a police officer. There is an opposition between law enforcement and intelligence, because the two entities are very different. In his research paper, Dr Bidanda M Chengappa has argued that ISI is mainly controlled and used by military against democratic government in Pakistan: "Apparently the ISI is controlled either by the military or the political leadership depending on whichever is in power. The DG-I, as the head of the ISI is known, is an appointment made by the Prime Minister in consultation with the Chief of Army Staff (COAS). The DG-I reports to the Prime Minister considering the ISI has a political section to handle internal intelligence duties. However, the army appears to dictate the policy towards India even when the country has an elected leader. To that extent it would be appropriate to state that the PM has a degree of control over the ISI's involvement in internal affairs which the Chief of Army Staff oversees the external role of the agency."[20]

The greatest challenge Nawaz Sharif faced was on the national security front. The miltablishment was not happy with his national security approach. The Intelligence Bureau is the country's main civilian intelligence agency, and functions under the direct control of the Prime Minister, tackling terrorism, insurgency and extremism. Over the last four decades, the ISI operated in changing security environment, but it mostly targeted democracy and political parties, strengthened miltablishment and its illegal business. The ISI, the MI and the IB assumed more controversial proportions than ever before. Journalist and expert Abbas Nasir (Herald, January 1991) describes the way intelligence targets politician in many ways to retrieve information:

"On a freezing December day in Islamabad, MNA Dr. Imran Farooq, ordered the maintenance staff of the MNA hostel to service his room heater. The staff took down the gas heater, only to discover a device that didn't belong there taped to its back. Noticing that there were batteries attached to it, they immediately became alarmed and summoned the bomb disposal squad. Being experts at their job, the members of the bomb squad soon allayed the perturbed MNA's fears that the device was not a bomb of any sort. Instead, they said, they had discovered a powerful transmitter that was being used to bug the MQM MNA's room. While the federal interior minister was quick to order an inquiry into the affair, the MQM blamed the former PPP government for bugging Dr. Farooq's room. The real culprit, however, is still to be identified. A few days earlier, a heated debate in parliament had focused on the activities of our intelligence agencies as being "rather over-extended". As the range of intelligence operations came under discussion, the fact that their agencies were maintaining files and tapes – not only on all politicians in the country, but many non-political civilians as well – drew the wrath of many MNAs of all political shades."[21]

Abbas Nasir is a senior journalist who knows how Pakistani intelligence agencies were spying on citizens and politician, and how they violate their right of privacy. The evolution of ISI through different states made the agency capable to adopt a professional approach in countering national security threats. Former Prime Minister Zulfiqar Ali Bhutto was the only person who realized the importance of a strong and competent intelligence agency in enhancing the goal of foreign policy. Abbas Nasir noted the zeal of Mr. Bhutto to make professionalize: "According to him, Bhutto chose the ISI to be the premier agency because he could accomplish two tasks with it. The first related to the country's foreign policy and the second to self-preservation, as only a services intelligence agency could look into the army itself and keep Bhutto abreast with the mood and the sentiment in the forces. This part of history also had its ironical twists. It is widely believed that Bhutto promoted General Zia as the army chief, superseding several far more senior and well-reputed lieutenant generals, because the

DG of the ISI had recommended him as the most "reliable and loyal" choice for the coveted post. It was no coincidence then, that when Bhutto was overthrown, Lt General Ghulam Jilani was retained as the DG of the ISI. Jilani remained one of the most trusted Zia lieutenants for a number of years, both as DG and later as the governor of Punjab. While Jilani was the governor of Punjab, he made a decision that would create obstacles in the path of the PPP for years to come. He plucked a young industrialist from relative obscurity and nurtured him as a civilian alternative to the PPP leadership. The young man would be prime minister one day. To this day, Jilani remains Nawaz Sharif's key mentor".[22]

Prime Minister Benazir Bhutto strengthened the role of the Intelligence Bureau (IB) to collect intelligence information for her government, and used it against opposition parties and ISI as well. There has been a clash of interest between the ISI and the IB management in 1990s. Both the ISI and IB were trying to get the favour of Prime Minister. Prime Minister Benazir created 20 senior positions at the joint director level to strengthen the management structure in the organization. Dr. Bidanda M. Chengappa had elucidated the role of ISI and IB against civilian government in Pakistan: "In post–Zia Pakistan, intelligence agencies were effectively used to topple governments. One such case pertains to how an intelligence agency was used to remove then Prime Minister Benazir Bhutto from office. It has been reported that on July 17, 1989 an intelligence agency clandestinely recorded the conversation between then Prime Ministers Benazir and Rajiv Gandhi while the latter was on a state visit to Pakistan. The room was bugged by the intelligence agency and the two leaders in the course of their private meeting at Islamabad discussed, among other issues, the possibility of mutual troop reduction. Apparently, Benazir was supposed to have agreed in principle to the proposal. Soon thereafter the Chief of Army Staff (COAS) General Mirza Aslam Beg and President Ghulam Ishaq Khan met each other on July 24, 1989 and decided to topple the Benazir government".[23]

The ISI's primary aim (Shuja Nawaz-2011) has been 'counterintelligence and espionage, especially aimed at India, where it has been fairly successful, but the IB was countering political parties. Prominent analyst B. Raman in his paper highlighted political confrontation and the role of the army in overthrowing the democratic government. Prime Minister Nawaz Sharif warned Mullah Omer to stop supporting Sepah Sahaba and cooperate with the United States. The army didn't like this way of treating their proxies by the Prime Minister. B.Raman has noted aspects of the whole saga: "The third instance was during the second tenure of Nawaz Sharif (1997-99) when his action in appointing Lt.Gen. Ziauddin, an engineer, as the DG ISI, over-riding the objection of Gen.Musharraf led to the first friction between the two. Gen. Musharraf transferred Lt. Gen.Mohammad Aziz, the then DDG ISI on his promotion as Lt.Gen to the GHQ as the CGS and transferred the entire Joint Intelligence North (JIN), responsible for covert actions in India and Afghanistan to the Directorate-General of Military Intelligence (DGMI) to be supervised by Lt. Gen.Aziz. It is believed that the JIN continues to function under the DGMI even after the appointment of Lt. Gen.Mahmood Ahmed as the DG, ISI, after the overthrow of Sharif on October 12, 1999. Gen. Musharraf, as the COAS, stopped inviting Lt.Gen Ziauddin to the Corps Commanders conferences. He kept Lt. Gen.Ziauddin totally out of the picture in the planning and implementation of the Kargil operations. After the Kargil war, Nawaz Sharif had sent Lt.Gen.Ziauddin to Washington on a secret visit to inform the Clinton Administration officials of his concerns over the continued loyalty of Gen.Musharraf".[24]Prime Minister Nawaz Sharif experienced the same challenges as a head of the IJI-led government which also resorted to using intelligence agencies to gain unfair advantage in domestic politics. The IB spied on MQM leaders and installed intelligence monitors devices in their rooms and houses."[25]

Chapter 6

Dematerialization of Civilian Intelligence and a War of Strength between the ISI and the IB

Pakistan's war crimes in Afghanistan caused challenges, trouble and fear in Central Asia and South Asia. General Pervez Musharraf admitted that during his tenure as the head of state, Pakistan had tried to undermine the government of former Afghan President Hamid Karzai because he had helped India cooking words on Pakistan's back. The former army chief said spies in Pakistan's Inter-Services Intelligence (ISI) had given birth to the Taliban after 2001 because the government of Ghani's predecessor had an overwhelming number of non-Pashtuns and officials who were said to favour India. "Obviously we were looking for some groups to counter this Indian action against Pakistan," he said. "Kashmiris Mujahideen who came to Pakistan received a hero reception here. We used to train them and support them. We considered them as Mujahideen who will fight with the Indian Army. Pakistan provided terrorist training to Kashmiris, Osama bin Laden was our hero. Terrorists like Osama bin Laden, Ayman al-Zawahiri, Jalaluddin Haqqani, and others were always considered to be "Pakistan's heroes", Parvez Musharraf said.

The challenges of democratic consolidation and security sector reform lies in the fact that in Pakistan, there is little public awareness about the function and operation of intelligence agencies. Major political and religious parties have no basic knowledge of the organization of intelligence. For this reason, this book will be the prime source of knowledge for politicians and civil society-containing basic knowledge of the manner of intelligence operation and its role in politics.[1] Thus, ignorance about intelligence communities is combined with fear, which perpetuates inadequate dissemination of information.[2] In modern states, security and intelligence agencies play a vital role in support of government in its domestic, defence and foreign policies by supplying and analyzing relevant intelligence and countering specified threats.[3]

Pakistani intelligence agencies have been shaping governments, parliaments, and dissolve it while the interests of military establishment is not served. This is a catchphrase, and a verbalism appearing in newspapers and intellectual debates since 1980s.[4] International media have also published numerous articles that highlighted the role of intelligence agencies in politics and judicial matter in Pakistan. I am not going to discredit ISI or criticize the IB to make my debate engrossing, because ISI is a professional intelligence agency of the country, and the IB stakeholders need to fix some cleft in the wall.[5] On 22 October 2019, Dr Niaz Murtaza in his article, sternly criticized military rulers and their involvement in politics. Dr. Murtaza also argued that policies of dictators caused extremism and social alienation; "Zia ruled for 11 years with absolute powers, guided by security-phobic lenses and with little regard for public welfare. Obviously, it would take highly capable rulers with a concern for public welfare, long tenures and full powers to undo this harm. No civilian has had the longevity or full powers to do so. His army successor Musharraf had these luxuries. But despite his enlightened moderation mantra, his policies turned Zia-era extremism into huge terrorism as he too was guided by security-phobic rather than public welfare lenses. Today, Pakistan has a sullied global reputation. The economy is industrially stagnant and suffers large deficits and debt. Politics suffers from instability, corruption, incompetence and agencies' control. Society is bigoted and intolerant with little space for freedom of thought and speech. All these reflect the corrosion of basic societal structures and the undermining of social, political, economic and national capacities primarily under Zia".[6]

Criticism is not resentment. Criticism builds societies and improves the capacity of state institutions. Not only Pakistan, intelligence in every South Asian state has weaknesses and lack of professional approach to national security challenges, but it doesn't mean they are unable to protect the interests of their own states.[7] On 25 September 2017, New Delhi Times Pakistan Bureau noted elements of state within state in Pakistan, and argued that IB and ISI spy on all parliamentarian, politicians, and opposition parties.[8] The newspaper also elucidated that their way of business has caused consternation among social and political stratifications:

"The three key agencies- the ISI, the MI and the IB–have assumed more controversial, undercover roles invariably at odds with even each other. The parliament hotly debated their 'rather over-extended' activities like maintaining files and tapes on all politicians and many non-political civilians. Politicians either ordered spying on the opposition or were themselves the target of such 'special attention'. Speaker admitted 'we have all been the target of intelligence agencies' before ordering a select committee to look into the matter. The intelligence set up is a well-oiled, super-efficient machine, and one of the best organized befitting strategic geo-political situation of Pakistan whose very creation and the consequent sub continental environment generated hostility. Its security and survival depended on their efficiency but the civilian psyche now detests their role in foreign and domestic policies as secretive agencies are anathema to the open, consultative or accountable nature of democratic systems. The concession to intelligence agencies enhanced the size and scope of their activities. The Inter-services Intelligence Directorate existed before but evolved and grew tremendously during Bhutto's regime after the humiliating 1971 war leading to Bangladesh separation. Bhutto utilized the ISI for two tasks- the foreign policy and self -preservation by constantly monitoring the pulse of the army and keeping abreast of their sentiments. Nuclear programme facilitated more funds and leeway for ISI. The irony is, Bhutto promoted General Zia as the army chief, superseding several far more senior, reputed generals, based on ISI recommendation that Zia is the most 'reliable and loyal' choice. Jilani, DG of ISI, as trusted Zia lieutenant, survived Bhutto's ouster.".[9]

The political role of Pakistan's intelligence agencies has become even more crucial for the military domination. On 22 July, 2018, Mr. Justice Shaukat Aziz Siddiqui levelled serious allegations against ISI that the agency's interference in judicial affairs badly affected independence of judiciary. Addressing the Rawalpindi Bar Association, Mr. Justice Siddiqui professed that the Inter-Services Intelligence (ISI) "manipulating judicial proceedings as its officials manage to constitute benches at its will and mark cases to selected judges".[10] "The ISI approached the Chief Justice of the Islamabad High Court (IHC) and told him that the agency don't want release of Nawaz Sharif and his daughter before elections." He said. Mr. Justice Siddiqui divulged: "I know how messages have been conveyed to the Supreme Court; I know where the record of proceedings of the accountability court was dispatched every day and why the statutory provisions allowing the IHC to exercise administrative control of the accountability court was ceased. This was to stop the IHC judges to monitor the trial proceedings."[11]

The Secretary of the Supreme Judicial Council (SJC), and the registrar of the Supreme Court of Pakistan, submitted a note to the SJC to consider the allegations levied by Justice Shaukat Aziz, in particular the manipulation of the judiciary by the ISI. This was accepted by the Chairman of the SJC as a matter requiring attention and he directed the Chief Justice of the Islamabad High Court to respond to the allegations made against him by Justice Shaukat Aziz.[12]The judge said that officials of the secret agency were expecting a favorable response from him over their offer "but he flatly refused and replied that he would prefer to die than sell his conscience." "I don't care about my job. I even know the consequences of sharing the truth with you but I am not afraid even if I am assassinated," Justice Siddiqui said.[13] He also said that the bar and the bench were from the same family "but our home has been invaded by armed men and independence of the judiciary has been usurped". Consequently, after two months, President Dr. Arif Alvi removed Justice Shaukat Aziz Siddiqui on the recommendations of the Supreme Judicial Council (SJC).[14]

The SJC headed by Chief Justice of Pakistan Mian Saqib Nisar. Mr. Nisar ruled: "This council is unanimously of the opinion that in the matter of making his speech before the District Bar Association, Rawalpindi, on July 21, 2018, Mr, Justice Shaukat Aziz Siddiqui, Judge of Islamabad High Court, had displayed conduct unbecoming of Judge of a High Court and was, thus, guilty of misconduct and he is, therefore, liable to be removed from his office under Article 209(6) of the Constitution of the Islamic Republic of Pakistan, 1973.[15]" Mr. Justice Siddiqui said that SJC took up 'baseless reference' against him about the renovation of his official residence. Dawn reported[16] On 30 April 2019, Dr. Faqir Hussain (Pakistan Today) in his article noted some aspects of Mr. Justice Siddiqui's allegations against the Inter Service Intelligence (ISI):

"The Supreme Court admitted for hearing the petition of Mr Justice Shaukat Aziz Siddiqui, former Judge of Islamabad High Court, who had challenged his removal by the Supreme Judicial Council (SJC). It is somewhat unprecedented because of the prohibition, imposed by Article 211 of the Constitution, which debars the jurisdiction of "any court" in the matter. Further, the Karachi Bar Council decided to become a party to the case and deputed two of its eminent members to argue the matter. Mr. Justice Siddiqui was a vocal critic of the government and establishment, often making remarks against them for exceeding authority and committing excesses, which came to light during the hearing of cases. Such criticism was not well received. As a judge, he possessed some unique qualities. He could stand pressure from the high and mighty, and reprimanded lawyers for coming unprepared, spurning their demands for strikes or requests for undue adjournments. Certainly, he was not amongst the special breed of judges who only "speak through their judgments". Giving a media-savvy appearance, he often expressed himself during hearings, and had the knack to drag religion into sociopolitical matters, which attracted public rebuke/criticism.[17]

Moreover, social media and newspapers criticized the removal of Justice Siddiqui. All political circles and opposition parties' regretted and warned that these traditions must not prevail in Pakistan. If we look at the structure and policies of Prime Minister Imran Khan's government, we can easily guess and calculate the interests of establishment. Global Village (21 October, 2018) in its news analysis also highlighted details of the removal of Mr. Justice Siddiqui by President Dr. Alvi:

"The decision was taken under Article 209(5) on the SJC's recommendation under Article 209(6) read with Article 48(1) of the Constitution, read a notification issued by the Ministry of Law and Justice. "Consequent upon proceedings under Article 209(5) and recommendations of the Supreme Judicial Council of Pakistan under Article 209(6) read with Article 48(1) of the Constitution of the Islamic Republic of Pakistan, 1973...... The President of Pakistan has been pleased to remove Justice Shaukat Aziz Siddiqui, Judge, Islamabad High Court, Islamabad, from his office with immediate effect," reads the notification issued by the Ministry of Law and Justice. A few months ago, Mr. Siddiqui lambasted at spy agencies of the country and held them accountable for many upsetting political and security challenges in Pakistan. Hearing the case of missing persons, the high court judge appealed to Chief of Army Staff General Qamar Javed Bajwa for "barring his persons from intervention in the matters of other institutions," adding that the army chief should take notice of the alarming situation. He claimed, "Judges' lives are in danger as their telephones are being tapped by the officials of the security agencies". Addressing a representative of the Inter-Services Intelligence (ISI), who appeared in the court, Mr. Siddiqui said: "Your personnel try to form a court bench of their own wish and the army chief should be aware of the misdeeds committed by them". [18]

On 08 June 2021, Hasanaat Malik reported (Express Tribune) Islamabad High Court's deposed judge Shaukat Aziz Siddiqui's stance on his statement against the ISI and military establishment that caused his removal. "Through that speech, I wanted to remove the security apparatus' pressure on courts. "However, my dilemma was that two senior Supreme Court judges – Mian Saqib Nisar and Asif Saeed Khosa – were against me since 2015," Siddiqui told a five-judge larger bench on Tuesday in response to one of the bench members' query as to what motivated him to made that speech. The bench presided over by Justice Umar Ata Bandial-hearing the former judge's petition against the Supreme Judicial Council's (SJC) decision of October 2018. "The SJC on October 11, 2018 recommended sacking Justice Siddiqui in view of his July 2018 speech at Rawalpindi bar–a speech in which he had accused the top intelligence agency of manipulating courts. The SJC, the constitutional forum that can hold superior court judges accountable was then headed by former chief justice Mian Saqib Nisar and included Justice Khosa, Justice Gulzar Ahmed, Lahore High Court Chief Justice Yawar Ali and Sindh High Court Chief Justice Ahmed Ali Sheikh. The former judge's comment about the two former chief justices, however, irked two of the bench members who left the proceedings in protest. Malik Hasanaat noted. Malik Hasanaat reported.

On the second visit on 19 June, 2018, Maj Gen Faiz Hameed told [me] that on passing of order dated 18.07.18 by me, he was summoned by General Qamar Javed Bajwa, Chief of Army Staff [COAS] and his job was at stake because the COAS showed great annoyance and displeasure on his inability to handle a judge of high court, Siddiqui noted. Justice Siddiqui exposed the ISI Chief on his agency interference in judicial matters. He disclosed that the COAS directed him to hold a meeting with me to know 'what Judge Sahib wants?' "In reply, I stated that I need nothing except that all organs of the state and the respective departments of the executive may remain within the limits prescribed by the Constitution and the law of the land". Mr. Justice Siddiqui further brought to light Mr. Hameed's forgiveness and said; On this, he stated: Sir, it is better to forgive bitterness as you are considered as a very upright and loyal Pakistani even in the ranks of army except a few individuals, therefore, good working relations may be in the interest of Pakistan. Justice Siddiqui said.

Civilian control over intelligence agencies and parliamentary oversight in Pakistan is impossible without the consent of miltablishment. War criminal have no social, political and military ethics as they are acting like warlords. Musharraf was passionate to make ISI a strong arm of his government.[19] He often mentioned the support of ISI to his illegal military government in every forum, interview and statement, but he also knew that he illegally expelled more than 100 competent, educated, and religious officers of ISI from 2002-2005. This author is witness to the expulsion of 1600 honest and religiously committed officers of ISI in four provinces. In September 2001, Pervez Musharraf appointed a new Director-General for ISI, Lieutenant General Ehsanul Haq who was later on replaced by Lieutenant General Shuja Pasha, because Gen Ehsan was close to China.

On 3 November 2007, Musharraf declared emergency rule across Pakistan and suspended the Constitution, imposed a state of emergency, and fired the Chief Justice of the Supreme Court again. In Islamabad, troops entered the Supreme Court building, arrested the judges and kept them detained in their homes. Independent and international television channels went off air. Public protests were mounted against Musharraf.[20] Research scholar Frederic Grare (18 December 2015) highlights political developments after the departure of General Musharraf in 2008:

"Following the 2008 elections, the Pakistani military successfully inserted itself into the political sphere during the post-Musharraf administrations. This is evident in military's consolidation of power during the civilian regimes of Asif Ali Zardari and Nawaz Sharif. Pervez Kayani, Chief of Army Staff (COAS) during the presidency of Asif Zardari, "was very much part of Pakistan's political machinery even while cultivating meticulously the impression at home and abroad that he [was] a professional officer waiting for the civilian to lead" (Fair 2011: 580). He never ceased to manipulate the system, shrewdly using the judiciary to pressure the president and make him more amenable to the army's desires. A similar game is currently in play against the administration of Nawaz Sharif. In both cases, the military's resentment of the mainstream political establishment stems from the attempts of the civilian government to assert its control over foreign policy and, more specifically, over Pakistan's policy vis-à-vis India and Afghanistan. Relations with India in particular are viewed as an existential issue by the security establishment, and constitute a clear divide between the civilian and military authorities. The military has previously taken dramatic action to establish its autonomy over Pakistan's policy toward India".[21]

On 13 February 2015, Dawn newspaper reported former military ruler Gen (retd) Pervez Musharraf's yell for an end to militant proxies in Afghanistan while in his exclusive interview with Guardian newspaper (2015), Musharraf admitted that he had ordered ISI to train suicide bombers and send them back to Afghanistan to weaken the Karzai government in Kabul. "In President Karzai's times, yes, indeed, he was damaging Pakistan and therefore, we were working against his interest. Obviously, we had to protect our own interest," Musharraf said. He also admitted that: "Pakistan had its own proxies; India had its proxies, which is unhealthy. I do admit this, it is most unhealthy. It is not in favor of Afghanistan, or Pakistan or India. It must stop," he said. Former army chief wowed that ISI trained Taliban: "Obviously we were looking for some groups to counter this Indian action against Pakistan," he said. "That is where the intelligence work comes in. Intelligence was in contact with Taliban groups. Definitely they were in contact, and they should be."[22] Musharraf first used ISI against politicians and then discredited the agency in his interview with the British newspaper. He, however, purportedly involved ISI in training suicide bomber, and gave the impression that the agency was directly involved in acts of terrorism in Afghanistan. After Musharraf, the role of agencies in decision-making process remained strong; while President Zardari ordered the control of ISI under Interior Ministry, but his dream vanished due to a stern reaction of military establishment.[23] The military was making alliances through ISI' social and political contacts. This untraditional way of making alliances affected the popularity of the agency.[24] However; Dr. Suba Chandran (2008) has further highlighted the issue of civilian control over the ISI. He also elucidated weakness and fear of civilian government to bring ISI under Interior Ministry because the Zardari regime was threatened of dire consequences before the implementation of the plan he designed:

"On 26 July 2008, the Pakistan People's Party (PPP) led government surprised everyone by bringing the ISI under civilian control, through a memorandum. The memorandum placed the administrative, operational and financial control of both the ISI and the IB under the Interior Ministry. The stated objective of this change was to improve coordination among various intelligence organizations and the need to work with the civilian authorities; to avoid the army acquiring a bad name (by associating with the ISI). However, in reality, the notification was born out of fear, pressure and an anxiety to control the ISI. The PPP has always been uncomfortable with the ISI. Its role in assembling an anti-PPP coalition–the Islamic Jamhoori Ittihad (IJI)–in the 1980s to prevent Benazir from assuming power after the death of Zia is well known. Ever since the ISI has worked against the interests of the PPP. It played an important role in her removal from the post of prime minister – both in 1990 and in 1996. In turn, the PPP also attempted to curb the role and influence of the ISI. During her first tenure as prime minister, Benazir Bhutto attempted to bring the ISI under control. From Benazir's forced exile to Zardari's arrest and the attempts to split the party, the PPP considers the ISI as the main force behind all anti-PPP activities.[25]

Dr. Nasreen Akhtar in her desertion to The School of Politics and International Relations of Quiad-i- Azam University Islamabad, described civil military relations during the Zardari government in Pakistan with differnt perspectives. President Zardari strived to establish good relationship with the army, but due to his government's massive corruption and his personal resentment against the ISI clefts further opened up, and his government experienced irksome situation while military establishment threatened him of dire consequences. Dr. Nasreen also argued that President Zardari had pushed military establishment to the wall:

"In the background of four military interventions in Pakistan's politics and the emergence of security establishment as a center of power within the structure of the state, this study explores civil-military relation in the post-military regime (2008-2012). Unlike in the past, we witness that a weak and unpopular civilian government of Zardari, despite facing many challenges, survived and completed its tenure for the first time in the history of the country. The central question we address is how it became possible? Was it due to the structural changes in the society or on account of self-assessment of the military leadership of its role essentially as professional soldiers to provide security to the country? Actually, it is an expansive definition of national security that has brought the military into politics besides imbalance in the power of the military and the civilian sectors. For that reason, the self-reassessment is not what it seems would chart a new course for the military rather it provided the post-Musharraf civilian government led by Zardari, a space to flourish, watched its performance, orientations and handling of national security. In December 2009, the Supreme Court ruled that the National Reconciliation Ordinance amnesty was unconstitutional, and President Zardari had immunity from prosecution. The removal of NRO challenged the legality of his Presidency due to his massive corruption cases.[27] Dr. Nasreen Akhtar further highlighted his political journey and challenges:

"While combating the internal and external challenges and efforts to complete its tenure, the Zardari-led regime made a history in two important aspects. First, as indicated earlier, it completed its tenure of full five years, the term of the Parliament. Second, it transferred power to its rival party, the PML-N when the later won majority in the 2013 elections.......On the other hand, we see the military spreading out on several fronts in the country due to many internal security challenges with terrorism on the top of list along with insurgency in Balochistan and the proliferation of sectarian and Jihadi organization connected with transnational radical Islamic movements. There was an image problem for the military as well. Musharraf's decision to align Pakistan with the US in War on Terror and use of the military power to eradicate groups that were once the allies of the state in Afghanistan was not popular, at least with the religious sections of the society".[28] The real extent of the military's control over foreign policy and, by contrast, the degree of freedom of elected governments in conducting foreign policy cannot be determined without assessing the impact of public opinion on foreign policy matters.[29] The agencies and miltablishment have been hurting political leadership time and again to make a space in state institutions, but President Zardari never genuflected. Consequentially, he was openly threatened of murder and humiliation by military agencies and the GHQ. Major Pakistani newspapers published military intransigencies on their front pages.[30]

The ISI involvement in polities causes difficulties for political parties during the alliances making process when the agency pressurize candidate to change loyalties. On 24 October, 2012, the News International reported operation of the ISI cell under Lt Gen (retd) Ahmed Shuja Pasha, who was overwhelmingly involved in national politics and was frequently accused of conspiring against the PPP government, till his retirement in March 2012. "During his briefing Standing Committee of the Senate on Defence and Defence Production on October 22, Lt Gen (retd) Malik protected the agency by saying that it was not involved in politics. But the fact remains that Lt Gen Pasha was the only ISI chief to have been accused of hatching conspiracies not only against the PPP government but also against the mainstream opposition party–the PML-N, led by Nawaz Sharif. While the ruling party circles had accused Shuja Pasha of taking up the Memogate scandal to pressurize the government into granting him another extension in service, the PML-N leadership had described him as the worst ISI chief Pakistan has had since 1988. Addressing a press conference in Islamabad on March 11, 2012, Leader of the Opposition in the National Assembly, Choudhry Nisar Ali Khan accused Pasha of indulging in politics and misusing the political cell of the ISI to persuade several politicians to join Imran Khan's Tehrik-e-Insaf. That the ISI had been deeply involved in politics under Lt Gen Pasha's command ever since the 2008 general elections can be further gauged from a US diplomatic cable which was made public in December 2010. The newspaper reported.

The News International also reported General Pasha's visits to some Arab states to discuss possible coup against government. Involvement of some Pakistanis based in UK was also reported in support of the ISI Chief. "Another allegation against Shuja Pasha, which shows his involvement in politics, was his supposed tour of some Arab countries in the aftermath of the May 2 Abbottabad raid by the US Navy SEALs to discuss a military coup against the government. The charge had placed Pasha in a tight corner since it was levelled by none other than Mansoor Ijaz as reported by a British daily The Independent, on December 13, 2011. The Inter-Services Public Relations (ISPR) took a full week to rebuff the report, especially after Engineer Jameel Ahmed had approached the Supreme Court and sought Pasha's removal and a subsequent court-martial under the Pakistan Army Act, 1952. He had pleaded that the ISI chief had lost the right to remain in the military service for meddling in politics and conspiring against a democratically-elected government. Although, Pasha's close circles strongly refute all these allegations as a pack of lies, his critics insist that his tenure (October 2008 to March 2012) will be remembered for all the wrong reasons, mainly due to ISI's overwhelming involvement in national politics. The Newspaper reported.

Having quoted General Durrani's statement in his article, Journalist and columnist Zahid Gishkori (The News International-21 May 2018) argued that former ISI spy admitted involvement of ISI in politics ahead of election 1990. Both General Durrani and Army Chief Mirza Aslam Baig were engineering election by distributing millions rupees among their favourite candidates. General Durrani elucidated: "The [ISI] Political Cell was established by Zulfikar Ali Bhutto in 1975 according to the recommendations of different circles. A study was also carried out for this. It was possible that the mandate and name was different but it carried out political assessment [ahead of 1990 polls]". Moreover, Mirza Aslam Baig elucidated that he had vehemently warned the-then ISI Chief General Durrani against dragging the military into "politics. "I warned Durrani to be careful in handling of those [ISI] funds. After this, I never again discussed this matter with him [Durrani]. I gave him no names of politicians or the money to be distributed, because this was entirely his domain, and he was responsible to report to the president." Involvement of civilian intelligence agencies in politics raised important questions that this way of business can affect professional mechanism of the IB and CID. Mr. Nawaz Sharif once released a secret tape to make the Benazir government controversial, and the ISI distributed money among loyal candidates.[31] According to Dr. Bidanda argument, on 16 June 1997, Mirza Aslam Beg said that General Durrani had received the money and spent Rs 60 million for funding certain candidates and other operations. With the US intervention in Afghanistan, under heavy pressure from the Bush regime, General Pervez Musharraf, moved to bring the ISI into line. Those who resisted, including Mahmud Ahmed, were forced out. Gen. Musharraf shamelessly admitted that some retired officers of ISI were helping Taliban groups against the Karzai government in Afghanistan. Thus, he again discredited the agency.[32]

The nexus of Mullah and miltablishment was making situation even worse. The deep state was expanding its sphere of influence to all state institutions to gradually undermine democracy, and enrich its private enterprise. The nexus of jihadists, wealthy individuals and serving and retired bureaucrats, as well as opportunistic politicians, had lent support to the invisible forces of disorder so that the deep state could be able to preserve and continue a lucrative business enterprise. Pakistani intelligence agencies were undergoing a deep crisis of confidence, professional credibility, lack of modern intelligence collection technology, and national security management.[33] A contest of strength between the Inter-Services Intelligence (ISI) and the Intelligence Bureau (IB), and their joint fight against the policing agencies, a misplaced sense of patriotism, poor, politicized, and sectarian management; and an inefficient approach to national security and national integration, prompted tug-of-war, scorns and regional alienation.[34]

Pakistan's military leaders most often used the ISI's political wing against the civilian leadership of political parties. Indeed, within Pakistan, the implications of the move are seen as being almost entirely domestic. But Pakistani President Asif Ali Zardari's civilian government claims that taking the military spy agency out of domestic politics will also allow it to focus more on counterterrorism operations. But Zardari's government has acknowledged publicly that elements within the ISI are sympathetic to Islamists in Pakistan and the insurgency in Afghanistan. Those agents have been portrayed by Islamabad as "rogue" operators pursuing their own private agendas. In October 2008, President Zardari received stern domestic criticism for repeatedly calling Kashmiri Mujahedeen terrorists, which gave more pain to the military establishment. In November 2008, the President proposed no-first-use nuclear policy between Pakistan and India. It was a good proposal to normalize relationship between the two states, but the army didn't support his plan. The relationship between the two nations was damaged by the Mumbai attacks in November 2008.[35]

Dr. Nasreen Akhtar (2017) in her PhD thesis highlighted some aspects of relationship between President Zardari and the ISI. President Zardari and his party didn't like role of ISI in politic, while Prime Minister Bhutto used ISI for his political purposes. Dr Nasreen Akhtar highlights relationship between President Zardari and the armed forces: "Despite the fact that relations between Zardari, ISI, and the military were pernicious but Zardari as president completed his term and compromised with the military establishment. However, political cost was paid by his 'nominated'

Prime Minister Gilani who wanted to protect his party leader and the president Zardari. Zardari was considered 'master' to bargain and facilitate his opponents. However, the army and ISI both remained dominant factors in Zardari regime and played fundamental role in internal and external policies because democracy under Zardari's leadership was fragile, ineffective, and dysfunctional, which promoted corruption, lawlessness, and personal interests of the party leaders in power. Zardari appointed his close aides and trusted friends to important positions, both home and abroad, and made a few attempts to curtail military's power in the domain of national security".[36]

Pakistan's armed forces are among the most modern and well-funded in the world and the only ones in the Muslim world, while most analysts have tended to view Pakistan's political system as authoritarian and label it as a dictatorship. In every democratic government, the army retained a final say on sensitive issues such as regional policies, defence expenditures, and the nuclear sector, and refuses any interference in internal postings, transfers, and promotions.[37] The return to a civilian government in 1988 did not mark a reversal of the situation; in fact, Benazir Bhutto and Nawaz Sharif provided the military with even greater economic opportunities in order to appease it while trying to reduce its political role. Dr. Nitin Prasad (20 February 2016) highlights political and democratic development in Pakistan: "Pakistan has exercised different forms of Political systems like Presidential, Parliamentary, Federation and One Unit. Local Bodies system has also been influenced by these experiences. It has been facing Political, non-political, dictators and bureaucratic influence. Pakistan has poor facts of democracy. It has been ruled by the military, while the Military governments always generated mistakes with the politicians. Pakistan's capacity to protract the low cost conflict in Kashmir is beyond any doubt. Although the likely spillover effects of this on Pakistan's polity are obvious, they will be, to a great degree, manageable".[38]

The lack of security sector reforms in Pakistan prompted the surge of extremism and jihadism within the ranks of the agencies. In different political and intellectual forums, critics raised the question on the credibility of the country's intelligence and security infrastructure that they have been unable to maintain security and stability in the country. Pakistan's Supreme Court in 2012 remarked that the entire state machinery, including Frontier Corp and agencies failed in stabilizing Baluchistan province.[39] As we all know, capabilities of Pakistan intelligence agencies and their access to remote parts of the country, we are witnessed to the fact that they have been unable to even collect intelligence information from these regions. The fact is, they are mostly militarized and their operational mechanism is also militarized, their informers and officers have been unable to establish networks within civilian population. Intelligence information collection in remote regions needs friendly environment.[40] However, on 18 July 2012, the Daily Nation reported:

> "Chief Justice Iftikhar Muhammad Chaudhry, who was heading the three-member bench, told Attorney General Irfan Qadir that since the ISI was under the Prime Minister he should be informed about it and if any such cell was still operating, it must be closed. As the activities of the cell amounted to undermining the political process in the country, the Chief Justice warned that the court would not allow the strengthening of one institution at the cost of another, though no doubt would very much like to see Pakistan Army as a robust organization. As if recalling the government's obstinate defiance of judicial verdicts, Justice Chaudhry maintained that it would also not be possible to strengthen Parliament by weakening the judiciary. "There will be supremacy of the Constitution alone in the country" and nothing that was not legitimate under the Constitution would be tolerated, he asserted. Nor would any sort of Bangladesh model be tolerated". On 21 May 2018, Journalist Zahid Gishkori in his article reviewed the Asghar Khan case and its important players. Zahid has also highlighted other important aspects of the case: "Before this, Gen Mirza Aslam Beg claimed that he had vehemently claimed the-then spy chief Gen Durrani against dragging the military into "political engineering" ahead of the 1990 polls. "I warned Durrani to be careful in handling of those [ISI] funds. After this, I never again discussed this matter with him [Durrani]. I gave him no names of politicians or the money to be distributed, because this was entirely his domain, and he was responsible to report to the president," Gen Beg revealed in his written statement submitted to the FIA and the apex court".

The manifestation of war in public eye is missing persons, extra-judicial killings, body bags, corpses with torture marks, abductions, shooting sprees, ethnic and sectarian cleansing and selective/targeted assassinations of leadership. Gone unnoticed are hundreds of national, provincial and nationalist leaders, who have been assassinated, including Mohatrma Benazir Bhutto. Many times, despite compelling circumstantial evidence, the inability of the investigators to make a credible case allows these criminals to go scot-free and resume anti-state activities".[41] The Abbottabad

Operation remained controversial. Although, it was welcomed in the US and many European countries, and gave them an opportunity to cheer up, but for many in Pakistan was on the opinion that it was an attack on their sovereignty and integrity. It divided and embarrassed Pakistan institutions. On 11 July 2011, in reaction to series of events and actions of agencies against journalists and human rights activists in Pakistan, Mr. John R. Schmidt repudiated the extrajudicial killing of journalists by the Inter-Services Intelligence. He noted in his analysis the brutal murder of Salim Shahzad in Islamabad:

"But now there are accusations, publicly embraced by U.S. officials (including Joint Chiefs chairman Admiral Mike Mullen), that ISI ordered the murder of Pakistani journalist Saleem Shahzad, whose tortured and severely beaten body was found outside Islamabad on May 31. Shahzad had recently written a piece for the Asia Times alleging that the Pakistani Navy had arrested several naval personnel for helping al-Qaeda attack the Pakistani naval base in Karachi on May 22. Suspicion that ISI may have been responsible for his death surfaced after it was revealed he had earlier told colleagues he had received death threats from the intelligence agency. These threats had allegedly come in the wake of a previous article he had written accusing Pakistani authorities of releasing Afghan Taliban deputy leader Mullah Baradar in October 2010 after eight months in custody. According to Shahzad, senior flag rank ISI officials had pressed him to reveal the source of his information and, when he refused, had made a point of telling him they had recently gotten a hold of an Islamic terrorist hit list and would let him know if his name was on it. Shahzad interpreted this as a threat. The speculation following his death was that the Karachi-naval-base story was the last straw and that ISI had ordered his murder, not just in retaliation, but as a warning to the entire Pakistani journalist community, whose criticisms it believed had gotten out of hand".[42]

For decades, (Dhruva Jaishankar, Foreign Policy, 15 February 2019) 'Islamist terrorists belonging to groups like Jaish-e-Mohammed and Lashkar-e-Taiba benefited from recruitment, financing, training, and other forms of support provided by Pakistan's security establishment. Groups targeting India and Afghanistan continued to operate with relative impunity inside Pakistan, which has only cracked down on militancy against the Pakistani state'.[43] The killing of Osama Bin Laden near Islamabad painted an ugly face of Pakistani intelligence for their involvement with al Qaeda and its leader. Mr. Salim Shahzad's Karachi Naval Base story also occurred irksome, but Salim didn't accused ISI for its improper action. Mr. Davis was protecting a CIA cell that was trying to collect information on the terrorist group Lashkar-e-Taiba, one of the ISI's chief assets in its proxy war with India. The two men that Davis killed were alleged by Pakistani sources to have been tied to the ISI, likely as contractors. Mr. John R. Schmidt (2011) noted some aspects of the love and hate relationships between the two countries:

"Just two days after Admiral Mullen made his accusations on the Shahzad murder, the New York Times revealed the United States was suspending military assistance to Pakistan. Washington has been increasingly frustrated at Islamabad's unwillingness to go after those Afghan Taliban forces using the North Waziristan tribal area as a safe haven for conducting operations in eastern Afghanistan. The Pakistanis have refused to do so because they see the Afghan Taliban as a hedge against the emergence of a hostile government in Kabul allied to India after U.S. forces depart the region. Although little publicized in the West, the Indians have developed close ties to the Karzai government, flooded the country with aid workers and provided the Afghans with over a billion dollars in aid. Although the Pakistanis have no particular love for the Afghan Taliban—whose support for Osama bin Laden got them into their current fix—they fear the Indian presence in Afghanistan even more. Not only has the United States shown little sympathy for these Pakistani concerns, it has grown increasingly angry at Pakistani reluctance to do what it wants. Seen in this context, the U.S. decision to publicly accuse ISI of complicity in the Shahzad murder can be viewed as just another manifestation of American displeasure".[44]

Relationship between the two states remained strained, but after the killing of Osama Bin Laden, their relationship further complicated. "The death of bin Laden (Amir Hamza Marwan October 2015, PP-25) provided a reason to US to celebrate, and set a platform to claim that "Justice has been done" but the operation was perceived very differently in Pakistan, where the media outlets, politicians and several opinion leaders started questioning the one-sided US operation (considering it as violation of the sovereignty of Pakistan); expressing doubts about the role played by the Pakistani military and its intelligence agencies in helping the US to conduct the successful operation; the failure of the Air Force department of Pakistan to trace the US helicopters, which reportedly flew from Jalalabad (Afghanistan); and the inability of the Pakistani forces to counter the US forces, which remained in Pakistan for almost 40 minutes".[45]Whatever the ISI has done against al-Qaeda—and even the deepest skeptics about Pakistani motives do not deny that the ISI has at times been very helpful. On 12 May 2011, in his National interests' article, Mr. John R. Schindler argued that weak democratic control on intelligence agencies in Pakistan, jihad in Kashmir and war on terror in Afghanistan, and Pakistan's reluctant support to the US and NATO campaign caused funny feeling between the two states:

"The lack of Pakistani civilian control of the military generally, and the ISI specifically, should no longer constitute a pass for dubious conduct. The unspoken quid pro quo—that the U.S. and other Western partners would look the other way on certain ISI misdeeds, especially its support for "liberation movements" in Kashmir and Afghanistan as long as it worked with us against al-Qaeda—has been overtaken by events in Abbottabad and elsewhere. This alleged wall between acceptable and unacceptable jihads has existed only in the Western mind anyway. The ramifications of the Headley case have been one of the causes of the fraying of ties between Islamabad and Washington. Even more provocative, from the Pakistani viewpoint, has been the increasing number of U.S. intelligence operations run without coordination with the ISI, known as "unilateral" in the trade. While it is hardly unknown for the CIA and other agencies to run unilateral, especially against high-value targets, even in friendly countries, this has grated on Islamabad, which appears fearful of what our personnel might find if they start digging too deeply. Pushback culminated in early 2011 with the arrest of Ray Davis, a CIA contractor, who shot two armed Pakistanis—suspected intelligence operatives—whom Davis believed threatened him. Davis was released after payment of blood money to the families, but this public spectacle brought the always-touchy relationship between Islamabad and Washington to a new low. They have descended further still with the outrage in Pakistan over the Abbottabad raid, the ultimate unilateral. The embarrassment of the Zardari government, which has had trouble knowing quite what to say to the global media, has been matched by the fury of the ISI, now that it is obvious to all that they were either sheltering bin Laden or were so incompetent as to have had no idea the world's most wanted man was living, barely concealed, practically in a Pakistani Army base".[46]

Chapter 7

President Zardari, the ISI Double-Dealing and Miltablishment

President Asif Ali Zardari (Financial Times-12 January 2012) was locked in an interminable battle with the army, ISI and judges. His conflict with judges and generals intensified on both fronts-precipitating a session of puffing speculation by television channels that his government was on the verge of collapse.[1] There were different perceptions about the performance of Pakistan's intelligence agencies in war and peace, but one couldn't deny the fact that the agencies were deeply politicized and their loyalties were with their private and bureaucratic stakeholders.[2] They were protecting their masters and kept sharp-eyed about the political developments in the country. The political leadership had serious apprehensions about the working style of the intelligence agencies. According to Brigadier (r) Shaukat Qadir, the ISI, under Gen Mehmood from 2000-2001, completely went out of control until he was sacked. It was more of an ego problem, where Gen Mehmood, the ISI Director General, considered him unaccountable. Ali K Chishti, Pakistan's security analyst, highlights the whole story of distrusts, tug-of-war and mismanagement with the intelligence agencies:"

"The civilian-military distrust could also be witnessed in the intelligence community where it is part of the book by the uniformed intelligence agencies, the Military Intelligence and the ISI to seals off the K-Block or the IB's Headquarters as a routine whenever there's a coup which shows a thread of animosity and mistrust between the civilian and military institutions. The politicisation of the intelligence agencies could be judged with the fact that at least 4,000-5,000 sacked Intelligence Bureau officials, who were previously profiled to be "unfit for service" due to political connections, were reinstated by the Pakistan People's Party (PPP) government with back pay and benefits only recently. The IB often accuses other intelligence agencies of interfering in its affairs remember only in recent years more IB operatives have gone down than anyone else. So, how do our intelligence agencies work? They send out a daily report to the president and the prime minister via COAS, titled "eyes only" mostly "googled stuff" and constantly play up threat levels apart from nagging for more funds. While the three big intelligence agencies have received all the latest tech and surveillance equipment from the United States, including serious investments in a new field, quantum computing to break terrorist codes, it is the human intelligence which the Pakistani intelligence agencies normally rely upon but lacks training in".[3]

In 2013 and 2015, Prime Minister Nawaz Sharif faced challenges when he criticized the involvement of military generals in politics. Mr. Nawaz Sharif extended hands of friendship to India and invited Prime Minister Modi to Lahore to further strengthen relationship between the two states, but miltablishment and its political cronies launched a campaign against his government in the pretext that he might possibly wanted to establish the RAW networks in Punjab.[4] Moreover, intelligence agencies requested Dr. Tahirul Qadri to help them in undermining the PML-N government. This unending resultant tussle between civilian and military intelligence agencies forced former Prime Minister Nawaz Sharif to restructure the IB and make it more effective to counter ISI's influence in political institutions. The Prime Minister allocated huge funds to the IB to recruit and employ more agents to meet the country's internal and external challenges. The greatest challenge Nawaz Sharif faced was on the national security front he decided to control policymaking process of Kashmir and Afghanistan. The miltablishment was not happy with his national security approach. The Intelligence Bureau was consecutively receiving instructions from the Prime Minister office to keep tightrope around the ISI and GHQ. Research scholar Frederic Grare (18 December 2015) highlights the role of Qadri in humiliating the Nawaz government:

"The so-called "Qadri episodes" are viewed by many in Pakistan as illustrative of the relationship between the army and the intelligence services. Tahirul Qadri is a Canadian cleric of Pakistani origin who, in December 2012, returned to Pakistan and initiated a political campaign "calling for a democratic revolution through electoral reforms aimed at preventing corrupt candidates from participating in the forthcoming elections" (Grare 2013: 989). Qadri, who also had apparently unlimited access to resources of vague and unclear origin, called for the resignation of Asif Zardari, the dissolution of the parliament, and the participation of the military in the caretaker government. Many Pakistani observers

117

interpreted Qadri's anti-corruption campaign as an attempt by the security establishment to create the conditions of an indefinite postponement of the elections, thereby facilitating the replacement of the existing government by a body composed of technocrats and military leaders. Such was the case in the 1990s, when the army repeatedly felt the need to get rid of the Prime Minister of the moment, alternately Benazir Bhutto and Nawaz Sharif. The 2013 Qadri plot ultimately proved to be a failure. The government made no concession, and although Tahirul Qadri was allowed to save face, he had to back off, only to consequently reemerge with Imran Khan, leader of the Pakistan Tehreek-e-Insaf (PTI) and a favorite of the security establishment. The two initiated a campaign against the Nawaz Sharif government, which began in the summer of 2014. Starting in August 2014, Islamabad, Pakistan's capital city was paralyzed by tens of thousands of protesters led by Imran Khan and Qadri, who not only called for the resignation of the Prime Minister on the allegation that he had rigged the May 2013 general elections, but also repeatedly threatened him and his ministers with violence (Siddiqi 2014)."[5]

On 07 February 2019, Agence France-Presse reported Pakistan's Supreme Court called on intelligence agencies for upholding free speech and staying out of politics. This strong criticism was issued in a judgment criticizing the role of the intelligence agencies in anti-blasphemy protests which paralyzed the capital Islamabad for several weeks in 2017.[6] "If any personnel of the Armed Forces indulges in any form of politicking or tries to manipulate the media he undermines the integrity and professionalism of the Armed Forces," stated the judgment.[7] The 2017 protests were led by the then little-known Islamist group called the Tehreek-e-Labaik Pakistan (TLP), and were only dispersed after violent clashes led to a military-brokered deal which forced the resignation of the country's law Minister. France Presse reported".[8] On 26 January 2020, daily Dawn quoted the report of a local think tank which noted challenges of Pakistan's external environment throughout 2020. The Islamabad Policy Institute warned that the country's tense relations with neighbouring states might consume much of Pakistan's strategic and diplomatic interaction.[9]The report (Pakistan Outlook 2020: Politics, Economy & Security) highlighted persisting trends in external environment, economy, political stability, and security and on the basis of that made short-term projections in these areas. Pakistani state has been weak and fragile since 1947.[10] Since 1990s the state has been trying to showcase its divergent approach to religion and religious institutions from its previous position. The United States and European Union have already pressed successive Pakistani governments to reform the country's intelligence agencies to counter their influence on civil society and politics, but agencies further intensified their watchdog campaign against civilian population.[11] Privacy International (July 2015) in its research paper has highlighted the role of agencies in changing surveillance mechanism in Pakistan:

"The Pakistani government is engaged in a protracted conflict against armed militant groups within its borders and outside its borders, it is a key player in the global 'war on terror'. Communications surveillance - of phone and internet protocol (IP) traffic, domestically and internationally- and other forms such as biometric or device registration, is justified by the government as necessary to counter these internal and external threats, even as it becomes less and less targeted and more widespread against ordinary civilians. The military's defence budget has ballooned in recent years as result of significant levels of international assistance, with the military's access to sophisticated technologies having increased in turn. Attacks against civilian targets in Pakistan's cities have also fed popular support for communications surveillance and other efforts to register and monitor the civilian population, including national databases and mandatory SIM card registration. Pakistan's intelligence agencies have abused their communications surveillance powers, including by spying on opposition politicians and Supreme Court judges. Widespread internet monitoring and censorship has also been used to target journalists, lawyers and activists. This report outlines the state of communications surveillance in Pakistan. It compares the vague and imprecise laws that govern it against international human rights law standards. The report also gives an overview of the international intelligence operations that Pakistan has participated in and been subject to, including programmes operated by the US National Security Agency (NSA) and the UK Government Communications Headquarters (GCHQ)".[12]

Pakistan's intelligence agencies have long faced accusations of meddling in the privacy affairs of its civilian population. Intellectual forums and newspapers have often stepped up suggestions that this way of watchdog might alienate citizens from the state. In June 2013, the Inter-Services Intelligence (ISI) developed a mass surveillance system by directly tapping the main fiber optic cables entering Pakistan that carried most of the nation's network communication data.[13] These and other intransigencies of the agencies in 2008, forced the PPP government to bring ISI under democratic control, but faced tenacious resistance from the armed forces. Privacy International (July 2015) in its report noted the import of surveillance technology by Pakistani government to intensify incarceration of civilian population, political and religious leaders in their house:

"Mobile monitoring equipment for identification and/or interception is particularly widely used by law enforcement agencies across Pakistan. The Pakistani government has imported many of these tactical communications surveillance technologies from Europe. In 2010, Germany granted German companies export licenses valued at € 3.9 million to export "monitoring technology and spyware software "to Pakistan. Between 2012 and 2014, Swiss companies were granted licenses to export dual-use communications surveillance technology to Pakistan. The total value of the three exports based on the category provided was over CHF 1 million, according to records obtained by Privacy International. Finland, too, granted licenses to companies based in Finland, exporting surveillance technologies to Pakistan. For instance, the Finnish export authority authorized four export licenses to ABB, a Finnish automation technology company, to provide "waveform digitizers and transient recorders" in Pakistan, which are used to analyses audio and remote sensing data. The Pakistani government is also a confirmed user of intrusion technologies which enable the remote hacking of targeted devices. Intrusion technologies are capable of collecting, modifying and extracting all data communicated and stored on a device. To do this, malware, short for malicious software, must be installed on the device. The installation often occurs when the user inadvertently installs a Trojan, which is a disguised or concealed programme".[14]

On 25 July 2019, Prime Minister Imran Khan on his official visit to the United States claimed the presence of 30000-40000 armed terrorists in the country. The agencies established links with fundamentalist parties such as the Jamaat-i-Islami and its offshoots, the Tableghi Jamaat and Markaz Dawa-al Irshad. This interaction also allowed the Islamic fundamentalist parties in Pakistan to extend influence over armed forces personnel.[15] The U.S. Country Reports on Terrorism described Pakistan as a "Terrorist safe haven" where terrorists are able to organize, plan, raise funds, communicate, and recruit fighters, while the ISI, has often been accused of playing a role in major terrorist attacks across India including terrorism in Kashmir. President Hamid Karzai was regularly reiterating allegations that militants operating training camps in Pakistan have used it as a launch platform to attack targets in Afghanistan.[16] Alexandra Gilliard (18 December 2018) the role of Pakistani intelligence agencies in using terrorists against Afghanistan:

"The ISI Directorate in Pakistan has enjoyed unparalleled power since its creation in 1948. As the ISI Director-General is selected by the Military Branch, the agency has remained steeped in army and military affairs for seventy years. From its outset, the ISI has backed terrorist organizations that provide strategic depth within India and greater influence in Afghanistan. These efforts are designed to promote Pakistan's regional hegemony— all while wreaking havoc on the national security interests of both India and Afghanistan. ISI support and aid for several terrorist organizations, including the Afghan Taliban and the Haqqani network, have resulted in international condemnation of the ISI's failures to prevent "systematic and persistent human rights violations," albeit with little effect. Within Pakistan, terrorist attacks have declined in recent years following legislation and ISI counter-terrorism policies enacted between 2013 and 2016. However, the ISI's continued covert support for extremists has fostered a growing radical community and new splinter groups that have spread throughout the region. After former President Musharraf's pledge to join the War on Terror, the ISI vacillated between continued sponsorship of extremist groups in support of its interests and cracking down on radical anti-ISI groups within Pakistan. Ultimately, due to inconsistencies in its counter-terrorism campaign, Pakistan's intelligence agency was quietly listed as a terrorist organization in U.S. military documents, instructing that ISI officers be treated the same as terrorists".[17]

However, Dawn newspaper reported former Prime Minister Nawaz Sharif directions for fresh attempts to conclude the Pathankot investigation and restart the stalled Mumbai attacks-related trials in a Rawalpindi antiterrorism court.[19] Those decisions, taken after an extraordinary verbal confrontation between Punjab Chief Minister Shahbaz Sharif and the DG ISI, appeared to indicate a high-stakes new approach by the PML-N government. However, during the meeting, Gen Akhtar offered that the government should arrest whomever it deems necessary, but Shahbaz Sharif told Gen Akhtar that whenever action has been taken against certain groups by civilian authorities, the security establishment has worked behind the scenes to set the arrested free. Dawn reported.[20] The uninterrupted militarization of society, and the enfeebled operational mechanism of civilian intelligence in the country resulted in a popular mindset where every movement, action and way of thinking of Pakistan's political leadership as well as a common man have become militarised, and accordingly, seeks a military solution for every major or minor issue.[21] Expanding the spectrum of their illegal business of forced-disappearance to cover major foreign and domestic policy areas, the agencies assumed

121

a more controversial position than ever before. Normally, the prime task of intelligence agencies is to lead policy makers in the right direction, based on detailed and reality-based intelligence, but the case in Pakistan is different.[22] The agencies were misleading political leadership and policy makers, driving them into the wrong direction, and making alliances with radicalized elements in support of the miltablishment's business of forced disappearances and torture.[23] In all previous democratic governments of the country, even Ministers of Cabinet rank never dared to question the secret agencies about their illegal prisons, and kidnapping for ransom.[24]Nevertheless, civilian and military intelligence agencies in Pakistan faced numerous challenges, including widespread lack of civilian support, faith in themselves, sectarian and political affiliations, as well as the war in Waziristan and Balochistan, where the circle of intelligence information collection has contracted drastically[25]

Over the past two decades, the role and scale of Pakistan's intelligence agencies was grown over and above their prescribed functions, to the degree that their operations, often undercover and at odds even with each other, have earned them the repute of being a "State within a State".[26]In most parts of the country, intelligence information collection faced numerous difficulties since the Taliban and other militant groups returned to important strategic locations. Having faced serious difficulties in dealing with insurgent forces in Balochistan and Waziristan, the agencies started translating their anger into the killing and kidnapping of innocent civilians with impunity.[27]A secret war goes on between the ISI, and the IB which painted a murky picture of concordance and cooperation. It is known that the officials from the military's ISI agency had their phone calls eavesdropped at the height of civil-military tension in 2014.[28]

The Intelligence Bureau (IB) was established by the British Army's Major General Sir Charles MacGregor who, at that time, was Quartermaster General and head of the Intelligence Department for the British Indian Army at Shimla, in 1885.[29] Appointment for IB's Director-General is made by the Prime Minister and confirmed by the President. The IB, which was patterned after the IB of British India, used to be a largely police organization, but the post of Director-General (DG), IB, is no longer tenable only by police officers as it was in the past. Serving and retired military officers are being appointed in increasing numbers to senior posts in the IB, including to the post of DG. In the 1990s, the IB remained actively involved to curb sectarianism and the fundamentalism in the country. Many of its operations were directed towards infiltration, conducting espionage, counterespionage, and providing key information on terrorist organizations.[30] The IB has been using by successive governments in Pakistan since 1970s, while former Prime Minister Benazir Bhutto and Nawaz Sharif painted a controversial picture of its operational mechanism.[31] The intelligence community of Pakistan was once described by the daily Frontier Post (May 18, 1994) [32]as an invisible government[33] and by the daily Dawn (April 25, 1994)[34] as secret godfathers consists of the Intelligence Bureau (IB) and the ISI. After PTI Chief Imran Khan became Prime Minister, the IB started dancing to his tango. Analyst Azaz Syed (28 September 2018) noted some developments within the intelligence infrastructure, and the IB loyalties to Imran Khan who used the agency against the deposed Prime Minister Nawaz Sharif:

"Amid a major reshuffle within the premier civilian intelligence outfit, the Intelligence Bureau (IB) has been directed to concentrate on fighting corruption instead of countering terrorism, The Friday Times has learnt. Although IB chief Dr Suleman Khan denied this development while talking to TFT, sources within the agency insist that they have been tasked to bring forward corruption cases against prominent political figures and pay attention to these areas. "There are other agencies and organizations which were trained for anti-corruption efforts. IB should not do this. Its expertise is in countering terrorism and its focus should not be redirected towards corruption," said Ehsan Ghani, a recently retired former chief of the IB while talking to TFT. Dr Suleman, who has also served the agency in Khyber Pakhtunkhwa, is counted among those who played a vital role in countering terrorism in the province with the help of the police and the Counter-Terrorism Department (CTD). Now, sources say, he has agreed to shelve counter-terrorism as a subject of the agency, as another agency has been tasked to deal with it. Dr Suleman was appointed chief of the agency by former Prime Minister Shahid Khaqan Abbasi on the recommendation of Aftab Sultan, the then IB chief. But in a conversation with TFT, Dr Suleman denied this. "I come from a background of counter-terrorism, how can I abandon something I have worked on for years?"[35]

All civilian and military agencies have adopted a specific mindset[36]. Their sectarian affiliation and dearth of electronically trained manpower, lack of professional surveillance approach, and the absence of a proper intelligence sharing culture raised serious questions about their credibility, and weak national security approach[37] These and other things also caused the failure of the National Counter Terrorism Authority (NACTA) to effectively counter the exponential growth of radicalization and extremism within

Pakistan.[38]Military and civilian intelligence agencies did not cooperate with NACTA in its war against radicalized forces.[39] As a matter of fact, NACTA established a Joint Intelligence Directorate (JID) with officers from ISI, MI, IB, and Law Enforcement Agencies (LEAs) to fight terrorism and extremism in close cooperation of these agencies, but couldn't succeed in winning their loyalties.[40]The NACTA Act 2013, Section 4 (a) mandates the Authority to receive, collate and disseminate intelligence and coordinate between all relevant stakeholders to formulate threat assessments.[41] Section 47 of the National Internal Security Policy 2014-2018 spelled out the need for establishment of Directorate of Internal Security (DIS) under NACTA[42] where thirty three civilian and military intelligence and operational agencies are represented, having clear articulation of command and control by integrating all grids of tactical, operational and strategic intelligence, civil and military, under one roof. In this context, a Joint Intelligence Directorate (JID) was established under the National Coordinator, NACTA, at its headquarter.[43]

The JID's goal was to manage and pool effective intelligence works undertaken by both civilian and military intelligence agencies of the country, and to increase intelligence sharing with Police Departments, Provincial and Federal LEAs.[44] The JID was to help the democratic government in dealing with extremism and Talibanisation in four provinces, but the government didn't pay long-term attention, nor did it receive sufficient financial support. The military establishment, moreover, failed to help train its operational managers.[45] Under the NACTA Act, the agency was entrusted to the Board of Governors (BOG).[40] The Prime Minister was the Chairman, and its members included defence, finance, foreign and law ministers, members of the Senate and National Assembly, Chief Ministers of the four provinces, the Prime Minister of Kashmir, the Interior Secretary, Director General of Federal Investigation Agency (FIA), all chiefs of intelligence agencies, and chiefs of Police department from all provinces.[46] On September 25, 2018, Prime Minister Imran Khan chaired the first meeting of the BOG.[47] Expressing dissatisfaction over the NACTA's performance, he ordered the establishment of a special committee to oversee its performance and make it competent.[48]

Pakistani establishment never allowed controlling the hydra of intelligence agencies[49] to introduce security sector reforms, and make them fit to the fight against radicalization, terrorism and jihadism.[43] Consequentially,[50]the agencies became militarised and a tool of miltablishment to harass political leaders[51] and those who write against the corruption of military Generals.[52]

Scholar Frederic Grare (18 December 2015) has painted a nice picture of the business of military establishment in his well-written paper: "Despite more than eight years of continued civilian power, Pakistan can be labeled as a transitional democracy at best. True, the country has experienced two successive and relatively democratic elections in February 2008 and May 2013, and the mainstream political parties--essentially the Pakistan Muslim League Nawaz faction (PML-N) and the Pakistan People's Party (PPP)--are no longer willing to let themselves be played off the other by the military, thereby limiting the margin of maneuver of the security establishment. Today, as much as in the past, "operations against dissenting politicians, objective intellectuals, and other activists, are still carried out through systematic harassment, disinformation campaigns, fictitious trials, kidnap, torture, and assassinations", as demonstrated by the de facto genocide in Balochistan."[53]

In 2017, the then Prime Minister Nawaz Sharif tried to take control of foreign and internal policy of the country, but was disqualified from his post by the Supreme Court.[54] He sought to lead Pakistan's India and Afghan policy in the right direction; but was intercepted, humiliated, and his movements were salami-sliced when former President Asif Ali Zardari tried to bring the ISI under democratic control, he faced the same fate. He was pushed around and his crippled and tortured body would be shifted to hospital in an army ambulance. On November 27, 2013, the then Prime Minister Nawaz Sharif appointed General Raheel Sharif as Chief of the Pakistan Army, but Sharif later resisted his governments pressure to introduce security and intelligence sector reforms.[55] This change of face ensured that any action against the Taliban would be ineffective, even as General Sharif's mission of killing Pashtuns in Waziristan failed to eradicate domestic militancy. Moreover, a large number of General Sharif's Army officers and soldiers refused to fight against the civilian population.[56] The Army Chief declined to negotiate with tribal leaders, and refused to respect Parliament and democratic norms. Instead, he designed the policy of shoot to kill in Waziristan, causing death of large numbers of innocents, including women and children, with impunity, and the kidnapping of tribal elders[57].

On 15 July2016, New York Times reported a poster aiding General Raheel Sharif to take over the country in a military coup. The posters immediately sparked all-too-familiar speculation. Was the military planned a coup? Were the generals tired of prodding the civilian government, saddled by one crisis or another? However, journalist Imad Zafar recently reviewed

Mr. Shuja Nawaz new book, which appeared in US market: "The downfall of military dictator General Pervez Musharraf, General Ashfaq Parvez Kayani's role in restoring the judiciary is a well-known fact, but Nawaz summarizes this with details. Nawaz' most startling revelation about politics in Pakistan is the reference to former US ambassador to Pakistan Richard Olsen.[58] According to Nawaz, Olson had information that General Zaheer-ul-Islam, then the director-general of ISI, was planning to stage a coup against Nawaz Sharif's government during the 2014 sit-in organized by Imran Khan. However, General Raheel Sharif stopped him from doing that.[59] This revelation was first made public by Pakistan Muslim League-Nawaz (PML-N) stalwart Senator Mushaid Ullah Khan, who in an interview to the British Broadcasting Corporation claimed that Zaheer-ul-Islam was the main architect of Khan's sit-in. Mushaid Ullah Khan had to resign from his ministry after the interview, as the military establishment did not like it".[60]

The consecutive militarization and Talibanisation of society, and instability led to the catastrophe of disintegration and failure of the state, which was further inflamed by the US war on terrorism, and involvement of NATO forces in Afghanistan.[61]Pakistan's weak and unprofessional diplomatic approach towards Afghanistan prompted a deep crisis, including the closure of trade routes and a diplomatic impasse.[62] One can easily focus on the Army's political and bureaucratic role in state institutions. According to the Constitution of Pakistan, every democratic government is answerable to the people of Pakistan. But in reality, they are actually answerable to the Army headquarters in Rawalpindi. Every single Prime Minister in Pakistan can only do his or her job smoothly if they completely surrender defence, interior, strategic decisions and foreign policy to the Army.[63]

It means the rules for civilian governments are pre-planned and they have been told to go by the book and not cross the red-lines defined by the military establishment. This makes it a "State within a State" that, instead of ruling the country from the front, prefers that the politicians and civilian governments implement its decision and exercise power.[64]To punish Afghanistan's National Army, Pakistan's intelligence agencies provided sophisticated weapons to the Taliban and other extremist organizations to make the war in Afghanistan disastrous and unfavorable to Kabul since 2001. Pakistan's military establishment continues to train, arm, and transport terrorist groups inside Afghanistan to target civilian and military installations, and make the lives of civilians, including women and children hell. The ISI has often been accused by the Afghan Army and Government of playing a role in major terrorist attacks. Scholar Frederic Grare (18 December 2015) has reviewed the power and operational mechanism of Pakistani intelligence agencies. Their relationship with journalists and their newspapers is irksome for politicians and civil society:

"Pakistan's three most powerful intelligence outfits–the Inter-Services Intelligence (ISI), the Military Intelligence (MI), and the Intelligence Bureau (IB)—are known to recruit informants among journalists (Grare 2008: 24). But the link between journalists and the intelligence agencies is a complex one, and cannot be reduced to a simple power dynamic in which the journalists are merely the victim. Journalists need information, and thus have an interest in maintaining a good relationship with intelligence agencies. In return, journalists are often asked to provide information themselves to intelligence agencies. This connivance sometimes results in a collusion that extends beyond appropriate journalistic conduct. Pakistani journalists are a diverse lot with a vast range of opinions--some of which are closer to the security establishment than others--but in Pakistan, like everywhere else in the world, proximity to power is an efficient way to climb the social ladder".[65]

Chapter 8

The ISI War against Journalists, Bloggers, and Social Media Anchors

Freedom of press and freedom of expression in Pakistan is, no doubt matchless. No Western democracy and kingdoms allow such critical news stories and articles on various political and social issues published in Newspapers and electronic media in Pakistan. In EU and Britain, I have a considerable experience of writing and publishing books, comments, analysis and critical notes, but the way criticism is allowed in Pakistan, is unsupportable in EU and Britain. If one writes such stories, he would face the wrath of police, government and intelligence agencies. Notwithstanding all this freedom of press and Media, the ISI and civilian intelligence agencies, torture, kidnap and disappear journalists, writers and bloggers to their illiterate ferment into a violent and inhuman action. The IB, CID, Special Branch and the ISI's understanding of national security and domestic governance is audaciously negative and gloom-ridden. They have failed to address issues of national security, national alienation and geographical fault, but they have been addressing these issues through torture, disappearance and murder since 2001. The US Department of State in its report (Country Reports on Human Rights Practices: Pakistan-2020, March 30, 2021) highlighted a weak and shameless approach of Military Establishment and civilian government towards print and electronic media:

"Authorities used this technic to prevent or punish media criticism of the government and armed forces. To publish within Pakistan-administered Kashmir, media owners had to obtain permission from the Kashmir Council and the Ministry of Kashmir Affairs, and journalists had to depend largely on information provided by the government and military. There were limitations on transmission of Indian media content. Journalists also protested their inability to report freely on rights violations and forced disappearances in Baluchistan, the Pashtun movement's activities and protests, and the military's involvement in business enterprises. In January, the Ministry of Information Technology and Telecommunication approved the Citizen's Protection (Against Online Harm) Rules to regulate content on social media platforms. In October, the government used those rules to briefly ban the TikTok application, lifting the ban once the application's company agreed to block users who upload unlawful content. Rights activists reported the government contacted Twitter and asked them to take down accounts of activists deemed problematic. Journalists alleged PEMRA issued editorial directives to television stations, and media outlets claimed the government pressured stations to halt broadcasting of interviews with opposition political party leaders. In March, the Committee to Protect Journalists reported PEMRA contacted cable distributers throughout the country and ordered them to stop transmitting Geo TV or switch its broadcasts to higher channels that are harder for viewers to find. This action followed the arrest of parent company Jang Media Group's CEO and editor in chief. The Islamabad office of Radio Mashal, the Pashto language service of Radio Free Europe, which the Interior Ministry closed in 2018, remained closed at the end of the year. Violence and Harassment: Security forces, political parties, militants, and other groups subjected media outlets, journalists, and their families to threats and harassment. Female journalists in particular faced threats of sexual violence and harassment, including via social media, where they had a particularly strong presence".[1]

Lahore, Karachi, Peshawar, Baluchistan, and Islamabad based journalist paid high price for their writings, struggle, and campaign to keep freedom of expression intact and keep military establishment and its intelligence agencies to one side. They were incarcerated, and their families were harassed. Countless journalist, bloggers and analysts have been arrested, tortured, harassed and disappeared for their literary contribution. Journalists of Khyber Pakhtunkhawa and Baluchistan are living in consternation and fear. The US Department of State in its report (Country Reports on Human Rights Practices: Pakistan-2020, March 30, 2021) has documented all these atrocities of Pakistani establishment against civilian population:

"On July 21, a journalist and outspoken critic of the military establishment, Mr. Matiullah Jan, was kidnapped by heavily armed men in Islamabad and released 12 hours later. The abduction was caught on closed-circuit television cameras, images from which were shared widely on social media. The Committee to Protect Journalists said Jan was among the journalists the army accused of sharing anti-state remarks on social media in 2018. On September 4, Sajid Gondal, a former journalist and a joint director of

Pakistan's Securities and Exchange Commission, disappeared after being "kidnapped by unidentified persons;" on September 8, Gondal tweeted that he had returned home safely. On September 12, police charged another journalist, Asad Ali Toor, with allegedly spreading "negative propaganda against the state, Pakistani institutions and the Pakistan Army," citing the Pakistan Electronic Crimes Act. Journalists Saeed Ali Achakzai and Abdul Mateen Achakzai alleged, according to Committee to Protect Journalists reporting, that agents of the Baluchistan Levies, a paramilitary gendarmerie that operates as a primary security agency in the province, detained them on June 19 without charges, held them for two days, and beat them. On June 8, the journalists had reported on poor conditions at a COVID-19 quarantine center. Censorship or Content Restrictions: Media organizations generally engaged in self-censorship, especially in reporting news regarding the military, religious extremism, and abuse of blasphemy laws; journalists stated they were under increased pressure to report the predetermined narrative during the year, and PEMRA issued editorial directives to media outlets. For example, some stated they were pressured to publish or broadcast military statements or rebuttals of stories that reflected badly on government officials prominently in their newspapers and news bulletins. Journalists reported regular denial of permission to visit conflict areas or being required to travel with a military escort while reporting on conditions in conflict areas".[2]

Journalist and editor *Friday Times* Lahore Pakistan, Najam Sethi (The Friday Times, 04 June 2021) in his editorial page described painful story and humiliation of Pakistani journalist by the ISI and policing intelligence agencies. He also highlighted the role of Military Establishment in harassing, torturing and kidnapping journalists, bloggers and writers. Mr. Najam Sethi has long challenged military establishment to protect people of Baluchistan. He, however, was imprisoned, tortured and intimidated. Mr. Sethi has criticized the illegitimate, insecure and authoritarian laws enacted by successive governments to harass, intimidate and humiliate media and intellectuals. Pakistani media is now facing an unprecedented threat from the Niazi government and rogue intelligence units:

"Currently, two institutions representing the civil-military hybrid regime are being manipulated to manage and control the media. The ISPR is the Miltablishment boot while PEMRA is the civilian arm of this joint exercise. The FIA has now been brought into the loop of repression to put down social media activists. Hovering above are the invisible, unaccountable civil-military intelligence agencies obsessed with notions of 5th Generation

Warfare in which elements of the independent media are constantly accused of being in the pay of foreign masters and following "enemy agendas". Together these state institutions account for all the threats, warnings, legal notices, fines, closures, beatings, arrests and disappearances that have now become commonplace. The evidence of this is piling up and spilling into the international media. The physical assault on journalist Asad Ali Toor last week has opened up all the wounds and compelled relatively independent sections of media and civil society to stand up and resist. The list of brave media warriors who have paid a high, often brutal, price for demanding free-speech and constitutional rights reads like a Who's Who of prominence. Hayatullah (2003, kidnapped and killed); Umar Cheema (2010 kidnapped, beaten up); Saleem Shahzad (2011, disappeared, tortured to death and dumped in a canal); Hamid Mir (2014, shot and injured); Ahmed Noorani (2017 kidnapped, beaten up, exiled); Taha Siddiqui (2018, kidnapped, beaten up, exiled); Gul Bukhari (2018, kidnapped, intimidated, exiled); Matiullah Jan (2020, kidnapped, warned); Absar Alam (2021, shot, injured) and now Asad Toor (assaulted at home). Shockingly, not a single assailant or perpetrator has been caught by the mighty intelligence agencies without whose permission a leaf dare not stir. The Owner-Editor of the Geo-Jang Group, Mir Shakilur Rahman, has just spent seven months in solitary confinement in NAB quarters for not heeding the advice of these invisible agencies. Now Hamid Mir has been banned from Geo TV following his outburst against an alleged oppressor. In between, several prominent journalists are out in the cold, facing sedition charges filed by faceless complainants".[3]

Moreover, Amnesty International (Pakistan: Enduring Enforced Disappearances-27 March, 2019) has noted some aspects of enforced disappearances in Pakistan. In April, 2017, a school teacher Hydayatullah Lahor was kidnapped by intelligence agencies from Sindh province. His family registered a case with Larkana High Court against the kidnappers. His daughters, Sausui and Sorath Lahor initiated a campaign against enforced disappearances in Sindh Province. The Joint Investigation Team also registered this case. The Joint Intelligence Team consisted of government agents, Ministry of Interior, police department and representatives of all intelligence agencies:

"Enforced disappearances have long been a stain on Pakistan's human rights record. Despite the pledges of successive governments to criminalize the practice, there has been slow movement on legislation while people continue to be forcibly disappeared with impunity. The Commission of

Inquiry on Enforced Disappearances (COIED) has 2178 cases unresolved as of now. As per the Commission's recent monthly report, 48 cases disposed of in the month of January 2019, included 46 traced persons out of which 29 were returned home, 10 were traced to internment centers, five are in jails on terrorism charges and two were described as "dead bodies"......
While marching against enforced disappearances, Sasui and Sorath Lohar have spent Eids in hunger strike camps outside the Karachi Press Club with other families of the "missing persons", as the victims of enforced disappearance are commonly referred to in Pakistan. In May 2018, during a violent dispersal of the protest they were part of in Sindh, Sasui says she was assaulted by a law enforcement officer. In November 2018, a peaceful march of the missing persons of Sindh was interrupted repeatedly by the Sindh Rangers and by officials in plain clothes – who are thought to be from the intelligence agencies. On 12 January 2019, Sindh Rangers attempted to detain one of Lohar's sons, Sanghaar Lohar, without search warrants, from his mobile shop in Karachi. The sisters and mother resisted and raised enough noise to gather neighbours and managed to halt the detention. The video evidence of the entire incident shows men in uniform claiming that their brother was involved in wrongdoing, without specifying any allegations or charges. In 2017 and 2018, the family of the blogger Ahmad Waqass Goraya were repeatedly harassed by intelligence agencies. In 2017, Goraya was forcibly disappeared from January 4 till January 27, along with three other bloggers in Punjab for running Facebook pages critical of Pakistani military's policies. Goraya's father, Liaqat Goraya, told Amnesty International .[4]

Journalists in Pakistan are under threat from a variety of actors, with rights groups decrying increasing government and military censorship, intimidation and harassment of journalists in recent years. Further, as previously documented, enforced disappearances have been used as a tool to muzzle dissent and criticism of military policies. Pakistan's human rights groups reported the abduction of a 26-year-old political activist Mohammad Amin who was allegedly abducted by the country's security forces. Amin was forcibly taken from his residence in Shah Faisal Colony in Karachi on 14th July 2020. Amin was associated with the Progressive Youth Alliance and is an advocate of students' rights. On 06 April, 2021, columnist Jaffer A. Mirza in his article (The Diplomat) noted Pakistan's anti-Shia policies, but conversely, Nasrullah Baloch (Ending Pakistan's epidemic of enforced disappearances-Al Jazeera 9 Mar 2021) documented incidents of enforced disappearance in Pakistan:

"In February 2020, Haseeba Qambrani, a young woman living in Pakistan's southwestern province of Baluchistan, received chilling news: Her brother Hassan and cousin Hizbullah had gone missing. This was not the first time her family had experienced such a tragedy, just a few years earlier, in 2015, Haseeba's other brother Salman and cousin Gazain went missing. One year later, Haseeba's family discovered their mutilated dead bodies. The whereabouts of Hassan and Hizbullah are still unknown a year later, and Haseeba is still trying to find them. She is not alone in her search for loved ones who have been abducted over the years in Baluchistan. Baluchistan borders Afghanistan and Iran. Full of mountains and deserts, I call this place my home. Here, thousands of men and boys have been forcefully disappeared, held in incommunicado detention for long periods, or extra-judicially killed in the last two decades. My own uncle, Ali Asghar Bangulzai, was abducted from Baluchistan's provincial capital, Quetta, in 2001. Twenty years on, we still do not know where he is. Deen Muhammad, a local doctor, suffered the same fate in June 2009, and his wife and two daughters Sammi and Mehlab are still searching for him. In October 2016, a student leader, Shabbir Baloch, was disappeared during a military operation. His relatives are still waiting for his return. I could go on. As a co-founder and chairperson of the Voice for Baloch Missing Persons (VBMP), a grassroots collective representing family members of Baluchistan's forcibly disappeared, I have registered more than 5,000 such cases. Other grassroots movements across the country have also collected chilling stories about fathers, brothers and sons who have been picked up by security forces in other parts of the country and vanished without a trace over the years. Several organizations, including the Human Rights Commission of Pakistan, Amnesty International, Human Rights Watch, and the UN Working Group on Enforced Disappearances, have confirmed that the security forces are the primary suspects behind these disappearances. In 2012, when I admitted cases to the Supreme Court on behalf of VBMP, a three-judge bench formally declared that based on the evidence, it is clear that law enforcement agencies have been behind the abductions".[5]

While six FC soldiers were killed by militants on 19 May 2020, intelligence agencies started crackdown and arrested innocent Baloch citizens. Baloch Liberation Army clarified in its statement that the Army officer killed in the attack was "directly involved in the formation of criminal gangs operated by the army" in the Kech region. The statement also accused the army officer of helping drug dealers and arming them to take on the rebels. Research Associate, Institute for Conflict Management, Tushar Ranjan Mohanty

(Balochistan: Violent Retaliation-16 Jun 2020) in his expert analysis noted some aspects of violence and disappearance in Baluchistan Province:

'Mar 22, 2021, ANI reported the death of four youths, whose mutilated bodies were found in the open field near an army camp, were allegedly picked on the pretext of espionage by ISI-backed TTP. Some say the army had direct involvement. People also suspect they were traumatized sexually before being hacked to death. Family, relatives and tens of hundreds of native Pashtuns held sit-in with their mutilated corpses in Jani Khel. On social media, Fazal Rehman Wazir warned: "GHQ guards are the killers of the Pashtun nation. A few days ago in Jani Khel, Bannu, and Good Taliban kidnapped four minor boys on suspicion of espionage and today their tortured bodies were found." "Heart-wrenching graphics of mutilated bodies of 4 minors were circulating on social media. Soon after discovering the bodies, a protest sit-in started in Jani khel. On 28 March 2021, about 10,000 protesters embarked on a long march from Jani khel to Islamabad along with the bodies to demand action against militants. On 27 June, 2021, talks between the committee of Jani khel protesters and district administration for ending the sit-in remained inconclusive. However, the protesters refused to end the sit-in and bury the body of the slain elder, saying that they wanted practical action for implementation of the agreement, including release of arrested residents, recovery of all missing persons, restoration of lasting peace to the area, compensation to the affected families and others. Jani Khel residents wanted the government to uphold its promises to rout out militants, investigate murders, pay compensation to victims of terrorism, and invest in regional development.[6]

On February 20, 2020, five Security Force (SF) personnel were killed and three were injured after militants attacked a check post in the Turbat District of Balochistan. Three militants were also killed in the subsequent exchange of fire between the SF personnel and militants. There was no claim of responsibility, but the attack took place an area where Baloch separatists frequently target Pakistani security convoys and checkpoints. On February 19, 2020, at least 16 Army personnel were killed in an attack by Balochistan Liberation Tigers (BLT) at an Army post in the Singsila area of the Dera Bugti District of Balochistan. BLT militants also seized all weapons and ammunition kept at the post and subsequently set the post on fire. This attack was the worst on SFs by a Baloch group. The previous worst attack by a Baloch group targeting SFs was recorded on February 1, 2012, when at least 15 FC personnel were killed and 12 were injured in an attack on four FC check posts near the Margat Coalmines in Mach District. Mirak Baloch, who introduced himself as the BLA spokesperson, claiming the attack declaring. Research Analyst at Manohar Parrikar Institute for Defence Studies and Analyses, Dr. Nazir Ahmad Mir (Abysmal Human Rights Situation in Baluchistan-20 May 2020) has documented human rights violation in Baluchistan province of Pakistan by the rogue intelligence units of the armed forces who kidnap, kill, torture and disappear innocent Baloch men, women and children with impunity. Some Baloch like Dr. Din Muhammad have never returned home since a decade. The Human Rights Commission of Pakistan (HRCP) has only condemned the way military establishment and the ISI and IB operate against civilian population. Pakistani state has a dismal record in handling the cases of enforced disappearances in Baluchistan. Dr. Nazir Ahmad Mir highlights all the above cited miseries of the citizens of Baluchistan:

"The Baloch have never felt safe inside Balochistan and now they do not feel safe even outside Pakistan. The case of the disappearance of Rashid Hussain Baloch from the United Arab Emirates (UAE) in December 2018, and the recent discovery of the dead body of Sajid Hussain Baloch in Sweden after he went missing in March 2020, only serves to demonstrate that the Baloch rights activists are being trailed even when they have quit Pakistan and are meeting the same fate as their ethnic cousins back home. According to Baloch forums worldwide, Pakistan's intelligence agencies are extending their influence and operations even in distant shores, especially in countries where the Baloch diaspora is actively propounding the case of Baloch marginalization in Pakistan. In the case of Rashid Hussain Baloch, he fled Balochistan after his close relatives were killed by the Pakistan security forces. His cousin, Abdul Majeed, was abducted on October 18, 2010 and his bullet-ridden dead body was found six days later. Two years later, Rashid's uncle and Majeed's father, Muhammad Ramzan, was shot dead on 02 February, 2012. Rashid had been working in UAE since 2017. While he was travelling to Sharjah in December 2018, his car was intercepted and he was arrested reportedly by the UAE intelligence agencies, and ever since he has gone missing. The online media run by Baloch activists allege that he was handed over to the Pakistani agencies. Sajid Hussain Baloch had fled Balochistan in September 2012 after he was targeted by the Pakistani establishment for investigating disappearances of the Baloch people".[7]

Journalist Hamid Mir's fought for media and journalists, has been widely acknowledged by the international community. In April 2014, he was attacked by ISI in Karachi. Dawn newspaper (27 April, 2014) reported attempt on his life in Karachi. Hamid Mir immediately blamed the 'ISI within ISI' for orchestrating the attack in an interview with BBC Urdu. Speaking during his first interaction with the media after the attack, Geo TV's senior anchor-person said that he has been threatened again to leave the country by the same elements who he alleged were behind the attack. He said he has been told to leave Karachi and Pakistan as "it will be a long fight." "People visit me in guise of friends but leave after conveying threatening messages of the foes," said the senior journalist answering a question about the source of the recent threats. "They say you better leave Pakistan…it's not safe for you anymore. Only yesterday a highly responsible person came to visit me and told me that I will be attacked again." Mir said the people who were threatening him had always been a part of the country's strong military establishment and they were conveying indifferent messages to him. He said those who keep an eye on journalists' movement and tape their telephone calls were behind the attack. "Only these people may know what flight Hamid Mir will take to reach Karachi. Which car will pick him up at the airport and at what time he will come out from the airport. They knew where to attack the car and chose a corner where CCTV camera wasn't functioning, DAWN newspaper reported.[8]

Hamid Mir has in the past criticized the Taliban and also Pakistan's armed forces, and media campaign group Reporters Without Borders said he had told it on April 7 that the ISI was "conspiring… to cause me harm." Pakistan's freewheeling private media has increasingly shown itself willing to challenge the military, once considered off-limits to criticism. On 06 June 2014, Dawn newspaper reported GeoNews served notice to the ISI for defamation over accusations of being anti-state. "Geo and Jang Group (have) served a legal notice on the Ministry of Defence, Inter-Services Intelligence and Pakistan Electronic Media Regulatory Authority for defaming and maligning the group," the channel said in a report published in a newspaper owned by the media house. "More than 8,000 journalists, workers and professionals attached to the group and their families are not only being harassed but also attacked and tortured across Pakistan." The suing by Geo News was followed by a suspension of the channel's license for 15 days along with a fine of Rs10 million. Moreover, the News International on 06 June 2014 reported the GeoNews notice served to the ISI and Pakistan Electronic Media Regulatory Authority (PEMRA) for defaming and maligning the group by accusing it of working on an anti-Pakistan agenda, inciting and fueling violence against the group, pressuring cable operators to black out Geo channels, the failure of Pemra to get the

Supreme Court order to restore Geo channels implemented, and has asked all to publicly apologize within 14 days and pay damages of Rs50 billion.[9]

The GeoNews served notice to the ISI under section 8 of defamation ordinance, 2002 and elucidated: "We, on behalf and instructions of the Independent Media Corporation (Pvt) Limited (IMC), Independent Newspaper Corporation (Pvt) Limited (INCL), News Publications (Pvt) Limited (NPL), Independent Music Group (Pvt) Limited (IMG), (hereinafter referred to as 'our clients') are writing to address you as follows: That subsequent to the above, ISI sent a complaint to the Ministry of Defence which without even providing any evidence/proof, contained baseless and untrue allegations that "Geo Network has a history of acting illegally in furtherance of anti-Pakistan agenda and upon receipt of the complaint of ISI, the Ministry of Defence immediately without verification of the allegations levelled in it, forwarded the said complaint containing the allegations regarding our clients having a history of acting on an anti-Pakistan agenda, as it is, to PEMRA seeking immediate suspension and cancellation of Geo News' license, and, after receiving complaints from the ISI through the Ministry of Defence, PEMRA too, without seeking any proof/evidence of anti-Pakistani activities of our clients, issued a show cause notice to our clients, accusing them of being involved in anti-Pakistan. Hamid Mir never relinquished his struggle against the ISI illegal interference in Media and journalism. Jyoti Malhotra (Hamid Mir's defiance of military, ISI and emergence of a new 'General Rani' in Pakistan: The Pakistani media may never undertake a full-throated challenge to the diktats of the deep state, but sometimes it is angry enough to let out a roar. The Print-01 June, 2021) documented atrocities of the ISI against journalists and media workers:

"When you fail to create a narrative about Israel in the Pakistani media, you get very angry. You pick up Matiullah Jan, shoot Absar Alam and enter the houses of people like Asad Toor. Then you say that your tanks are becoming rusty, so let's make peace with India...You called 'Madre-Millat Fatima Jinnah a traitor and today you call Asad Toor a traitor... Do not ever enter the homes of journalists again. We don't have tanks or guns like you, but we can tell the people of Pakistan about the stories that emerge from inside your homes. We will tell them whose wife shot whom inside the confines of their home. And which 'General Rani' was behind this. I hope you all have understood what I am saying."This was Pakistani journalist Hamid Mir of Geo News, speaking at the National Press Club in Islamabad over the weekend, in defence of his country's media and media persons........In the past ten years, journalists have increasingly fallen foul. In May 2011, the body of Saleem Shahzad was found "entangled" in the Upper Jhelum canal, a couple of hours away from Islamabad; his body bore signs of torture. In April 2014, four gunmen fired at Hamid Mir, as he drove from Karachi airport to his Geo News office – he received bullets in his stomach and upper legs. Mir had told his friends that if he was attacked, he would hold ISI chief Lt Gen Zaheerul Islam responsible. One month before, journalist Raza Rumi barely escaped with his life and now mostly lives abroad – along with other journalists like Ayesha Siddiqa (a columnist at The Print), Taha Siddiqui and Gul Bukhari".[10]

Mashal Radio noted several journalists in Pakistan left their job after being threatened. The GeoTV was forced off the air, and authorities disrupted the distribution of Dawn. However, Reporters without Borders termed Hamid Mir's suspension a step towards autocracy. Dawn newspaper on 02 June, 2021 quoted Global Media watchdog, Reporters without Borders (RSF) criticism against the Niazi government move to take veteran journalist and TV anchor-person Hamid Mir off air, terming it another step towards autocracy in the PTI-led government's rule. Hamid Mir had said earlier that he had been informed by the Geo News management that he would "not go on air" to host his five-days-a-week show 'Capital Talk'. Sources from the channel's management had confirmed that Mir had been sent on forced leave for some time.[11] Journalist bodies and human rights organizations strongly condemned the move, terming it an attack on the freedom of expression and press. In April in Islamabad, a gunman shot and wounded Absar Alam, another prominent media voice known for his critical views of the government and the military's meddling in politics. Criticism of the army has long been seen as a red line for the media, with journalists and bloggers complaining of intimidation tactics including kidnappings, beatings, and even killings if they cross that line. Dawn newspaper reported. Journalist Asma Shirazi, in her tweet, said: "If Hamid Mir is taken off air or banned from doing program, more fingers will point towards the powerful establishment and the government while resounding the words that he said." BBC reported the "Mir's fiery speech at the protest was noteworthy for an important subtext.[12]

As the anchor took on the military, he also appeared to be bringing attention to rumored internal divisions in the country's most powerful institution. The public outing of the personal travails of a serving general, even if he was not named, has likely ended this individual's ambition of climbing to the top of the pyramid". Retrospectively speaking. On 05 November, 2017, the

ISI had registered a case against Hamid Mir for his alleged involvement in the kidnapping and murder case of a top-ranked ISI officer in 2010. Hamid Mir faced threats from multiple quarters including the Taliban. Khalid Khawaja of the powerful spy agency Inter-Services Intelligence (ISI) and the army. Peoples Dispatch, formerly The Dawn News, is an international media organization with the mission of bringing to you voices from people's movements and organizations across the globe in its detailed study of enforced disappearance in Baluchistan has highlighted some important cases to exhibit that military establishment and intelligence agencies are operating illegally. In its recent report (Activists from Baluchistan province of Pakistan found dead in mysterious circumstances-05, 05, 2020:

"At least four rights activists from southwestern Balochistan province in Pakistan have been found dead in various places in the last four days. All four died under mysterious circumstances in separate incidents. Among them, two student-activists, Shahdad Balouch and Ihsan Balouch, were killed in Kelat a town in Balochistan on May 3. Earlier, on May 1, a gunman in Wana a town in Waziristan fatally attacked senior leader of the Pashtun Tahafuz Movement, Arif Wazir. In another incident, activist-journalist Sajid Hussain's body was found in a river in Sweden on May 1 after having gone missing two months ago. In the case of Shahdad and Ihsan, students of Quaid-e-Azam University, following their deaths mainstream media alleged that they had taken up arms against the Pakistani state. Both had been involved in student-related activism for several years, and had strong criticisms against the government. They had also sharply condemned state authorities for the continued exploitation of the natural resources of Balochistan. Their dead bodies were recovered in Kelat district after an army ambush in the region. Meanwhile, three more students, Shabbir, Zakir and Zahid, remain reportedly missing in the province. While the details of their disappearances have not led to a clear picture of who is involved, there are accusations hinting towards the role of state intelligence agencies, which have a shady reputation of being involved in and perpetrating mass disappearances"[13]

Chapter 9

Fair Trials Violations, Confessions without Adequate Safeguards against Torture, Rough-Handling of Prisoners, and Denial of Public Hearing

In 2014, the killing of innocent students in Peshawar by the ISI military unit fashioned good opportunity and an iron in the fire for the army to attack North Waziristan. War criminal General Raheel Sharif wanted to kill innocent women and children in Waziristan in a revenge mission. Later on, the army established their own courts to execute their darling militants. Prime Minister Nawaz Sharif and General Raheel forged a consensus 'to come down hard on the terrorists through a concerted national effort, and later on, it was changed into a so called twenty-point National Action Plan (NAP) approved by Parliament on 24 December 2014. Pakistan's military courts challenged the authority of the country's judicial system, and awarded death sentences to people in their custody.[1] Former DG ISPR Major General Asif Ghafoor favoured the continuance of military courts in Pakistan as a matter of "national requirement. Journalist Mohsin Raza Malik (22 January, 2019) in his article highlighted the controversial function of military courts:

"It was an important point in the National Action Plan (NAP) to establish some military courts in the country for the period of 2 years. After the unfortunate 2014 APS Peshawar incident, the Parliament passed the 21st Constitutional Amendment in January 2015, paving the way for establishing a number of military courts in Pakistan primarily "for speedy trial of certain offences relative to terrorism, waging of war or insurrection against Pakistan and prevention of acts threatening the security of Pakistan". Consequently, some 11 military courts were set up in the four provinces in Pakistan for 2 years. In March 2017, the Parliament extended the tenure of these courts for another 2 years. Meanwhile, the Supreme Court of

Pakistan also formally validated the establishment of these military courts through a landmark verdict. According to ISPR, military courts have taken up 717 cases, and 345 terrorists have given death sentences in four years. So, the conviction rate in these courts has been pretty high compared to civilian criminal courts in the country. The military courts established in Pakistan have constantly been criticized by various quarters for some reasons. Essentially rejecting the extraordinary-circumstances-warrant-extraordinary-measures reasoning, the critics find it hard to accord this 'parallel judicial system' with the tenets of human rights and due process of law. To them, the procedure adopted by the military courts is not strictly in accordance with the Article 10-A of the Constitution of Pakistan, which ensures the due process and fair trial to an accused person".[2]

On 24 November 2015, President amended the army act, and allowed intelligence agencies that they can detain civilians even before the passing of the 21st Amendment. The army was authorized to detain, kill, and torture suspects, and try them in military courts where no human rights organisation or journalist forum were allowed to cover the court proceeding. Dr. Muhammad Zubair, (28 January 2019) in his article noted the changing shape of the army act: "It also authorized military courts to hold in-camera proceedings and keep identities of individuals associated with the cases secret. Moreover, it gave protection and indemnity to court officers for any act done in 'good faith' in pursuance of the military trials. Contents of the presidential ordinance came to public knowledge only nine months later when it was placed before Parliament for approval, which was granted on 11 November 2015 through the Pakistan Army (Amendment) Act, 2015. The constitutional amendment included a sunset clause of two years, with the possibility of extension. The first two-year term of the military courts ended on 7 January 2017. In March 2017, under the watchful eyes of the military leadership, and after three months of negotiations, the government and opposition parties agreed to a two-year extension. It was claimed that the 'extraordinary situation and circumstances' continued to exist and that the extraordinary measures 'have yielded positive results in combating terrorism'".[3]

Pakistan's human rights commission was in hot water when the army tightens the rope around the neck of civilian government. The HRCP only expressed concerns over the planned extension of military courts. However, International Commission of Jurists (ICJ) also criticized the military trial of civilians as a 'disaster for human rights' in Pakistan. An Indian analyst and research scholar, D. Suba Chandran (NIAS, 11, December 2017) in his research paper on Pakistan's Military courts highlighted procedure of courts, and the involvement of military establishment in judicial matter:

"The military courts were established through the 21st constitutional amendment (Pakistan Army (Amendment) Bill, 2015) passed with huge support following the tragic terrorist attack on an Army Public School in December 2014 in Peshawar. The TTP led massacre witnessed the killing of nearly 140 persons in a School in Peshawar, most of them children. In January 2015, both houses of the Parliament passed the bill unanimously thereby establishing military courts for speedy trials of terrorists. The bill had a clause providing for the closure of military courts by 7 January 2017. The military courts also became a part of the Pakistan's National Action Plan (NAP); along with the Zarb-e-Azb, these three were seen as Pakistan's primary counter-terrorism strategy. While the Army is still continuing with the Zarb-e-Azb, the achievements and failure of the NAP have become a political issue during the recent months, whereas the military courts technically came to an end on 7 January 2017. According to media reports, close to 270 cases were tried by the military courts; of which majority of them (around 160) were sentenced to death (though a small number were actually executed) and the rest to prison. Despite a 90 percent conviction, civil society does complain about lack of transparency in the above trials. Though, there were discussions in the media during the late 2016 itself on the impending deadline, there were no political debates within the Parliament on providing an extension to the military courts. With no action, the tenure of the military courts automatically came to an end in early January".[4]

Some political circles supported the idea of military courts that high courts couldn't prosecute militants. The matter was not that simple. On a number of instances, civilian courts' judges were openly threatened by Islamic militant groups such as the Taliban and the Lashkar-e-Taiba. A number of lawyers were killed for prosecuting extremists. Many judges fled the country after receiving death threats. Military courts in Pakistan never convicted a single corrupt military official. These courts received tenacious criticism from civil society and international human rights organizations. Protection of Pakistan Act 2014 can easily deal with judicial matter, and can settle terror-related cases. Ayaz Gul (January 16, 2019) in his analytical article has reviewed operational mechanism of these courts and criticism of International commission of jurists:

The military tribunals have been in operation since January 2015. At that time, the Pakistani parliament authorized them for two years to conduct trials of suspected terrorists in a bid to deter growing terrorism in the country. The ICJ denunciation comes as Prime Minister Imran Khan's government consults with opposition parties on legislation to extend the tenure of the courts. The ICJ cited "serious fair trials violations in the operation of military courts, including: denial of the right to counsel of choice; failure to disclose the charges against the accused; denial of a public hearing; a very high number of convictions – more than 97 percent – based on "confessions" without adequate safeguards against torture and ill treatment."........The Pakistani army and civilian officials reject the charges and maintain the legislation allowing the trials binds the special tribunals to conduct "fair and transparent" hearings. Political parties have backed the military courts, noting Pakistan's regular judicial system does not offer protection to witnesses. Moreover, judges and attorneys prosecuting suspected hardcore militants have complained of receiving death threats or have come under attack. In January 2015, Prime Minister Nawaz Sharif's government promised to reform the civilian criminal justice system and presented the military courts as a temporary solution. Since then, the government has not taken any significant measures to reform the judiciary. From January 7, 2015 to January 6, 2017, military courts convicted 274 individuals and handed down 161 death sentences. At least 17 people have been executed after being convicted by a military court.[5]

Lawyer Kamaran Murtaza expressed deep concern over the apex court judgment and said: "Article 10 of the Pakistani constitution gives every citizen the right to an open trial, and this is not possible in the military courts. Forget about the fair trial, nobody even knows the names of the convicts the military courts have thus far sentenced, and he would appeal against the Supreme Court's decision as it violates fundamental constitutional rights of the people." The HRCP chairperson hammered political parties for not taking advantage of the consensus against Islamist militancy and surrendering their powers to the army. "It is unfortunate that the nationwide resolve against the Taliban and other extremist groups did not translate into political action. It remained a military affair. International human rights forums have deeply criticized the confession by torture in dark military cells and demanded the removal of this cruel justice system". On 16 January 2019, the International commission of jurists deeply criticized the illegal function of military courts in Pakistan. In its briefing paper, the ICJ documented serious fair trials violations in the operation of military courts and warned that high number of convictions–more than 97 percent–based on " confessions without adequate safeguards against torture and ill treatment:

"The trial of civilians by military courts is a glaring surrender of human rights and fundamental freedoms, found the ICJ in its Briefing Paper Military Injustice in Pakistan released today. The Pakistani Government must not extend the tenure of military courts to try civilians for terrorism-related offences, the ICJ said. "Military trials of civilians have been a disaster for human rights in Pakistan," said Frederick Rawski, ICJ's Asia Director. "As a recent judgment of the Peshawar High Court has confirmed, proceedings in these tribunals are secret, opaque, and violate the right to a fair trial before an independent and impartial tribunal," he added. In the briefing paper, the ICJ has documented serious fair trials violations in the operation of military courts, including: denial of the right to counsel of choice; failure to disclose the charges against the accused; denial of a public hearing; failure to give convicts copies of a judgment with evidence and reasons for the verdict; and a very high number of convictions – more than 97 percent – based on "confessions" without adequate safeguards against torture and ill treatment. The ICJ has also demonstrated how military courts are being used to give legal cover to the practice of enforced disappearances. The use of military courts to try civilians is inconsistent with international standards, the ICJ recalled. According to the military, in the four years since military courts were empowered to try terrorism-related offences, they have convicted at least 641 people. Some 345 people have been sentenced to death and 296 people have been given prison sentences. Only five people have been acquitted. At least 56 people have been hanged"[6]

On 12 January 2019, Dr. Mehdi Hasan, Chairperson of the Human Rights Commission of Pakistan (HRCP) expressed grave concern at the government's decision to table a bill in favour of extending the tenure of military courts, which were otherwise due to end their term. In a statement issued the HRCP categorically stated that 'the institution of military courts was an anomaly in any democratic order that claims to uphold the fundamental rights and freedoms of its citizens: "It is the state's duty to uphold the rule of law in a manner that ensures that every citizen is entitled to due process and a fair trial. Equally, it is the state's duty to uphold the rule of law to ensure the security of its citizens. These are not mutually exclusive obligations. Moreover, there is little evidence to show that military courts have succeeded in increasing respect for the rule of law. The perception of 'speedy justice' is no substitute for rooting out the militant extremism that led to the institution of these courts in the first instance or indeed for taking the time to train and equip domestic judicial and police mechanisms that are, and ought to remain, responsible for maintaining civilian law and order under a civilian mandate".[7]

In the aftermath of the December 16 school attack, Pakistan also lifted a seven-year-long moratorium on death penalties. The military, responding to public anger over the Peshawar killings, was moving fast. The military promised that it will not abuse its new powers by prosecuting politicians, journalists or rights activists, as happened in the 1980s. The mandate of the new courts was set to expire after two years, and the trials were subject to civilian oversight. Journalist Imad Zafar once argued that political system has been the target of milablishment propaganda machine. The hatred between the two political camps, Imad Zafar viewed it reaching boiling point and no one liked to be contradicted or criticized for his political affiliations or ideologies. The military establishment's power and control over state resources and institutions is immense. This means creating a counter-narrative has always been the toughest of jobs for the many political parties that have tried. Daily Dawn in its 06 March 2017 analysis of military courts highlighted consecutive conviction of military courts:

"Since February 2015, a total of 274 individuals have been convicted in military courts. So far, the army has sentenced 161 individuals to death, 12 of whom have been executed and 113 have been given jail terms (mostly life sentences). There are roughly 11 military courts that have been set up across Pakistan; three in KP, three in Punjab, two in Sindh and one in Baluchistan. With the sun today having set on Pakistan's military courts, Dawn.com recaps this paper's position against military courts with excerpts of past articles. In April 2015, Sabir Shah disappeared from Lahore's central jail. His family and lawyers did not know where he had gone. Five months later, the family was informed via an ISPR press release, that Sabir had been awarded a death sentence by the military courts. Sabir's lawyer claims he is unaware of the evidence that may have been used to convict his client. Sabir was originally indicted on murder charges. The trial was underway at the civilian courts when he was mysteriously moved to a military internment Centre. In August 2016, families of 16 civilians found guilty by the military courts filed a review petition at the Supreme Court of Pakistan in what turned out to be an iconic hearing. "These trials before the military courts need to be proceeded again after sharing complete evidence and the case record with the accused and also ensuring complete freedom to the accused to engage a counsel of his choice," argued Asma Jahangir before a five-judge Supreme Court bench, headed by Chief Justice Anwar Zaheer Jamali. At first the 21st Amendment, as it is popularly known, was met with much debate, but over time, military courts weaved themselves in to the fabric of Pakistan's criminal justice system". Pakistan's military courts-here's why it should never rise again: Murky procedures, no transparency or right to appeal in civilian courts-a snapshot of Pakistan's military courts.[8]

However, ISPR in 2016 issued a press statement in which its chairman indicated that 135 out of 144 people convicted in military courts had "confessed" to their crimes. That the confession rate was higher than 90 percent points towards a disturbing possibility; that confessions might be elicited using questionable interrogation methods. This statement was rejected by the International Commission of Jurists and noted: "suspects tried by military courts remain in military custody at all times, even after the magistrate records their "confessions". However, Amnesty international in its report (27 March 2019) noted some statements of victim families and the illegal disappearances of Pakistani intelligence agencies:

"We are repeatedly given advice that if we stop protesting, end our activism against enforced disappearances and sit at home, our Baba will come back." Sasui Lohar, daughter of Hidayatullah Lohar, forcibly disappeared since April 17, 2017 from Nasirabad, Sindh, Pakistan. In April 2017, Hidayatullah Lohar, school teacher (headmaster), blacksmith and political Sindhi activist was forcibly disappeared from the school where he taught. He was taken away in a "double-cabin grey coloured" vehicle by men in police uniform and civilian clothes. Since then the authorities have refused to disclose his whereabouts. Despite the presence of eye-witnesses, his family had to petition the Larkana High Court to order the area police station to register the First Information Report. Hidayatullah Lohar is one of Sindh's "missing persons". His family has been patiently seeking truth and justice through the courts and on the streets of Pakistan since his disappearance. His daughters, Sasui and Sorath Lohar are at the forefront of the campaign against enforced disappearance in the southern province of Sindh. Lohar's case was also registered in the Commission for Inquiry of Enforced Disappearances of Pakistan (COIED) and a number of Joint Investigation Team (JIT) (appointed by the COIED) hearings have taken place in the province on the commission's order but to no effect. The JITs comprise of government stakeholders, including the interior ministry, police officials, federal investigation agency officials and intelligence agencies.[9]Amnesty international on 27 March 2019, in its reports warned:

The issue of disappearances has been occasionally raised in public and parliament by political parties, including PPP, PML (N), MQM, BNP (M), and NP (when on Opposition benches). Initially, the media and courts were vocal on the issue. When Iftikhar Muhammad Chaudhry was Chief Justice of the Supreme Court of Pakistan, the apex court entertained a petition of the Balochistan Bar Council. Although, in Pakistan's power structure, law courts are not empowered to punish the Army personnel guilty of enforced disappearance of Baloch people, the Chaudhry-headed bench exerted pressure on the Pakistan Army, FC and intelligence agencies to release missing persons and stop inhuman practice of enforced disappearances. The said petition led to a tussle between the apex court and the Pakistan Army, which resulted in the dismissal and arrest of judges by General Pervez Musharraf. The Pakistan Army and intelligence agencies have been using enforced disappearances as a covert policy to bear down on the Baloch freedom movement and have been vociferously disputing the reports of enforced disappearances of people".[10]

However General Ghafoor admitted in a Press conference on 29 April, 2019: "We know you have a great attachment to missing persons (issue). We too have. We don't want any person to go missing but where there is a war, you have to do a number of (undesirable) works. It's said that everything is fair in love and war. War occurs to be ruthless."[11] The DG ISPR justified the enforced disappearances with his comments "everything is fair in love and war".[12] Moreover, Sayed Irfan Raza in his Dawn (30 January 2019) analysis noted standpoint of military courts about the missing persons. In 2019, Pakistani human rights defender Idris Khattak was forcibly disappeared, activist Muhammad Ismail was arbitrarily detained on trumped up charges, while his daughter and women rights activist Gulalai Ismail fled the country. The authorities also denied entry to a representative from the Committee to Protect Journalists' (CPJ), warned news anchors not to express their opinions, while journalists from the Dawn newspaper faced threats for their reporting. Student protesters including Alamgir Wazir were arrested and charged for their activism. In his Asia Times, (17 September 2019) article, Imad Zafar argued:

"Pakistani establishment is not simply powerful in its own right, with the controlled media and hegemony over state resources, but the current engineered discourse has been backed by Riyadh and Washington. Not a single analyst could have predicted that a regime backed by these superpowers could be defeated. However, all that changed when the establishment proved incapable of pre-empting India's annexation of Kashmir. That proved to be the last nail in the coffin of the current political discourse. According to whistleblowers in the power corridors who do not wish to be named, there is a rift within the security establishment, with many high-ranking officials wanting not only an end to military involvement in political matters but for certain heads to roll. The announcement by Fazal-ur-Rehman, president of the Jamiat Ulema-e-Islam (F) party, of a planned "long march" to Islamabad in October and to hold a sit-in there is not a coincidence by any means. It is believed by many whistleblowers that Fazal has the backing of certain quarters within the establishment who do not want the current dispensation to continue. These people are angry over the Kashmir fiasco and the political engineering that resulted in the current political and economic turmoil in Pakistan".[13] In January 2018, Human Right Watch in its report warned that notwithstanding the establishment of military courts, and an elected government of Prime Minister Imran Khan, cases of human right violation, rape, enforced disappearance, torture in darker prisons exacerbated:

"In March, parliament reinstated secret military courts empowered to try civilians after the term for military courts ended in January 2017. Pakistan human rights groups said that many defendants facing military courts were secretly detained and tortured to coerce confessions. Several remain forcibly disappeared. Authorities do not allow independent monitoring of military court trials. The Pakistan government failed to sufficiently investigate and prosecute allegations of human rights violations by security forces. Security forces remained unaccountable for human rights violations and exercised disproportionate political influence over civilian authorities, especially in matters of national security and counterterrorism. In March, parliament passed a constitutional amendment reinstating secret military courts to try terrorism suspects for another two years. Security forces were implicated in enforced disappearances and extrajudicial killings throughout the country. The government muzzled dissenting voices in nongovernmental organizations (NGOs) and media on the pretext of national security. Militants and interest groups also threatened freedom of expression. Women, religious minorities, and transgender people faced violent attacks, discrimination, and government persecution, with authorities failing to provide adequate protection or hold perpetrators accountable. The inclusion of the transgender population in the 2017 census and the first-ever proposed transgender law were positive developments. The human rights crisis in Balochistan continued with reports of enforced disappearances and extrajudicial killings of suspected Baloch militants. Baloch nationalists and other militant groups continued attacking non-Baloch civilians".[14]

On 22 May, 2020, OpIndia reported cases of abduction, torture, humiliation and organ trade by Pakistan's rogue military units in Baluchistan. Organizer paper reported alleged involvement of Pakistan field units in abduction, forced disappearances, torture and forced organ harvesting of people living in ethnic areas of Balochistan, Organizer reported. The report also claimed that corpses of such ethnic minorities were wrapped by the army in white cloth and family members were intercepted to see faces of their sons and brothers. Such dead bodies have been buried with missing organs. OpIndia reported that the army are burying the dead in dessert. The report of the Organizer claimed that the army covers the bodies such that the stitch marks are not visible to the family. Interestingly, the army also does not allow post-mortem to be conducted on such dead bodies. Organizer also reported that 'illegal organ harvesting has become a flourishing trade in the Islamic Republic of Pakistan. The country had, however, banned the commercial sale of human organs in 2010. As per the law, anyone found involved in organ harvesting and trade of organs can face up to a jail term of 10 years and a maximum fine of PKR 1 million'. Organizer reported.[15]

Chapter 10

The Political and Military Involvement of Inter-Services Intelligence in Afghanistan

D aily Outlook newspaper reported acknowledgement of Pakistan's military chief's official support to Taliban. Over the past few decades, people of Afghanistan have been the victim of continuous proxy wars of regional countries and world powers. Pakistan has specifically played a sinister role in keeping the war ablaze. The overwhelming majority of Afghans have come to the conclusion that the current war has never been fought for any higher value, rather it is a Pakistani proxy war for power. The ISI, and Taliban continue to ruin Afghanistan with the support of Pakistan army rogue units. These three brothers who are not only enemies of each but also indulging in a worst sin by killing innocent children and women in the name of Islam. In a Kabul girl's school, over 35 teenager girl students were killed and around 60 other were injured by the ISI proxies. Pakistani politicians have also expressed concern over the recent violent acts of the ISI and Taliban supported terrorist group. There is no justification either for the Taliban, the ISI and Daesh to continue terror acts while the US is going to withdraw its troops in accordance to Doha Qatar 2020 agreement. These three brother have been targeting Afghan health workers and female journalists since 2010. Healthcare workers were simply discharging their lifesaving polio vaccination and they were engaged in civic services. They were ordinary Afghans who wanted to make sure no children under age of five remain from two drops of vaccine as part of polio eradication initiative and also to prevent the children from being paralyzed.

Their crime was to stop the transmission of this virus and eradicate this scourge. The disgraceful targeting of health workers was an act of cruelty, and those who were behind such assassinations were the forces of destruction . In March, unknown gunmen killed three female polio vaccination workers in Jalalabad that forced the workers to suspend their operations. *Afghanistan Times*, (19 June 2021) noted the breaking point as millions live under the shadows of the war and devastation. "Afghanistan has been in the sticky wicket of conflict and foreign military entanglements for decades now. But, 2021 was the worse year as the US and NATO forces withdrawal emboldened insurgency in the country to levels hitherto unseen. They sharpened their teeth against civilians, massacring them in droves, ruining the modicum of normalcy here and ignoring a global call for ceasefire. What's worse is that the process and the outcome of peace talks inherently ambiguous which could be translated as a failure in the battlefield against the foes". The newspaper reported. The Canada Immigration and Refugee Board-Research Directorate, (23 November 1999) in its report spotlighted the ISI as state within a state, answerable neither to the leadership of the army, nor to the President or the Prime Minister. The result is there has been no real supervision of the ISI, and corruption, narcotics, and big money have all come into play, further complicating the political scenario. Drug money is used by ISI to finance not only the Afghanistan war, but also the proxy war against India in Punjab and Kashmir. The report noted:

"Staffed by hundreds of civilian and military officers, and thousands of other workers, the agency's headquarters is located in Islamabad. The ISI reportedly has a total of about 10,000 officers and staff members, a number which does not include informants and assets..........The Directorate for Inter-Services Intelligence is of particular importance at the joint services level. The directorate's importance derives from the fact that the agency is charged with managing covert operations outside of Pakistan -- whether in Afghanistan, Kashmir, or farther afield. The ISI supplies weapons, training, advice and planning assistance to terrorists in Punjab and Kashmir, as well as the separatist movements in the Northeast frontier areas of India. The ISI continues to actively participate in Afghan Civil War, supporting the Taliban in their fight against the Rabbani government". Allegations have been raised by international government officials, policy analysts and even Pakistani military officials that the ISI in conjunction with the military leadership has also provided some amount of support and refuge to al-Qaeda".

Former Indian parliamentarian and politician, Shashi Tharoor the Strategist, (09 June 2021) in his critical analysis noted: "The ISI has long been obsessed with the idea that controlling Afghanistan would give Pakistan the 'strategic depth' needed to challenge its main adversary, India. A Taliban regime (or even a Taliban-dominated coalition government) in Kabul is the best guarantee of that. The Taliban factions are so beholden to their Pakistani benefactors that, as Afghan President Ashraf Ghani acidly remarked, their decision-making bodies—Quetta Shura, Miramshah Shura and Peshawar Shura—are named after the Pakistani towns where they are based. And as the ISI knows, the problem with creating and sponsoring militant groups is that they do not always remain under your control. The lesson of Mary Shelley's Frankenstein—that the creatures we give life to can develop minds and needs of their own—has been apparent elsewhere as well, not least in Israel's role in building up Hamas as a rival to the Palestine Liberation Organization". The Inter-Services Intelligence (ISI) intelligence agency of Pakistan has been accused of heavily involved in covertly running military intelligence programs in Afghanistan since before the Soviet invasion of Afghanistan in 1979. Kamal Davar has documented involvement of the ISI with the Taliban and other terrorist groups. (The US withdrawal from Afghanistan: A strategic blunder in the making, June 17, 2021):

"In the complete mess existing in Afghanistan currently, the nation which appears to have the maximum gain from the ensuing political and security instability is neighbourly Pakistan. For years, its Inter-Services Intelligence (ISI) has trained, equipped and funded the Afghan Taliban and the other terrorist outfits operating inside Afghanistan. Pakistan senses, with the US exit, it will be able to exercise a hold on Afghanistan's internal affairs with a pliant regime in power in Kabul. It also hopes that its traditional strategy of keeping India out of any reckoning in Afghan affairs will bear fruition. The ISI would already be planning for out-of-work terrorists from Afghanistan to be redeployed for terrorist acts inside Jammu and Kashmir. Pakistan, however, with its myopic mind-set forgets the simple fact that a fiercely independent Pashtuni Taliban in Afghanistan, if and when it seizes power in Kabul, can turn the heat on its Pakistani mentors in working for assimilation of Pathan-dominated areas in Pakistan from the Khyber Pakhtunkhwa and Baluchistan provinces into Afghanistan. As is commonly known, no Afghan government in the past or any of its leaders or tribes have ever recognized the Durand Line, which was drawn by the erstwhile imperial British power in 1893 as the boundary between Afghanistan and Pakistan. Pakistan, as ever before, will continue to fish in the troubled waters of Afghanistan; this is a foregone conclusion. "Alexandra Gilliard (Global Security Review. Pakistan's Inter-Services Intelligence Contributes to Regional Instability 07 Jun, 2019) has also noted the role of the ISI in Afghan politics and its support to Taliban and the ISIS groups: "In Afghanistan, Pakistan's primary goal is to prevent India from gaining ground and obtaining too much influence. As the Taliban vies for more control, the ISI has provided it with military aid to ensure

Afghanistan remains in a state of perpetual instability. Should the Taliban gain power, Pakistan will have bought itself a staunch ally in the region, with the potential to form a strategic partnership against India".[1]

During the Afghan Jihad in 1980s, jihadists poured into Pakistan from across the Muslim world, including Palestinian teacher and preacher Abdullah Azzam, who had taught in Jordan and Saudi Arabia, preaching Muslims' duty to wage jihad against non-Muslims.[2] In 1990, The ISI diverted its attention towards Kashmir, and established training camps for Kashmiri mujahedeen to engage India in an unending proxy war. General Pervez Musharraf played an instrumental role in drafting Pakistan's role in the Afghan civil war. From 1996 to 2001 Osama Bin Laden and Ayman al-Zawahiri remained in Afghanistan. However, the US invaded Afghanistan in October 2001.[3] The Inter-Services Intelligence (ISI) intelligence agency of Pakistan has been heavily involved in covertly running military intelligence programs in Afghanistan before and after the US invasion. The United States, along with the ISI and Pakistan's government of Prime Minister Benazir Bhutto became the primary source of support for Hekmatyar in his 1992–1994 bombardment campaign against the Islamic State of Afghanistan. Hollingsworth, Christopher L and Sider, Joshua has noted changing political and military involvement of Pakistan in Afghanistan. Pakistan provided arms and financial support to Afghanistan, and in August 2021, its forces attacked Afghan cities:

"Pakistan's support of the Afghan Taliban has numerous layers that have morphed into the current relationship that exists today. This relationship originates from Pakistan's ties to the mujahedeen who fought the Soviet occupation of Afghanistan between 1979 and 1989. Following the Soviet withdrawal in 1989, Afghanistan was thrust into a civil war between the Soviet-backed Najibullah regime and Afghan warlords who fought to govern the country. This conflict left Pakistan caught between its rival, India, and an increasingly unstable Afghanistan. When the Taliban formed from these mujahedeen fighters in 1994, Pakistan viewed the organization as a possible method of stabilizing Afghanistan. Their support contributed to the Taliban rapidly seizure (90%) of Afghanistan between 1994 and 1996. The events between the Taliban's rise to power and today are well documented. The Taliban remained in control of most of the country until after the attacks on September 11, 2001. Since the U.S. and Northern Alliance removed them from power, the Taliban now control more territory than at any point since 2001. Many observers of the Afghan conflict have blamed poor security and governance in Afghanistan for the resurgent

Taliban. The Taliban benefits from the government of Afghanistan's lack of control, but the support of Pakistan remains a significant source of their resurgence".[4]

The ISI established relationship with numerous political organizations in Afghanistan, but its persisting policy inside the country causes distrust. The ISI wants Indian intelligence to curtail its presence in Afghanistan, and close terror training camps inside the country.[5] Indian intelligence RAW's proxy war against Pakistan prompted deep political and security crisis in Afghanistan. The ISI never tolerated the Indian RAW presence in Afghanistan, the reason that its role in managing several anti-India proxy networks was also unmistakable.[6] Pakistan's military establishment supported militant groups to destabilize the region and maintain Pakistan's sovereignty and national identity. However, civilian institutions also facilitated militants by routinely legitimizing expansive executive powers, limiting judicial oversight, and violating civil liberties in the name of the national interest.[7] Militants who sat across the table with American officials in Doha and Islamabad were trained in Pakistan.

Agreement for Bringing Peace to Afghanistan between the Islamic Emirate of Afghanistan which was not recognized by the United States as a state and known as the Taliban and the United States of America signed on 29, February, 2020. Afghans have only seen wars and there is little hope that their miseries will end soon. India has enjoyed a long period of primacy in Afghanistan but a growing Chinese interest in the war-ridden country is poised to upset that delicate arrangement. The China-India competition has many of the smaller neighboring countries in the region concerned about getting caught between the two Asian giants. China wants to build a small military base in Badakhshan to counter any insurgency spillover. In addition to its training efforts, India has also donated Mi-25 and Mi-35 helicopters to Afghanistan, which have proved invaluable for counter-militant operations. On 07 May 2018; Javid Ahmad in his article revealed some new things about the ISI role in Afghanistan:

"In Afghanistan, ISI's Afghan operations are undertaken by at least three units. The first is Directorate S, the principal covert action arm that directs and oversees the Afghan policy, including militant and terrorist outfits and their operations. The second unit is, the Special Service Group (SSG), also known as the Pakistani SS, and is the army's Special Forces element that was established in the 1950s as a hedge against the communists. Today, some SSG units effectively operate as ISI's paramilitary wing and have fought alongside the Taliban until 2001. In other instances, SSG advisors have allegedly been embedded with Taliban fighters to provide tactical military advice, including on special operations, surveillance, and reconnaissance. In fact, encountering ISI operatives fighting alongside the Taliban in Afghanistan has become a common occurrence that no longer surprise Afghan and American forces. The third ISI unit is the Afghan Logistics Cell, a transport network inside Pakistan facilitated by members of Pakistan's Frontier Corps that provide logistical support to the Taliban and their families. This includes space, weapons, vehicles, protection, money, identity cards and safe passage. Such ISI support networks have been designed to break Afghanistan into pieces and then remold it into a pliant state. The objective is to complicate Afghanistan's security landscape and drive its political climate into an uncharted constitutional territory to create a vacuum, which inevitably places the Taliban in the driving seat. These support actions have visibly made the group more effective. However, the Pakistani mantra is that they maintain contacts with the Taliban but exercise no control over them".[8]

However, after the Soviet intervention in Afghanistan, CIA and ISI established close relationship to fit their forces to the fight against Russian forces. General Abdul Rehman Khan further adorned the agency with modern intelligence technology, and benefited from the covert war operation of ISI. General Zia-ul-Haq was also trying to make the agency professionalize to counter the Indian influence in Afghanistan. He was committed to make the ISI one of the strongest intelligence agencies in South Asia, but unfortunately, he used the agency against political forces.[9] When Benazir took over as Prime Minister; she removed General Hamid Gul due to his jihadist concepts, and appointed General Shamsul Rehman Kallue as the Chief of ISI, but General Aslam Beg never allowed Benazir to manage the Kashmir and Afghan policy. Pakistan like other countries has professional management of its intelligence agencies. This is evident from the fact that in over five decades of nationhood, there have been six committees to review their function.[10] In his research paper, Dr. Bidanda M. Chengappa explains the strategies of ISI against democratic governments to protect the interests of miltablishment:

"During this period there was an uneasy relationship between the military and the political leadership when the country last experienced a decade of democracy. While the military did not directly intervene in the political process the generals used the ISI as a lever to manipulate the course of politics to suit their interests. Essentially the generals wanted a civilian government that would not curtail their power and to that extent such democracy came to be termed 'limited', 'guided' or Islamic democracy. The ISI was variously used to prop up friendly political persona who enjoyed good relations with the military leadership and conversely to minimize the chances of success for a hostile leader through the creation of unfavorable conditions. It was also involved with the creation of new parties or split existing ones in order to act as a counter-weight against other parties. Apparently, the ISI proved to be more useful to the military leadership—in the post-Zia decade—which could not exercise its power over state and society overtly but had to do so covertly.......However, Benazir said that the ISI was involved against her government which could be analyzed in terms of the power of information".[11]

There are different perceptions about the ISI and its support to Taliban in Afghanistan. Some politicians view the function of ISI in the country as interference in the internal affairs of Afghanistan, and some view it as a terrorist campaign against the country. On 19 September 2019, Afghan human rights activist Bilal Sarwary accused Inter-Services Intelligence (ISI) of providing institutional support to terrorist groups operating in Afghanistan. The activist—Bilal Sarway was addressing the tail-end session of the United Nations Human Rights Council (UNHRC) when he made this claim. According to a report by news agency ANI, Sarway said that the Haqqani Network, the Afghan insurgent group is a 'veritable arm' of ISI's and held it responsible for some of the worst attacks in Kabul. "Pakistan-sponsored terrorism has resulted in the deaths of the Afghan military personnel, international aid workers, civilians, children, and very often entire families have vanished due to these attacks. "Our cities, schools, clinics, funerals, and weddings have been targeted in these brutal terrorist attacks". Sarwary said.[12] Javid Ahmad (07 May 2018-The National Interests) in his article highlighted the ISI operations in Afghanistan through different units. He also spotlighted three important units of the ISI operating in Afghanistan in different directions:

"In Afghanistan, ISI's Afghan operations are undertaken by at least three units. The first is Directorate S, the principal covert action arm that directs and oversees the Afghan policy, including militant and terrorist outfits and their operations. The second unit is the Special Service Group (SSG), also known as the Pakistani SS, and is the army's Special Forces element that was established in the 1950s as a hedge against the communists. Today, some SSG units effectively operate as ISI's paramilitary wing and have fought alongside the Taliban until 2001. In other instances, SSG advisors have allegedly been embedded with Taliban fighters to provide tactical military advice, including on special operations, surveillance, and reconnaissance. In fact, encountering ISI operatives fighting alongside the Taliban in Afghanistan has become a common occurrence that no longer surprises Afghan and American forces. The third ISI unit is the Afghan Logistics Cell, a transport network inside Pakistan facilitated by members of Pakistan's Frontier Corps that provide logistical support to the Taliban and their families. This includes space, weapons, vehicles, protection, money, identity cards and safe passage. Such ISI support networks have been designed to break Afghanistan into pieces and then remould it into a pliant state. The objective is to complicate Afghanistan's security landscape and drive its political climate into uncharted constitutional territory to create a vacuum, which inevitably places the Taliban in the driving seat. These support actions have visibly made the group more effective. However, the Pakistani mantra is that they maintain contacts with the Taliban but exercise no control over them".[13]

Since 2001, posing as an indispensable ally in the war against terrorism, Pakistan has been benefitting from a lavish US military and development aid, while continuing to provide a safe haven for the Taliban and the Haqqani network. The ISI intelligence agency's grossly misguided Taliban project eventually gave birth to various groups of Pakistani Taliban. The unfortunate but crystalline reality of Afghanistan's future is that it hinges on the decisions made by Pakistani generals and whether their actions will be checked by a Coalition response. Mullah Abdul Salam Zaeef was arrested by Pakistan's ISI, with the help of their American counterparts, ignoring his diplomatic status and his application for political asylum in Pakistan to escape the wrath of Americans in Afghanistan. He was the senior most official of the Taliban government who could be arrested by the US forces with the help of Pakistan. Another mistake of Pakistan army was to trade in the lives of the Afghans-arresting and killing them, raiding their homes and illegally detaining their relatives and family members.

The arrest of Mullah Abdul Salam Zaeef by Pakistan's law enforcement agencies caused misunderstanding between the people of Afghanistan and Pakistan that a close and friendly neighbour intentionally violated international law. No doubt ISI has a prolixity list of friends in Afghanistan, but military dictator General Musharraf acted differently. Former Afghan Ambassador was arrested and handed to the US agencies. He was humiliated by the CIA in the presence of officials in Islamabad. John F. Burns 04 January 2002) published a detailed story of his humiliation and torture in New York Times. Pakistani analyst Ayaz Amir (daily Dawn. 22 September 2006) also noted some aspects of his painful instant:

"We know, to our lasting shame, how our overlords, dazzled by American power, and afraid of God knows what, handed over the ex-Taliban ambassador, Mullah Abdus Salam Zaeef, to the Americans in January 2002—in violation of every last comma of international law. But until now we have not been privy to the details: how exactly did the handing-over take place? Now to satisfy our curiosity, and perhaps outrage our feelings, comes Mullah Zaeef's own account, published in Pashto and parts of which have been translated into Urdu by the Express newspaper. To say that the account is eye-opening would be an understatement. It is harrowing and mind-blowing. Can anyone bend so low as our government did? And can behaviour be as wretched as that displayed by American military personnel into whose custody Zaeef was given? On the morning of January 2, 2002, three officials of a secret agency arrived at Zaeef's house in Islamabad with this message: "Your Excellency, you are no more excellency." One of them said, no one can resist American power or words to that effect. "America wants to question you. We are going to hand you over to the Americans so that their purpose is served and Pakistan is saved from a big danger." Zaeef could have been forgiven for feeling stunned. From the "guardians of Islam" this was the last thing that he expected, that for the sake of a few "coins" (his words) he would be delivered as a "gift" to the Americans. Under heavy escort he was taken to Peshawar, kept there for a few days and then pushed into his nightmare. Blindfolded and handcuffed, he was driven to a place where a helicopter was waiting, its engines running. Someone said, "Khuda hafiz" (God preserve you).[14]

Not only Mullah Zaeef was tortured by Pakistani agencies, many Pakistani citizens were detained incommunicado in undisclosed places of detention and tortured. Their families distressed about the lack of information on the whereabouts and fate of their loved ones. Ayaz Amir noted his painful journey, and mental and physical torture by the ISI and CIA, and noted Pakistan's constraints as well. This was Pakistan's biggest mistake that changed mind of every Afghan about the country's hostile attitude towards Afghanistan. Mullah Abdul Salam Zaeef, the Taliban government's ambassador to Pakistan in his book "My Life with the Taliban" has described his heartbreaking story:

"When we arrived in Peshawar I was taken to a lavishly-fitted office. A Pakistani flag stood on the desk, and a picture of Mohammad Ali Jinnah hung at the back of the room. A Pashtun man was sitting behind the desk.

He got up, introduced himself and welcomed me. His head was shaved —
seemingly his only feature of note — and he was of an average size and
weight. He walked over to me and said that he was the head of the bureau.
I was in the devil's workshop, the regional head office of the ISI. He told me
I was a close friend —a guest —and one that they cared about a great deal.
I wasn't really sure what he meant, since it was pretty clear that I was dear
to them only because they could get a good sum of money for me when
they sold me. Their trade was people; just as with goats, the higher the
price for the goat, the happier the owner. In the twenty-first century there
aren't many places left where you can still buy and sell people, but Pakistan
remains a hub for this trade. I prayed after dinner with the ISI officer, and
then was brought to a holding-cell for detainees.........Finally, after days in
my cell, a man came, tears flowing down his cheeks. He fainted as his grief
and shame overcame him. He was the last person I saw in that room. I never
learnt his name, but soon after—perhaps four hours after he left — I was
handed over to the Americans. Even before I reached the helicopter, I was
suddenly attacked from all sides. People kicked me, shouted at me, and my
clothes were cut with knives. They ripped the black cloth from my face and
for the first time I could see where I was. Pakistani and American soldiers
stood around me. The Pakistani soldiers were all staring as the Americans
hit me and tore the remaining clothes off from my body. Eventually I was
completely naked, and the Pakistani soldiers — the defenders of the Holy
Qur'an — shamelessly watched me with smiles on their faces, saluting this
disgraceful action of the Americans".[15]

Abdul Salam Zaeef was mentally tortured by Pakistani agencies. He was
sold by General Musharraf and ISI to the US just for handful money, and
never thought that his vivacity will alienate Afghans forever from Pakistan.
Before this occurrence, they killed former President of Afghanistan, Dr.
Muhammad Najibullah in Kabul. Analyst Ayaz Amir narrates Mullah
Zaeef's wearisomeness when he was undressed: "There were some people
speaking in English. "Suddenly I was pounced upon and flung on the
ground, kicked and pummeled from all sides. So sudden was the attack
that I was dumbfounded... My blindfold slipping, I saw a line of Pakistani
soldiers to one side and some vehicles including one with a flag...My clothes
were stripped from my body and I was naked but 'my former friends' kept
watching the spectacle. The locks on their lips I can never forget... The
(Pakistani) officers present there could at least have said he is our guest, in
our presence don't treat him like this. Even in my grave I will not be able to
forget that scene." Zaeef suffered unspeakable tortures at the hands of his
American captors. He was kept in Bagram, and then taken to Kandahar

and from there flown eventually to Guantanamo. He was released from Guantanomo and flown to Kabul in September 2005, charged with nothing, nothing having been proven against him. He remained in American captivity for close to four years".[16]

Mullah Abdul Salam Zaeef suffered inexpressible pain at the hands of ISI within Afghanistan and within the United States by CIA. Moreover, Pakistan perpetrated one more crime by killing former President Dr. Najeebullah inside the Presidential palace in Kabul in the presence of merchant of fear General Hamid Gul. This way of treating a neighboring state prompted bigger political and diplomatic challenges for Pakistan. On 26 September 2016, TolonewsTV reported an Afghan research center divulgence on the 20th anniversary of the death of former Afghan President Dr. Najibullah Ahmadzai. The TV report indicated that former leader was killed based on an intelligence plan, drafted by regional countries and adopted by Pakistan's Inter-Services Intelligence (ISI). Deputy Chief of Afghanistan's Strategic and Scientific Research Center, Aimal Liyan, said that evidence existed to this effect: "There is evidence which shows that famous Pakistani generals from Pakistan's intelligence agency such as Aslam Beg, Gen. Hamid Gul the former head of Pakistan's Inter-Services Intelligence (ISI), Nasirullah Babur and others and besides that, there were other intelligence officials from other countries. The plan to kill Najibullah was implemented by ISI," he said.

"Dr. Najibullah was in favor of unity among Afghans. He wanted peace in the country but he was killed." He added. Meanwhile, Suleiman Layiq, one of Najibullah›s supporters, said: "He [Najibullah] had good relations with people. He was an honest man." However, Aryan Khabir said that: "Twenty years after Najibullah's death we see that his demands which were unity among the people have not been fulfilled yet," Dr. Najibullah was President of Afghanistan from 1987 to 1992. He then lived in the United Nations headquarters in Kabul until 1996, when the Taliban took control of Kabul. Tolonews reported. Moreover, analyst Dr. Muhammad Taqi (September 2014, Daily Times) also quoted paragraphs from the book of US former special envoy to Afghanistan, Peter Tomsen who narrated story of Dr. Najeebullah murder in his book, 'The Wars of Afghanistan': "Four Taliban, including, by one account, a Pakistani ISI officer disguised as Taliban, drove directly to the UN compound in a Japanese Datsun pickup. Their mission was to lure the former Afghan President out of the diplomatically protected UN premises." Mullah Abdul Razzaq was the Taliban ringleader who carried out the torture, killing, mutilation and desecration of the corpses—a war crime by any definition—at the behest of his Pakistani minders".[17]

Pakistan's intelligence agencies and the Army support the ISIS terrorist networks inside Afghanistan and Pakistan. War in Afghanistan has inflicted catastrophe, displaced million people, and damaged the US artificial state and its institutions. Pakistan army played crucial role against the US and NATO forced, and forced to withdraw from Afghanistan. Pakistan army and the ISI support war in Afghanistan for the reason that it has gained a good experience of war and destruction in North Waziristan, where war criminal General Raheel Sharif and his rogue units killed women and children with impunity. Chris Alexander (Ending Pakistan's proxy war in Afghanistan. Chris Alexander (March 2021) in his research paper noted ISI's never closed training camps in Afghanistan.[18] Moreover, research scholars, Dr. Adrian Hänni and Lukas Hegi (Pakistani Godfather: (The Inter-Services Intelligence and the Afghan Taliban, 1994-2020, Small War Journal Tuesday, 04 February, 2013) have documented some aspects of the ISI involvement in Afghanistan and its support to Taliban:

"The involvement of the ISI in the early stages of the revolt against the Karzai government and international troops (2003-2005) has been widely documented. After the Taliban attacks in Afghanistan had increased in 2003, the ISI provided support again. U.S. and NATO intelligence shows a systematic and pervasive system of ISI collusion. The ISI held training camp for Taliban recruits north of Quetta, handing out money and weapons from the Gulf States and organized shopping tours in Quetta and Karachi, where the Taliban were able to stock up on material, buying hundreds of motorcycles, pickup trucks and satellite phones. Pakistani army trucks drove Taliban fighters to the border at night in order to infiltrate Afghanistan and were there to receive them when they returned several days later. In doing so, the Pakistani artillery provided fire protection as well as medical care near the border to the Taliban. Moreover, the Pakistani army officers upheld communications from the border with Taliban commanders in Afghanistan via mobile phone. Just like in the early days of the Mullah Omar gang, the Taliban, the ISI and the madrassas of Jamiat Ulema-e-Islam (JUI) were holding in place a well-organized system. Young militants in the madrassas first underwent "religious training" for several weeks before being recruited by Taliban recruiters - who often appeared in the company of ISI officers - and sent to the front. Every month, the heads of all JUI madrasas met with an ISI officer in Quetta to discuss the operational procedures and funding. The great double game soon proved to be an institutional difficulty for the ISI. Under the watchful eyes of Western intelligence agencies, it was almost impossible for them to help the CIA on the one hand and on the other hand to lead the Taliban. This challenge was overcome through privatization, specifically the construction of a new secret organization that was to operate outside the military and intelligence apparatus."[19]

Senator Jack Reed, Chairman of Senate Armed Services Committee warned that Pakistan's Inter-Services Intelligence supported the Taliban while 'opportunistically cooperating' with the US. PTI from Washington reported on April 16, 2021 Pakistan's role "on both sides of the field in Afghanistan, contributing to the Taliban's success, a senior US senator has reminded his colleagues, a day after Washington announced plans to withdraw all troops from the war-torn Asian country by September 11". "As the (congressionally mandated) Afghan Study Group noted, these sanctuaries are essential to the viability of the insurgency. Additionally, Pakistan's ISI aided and abetted the Taliban while opportunistically cooperating with the United States," Reed said.[20]

"This support of the Taliban runs counter to Pakistani cooperation with the United States, including as they have, allowing the use of airspace and other infrastructure for which the United States provided significant funding," he said.[21] Pakistan created and sponsored a Mujahedeen group calling themselves the Taliban, or 'students' of Islam, who swiftly took over Afghanistan and ruled it as a wholly owned ISI subsidiary," Tharoor argued. According to Tharoor, the Pakistan-Taliban axis remained robust until Osama bin Laden and al-Qaeda undertook the September 11 attacks against the US. "America's furious response resulted in the overthrow of the Taliban and the exile of bin Laden, under ISI protection, to refuge in a Pakistani military redoubt. The ISI had even less to crow about when US tracked down bin Laden to a secure compound in Abbottabad and Special Forces killed him there in 2011," Tharoor said.[22]

The United States intelligence reports claimed that Pakistani ISI had bombed Indian Embassy in Kabul in 2008. The Haqqani group carried out the attack. In response to the Afghan War documents leak, The Guardian newspaper had a very different take on allegations that Pakistan was sponsoring terrorism in Afghanistan. On 25 July, 2010, journalist Declan Walsh noted: "But for all their eye-popping details, the intelligence files, which are mostly collated by junior officers relying on informants and Afghan officials, fail to provide a convincing smoking gun for ISI complicity. Most of the reports are vague, filled with incongruent detail, or crudely fabricated. The same characters–famous Taliban commanders, well-known ISI officials–and scenarios repeatedly pop up. And few of the events predicted in the reports subsequently occurred. A retired senior American officer said ground-level reports were considered to be a mixture of "rumors, bullshit and second-hand information" and were weeded out as they passed up the chain of command".[23] In his Guardian interview, General Musharraf admitted that Kashmiri freedom fighters, Taliban, Hafiz Muhammad Saeed and Lakhvi were Pakistan's heroes. "We trained Taliban and sent them to fight against Soviet Union. Taliban, Haqqani, Osama Bin Laden and Zawahiri were our heroes then (during the Soviet-Afghan war). Later they became villains" says Pervez Musharraf". The ISI has often been accused of using Taliban against the Afghan government.[24]

Human Rights Watch in its report (2021) noted human rights violations in Afghanistan. The report documented important aspects of human rights in the country, and called for a broad representation of Afghans in the peace talks, including women. According to the United Nations Assistance Mission in Afghanistan (UNAMA), "the Taliban were responsible for 45 percent of attacks that caused civilian deaths and injuries in the first nine months of 2020. Pro-government forces were responsible for 27 percent. Attacks by the Islamic State of Khorasan Province (ISKP), the Afghan branch of the Islamic State (ISIS), declined, but the group was responsible for several deadly bombings. Women and children comprised over 44 percent of all civilian casualties". Human Rights Watch argued: "Although President Ashraf Ghani pledged to ban night raids in September 2019, such operations by Special Forces continued, including a December 2019 raid in which Special Forces killed a 15-year-old boy in Laghman. A January 7 operation by National Directorate of Security (NDS) forces killed a prominent politician, Amer Abdul Sattar, and five others at a house in Kabul. Government officials claimed to be investigating the killings of civilians in night raids by CIA-backed Special Forces, but no findings from these investigations were made public". Attacks against media workers and human rights activists were also carried out by Taliban.[25]

Human Rights Watch reported Fatima Natasha Khalil and Ahmad Jawid Folad, "employees of the Afghanistan Independent Human Rights Commission (AIHRC), were killed when an IED attached to their car in Kabul detonated on June 27. The AIHRC vehicle had government plates". Taliban appear to be on the verge of reconstituting the so-called Islamic Emirate of Afghanistan proto-state that was toppled in late 2001 by U.S., coalition and indigenous forces. Afghanistan Times (28 June, 2021) in its editorial page noted that Pakistan supports Taliban against the Afghan government: "Pakistan authorities have never admitted their support to the Taliban openly, but in some cases they didn't deny. Even in the recent interview, the foreign minister of Pakistan openly denied any bases or support to the Taliban. But here it comes opposite when Pakistan's Interior Minister Sheikh Rashid had exposed Pakistan support to the Taliban. He showed bravery and spoke about the truth and even said that Taliban are present in the outskirts of Islamabad........Even the Taliban are receiving treatment in Pakistani hospitals, maintaining sanctuaries, and their leaders are based in Pakistan and they were targeted in the Pakistani soil. Several Taliban and al-Qaeda leaders were killed there – and not more evidence needed. When the Pakistan Prime Minister Imran Khan himself gave martyr status to Osma bin-Laden, and his foreign minister don't answer this question that why Mr. Khan calls a terrorist a martyr, so why are the world leaders waiting for".[26]

Afghan newspapers on 25 December 2021 reported activities of insurgent elements and their leaders in Pakistani territory that clearly violate Afghanistan's national sovereignty, posing a serious challenge to achieving sustainable peace. "The visit of Taliban representatives to Pakistan and their negotiations with Pakistani officials raised further hopes for taking practical steps toward stopping the bloodshed and bringing about sustainable peace in Afghanistan, according to the statement. The leadership of the Government of Pakistan assured the Government of Afghanistan that it would employ all available means and potentials towards reducing violence, establishing a ceasefire, and paving the ground for a peaceful resolution of the Afghan crisis. To that end, the Ministry of Foreign Affairs of Afghanistan expressed its gratitude and appreciation for the Pakistani Government's recent efforts to advance the [Afghan] peace process. However, following the Taliban leaders' meetings with Pakistani officials, a series of video footages emerged in which the Taliban appeared among their followers, disclosing the existence of all Taliban leaders in Pakistan and acknowledging their continued activities in Pakistani territory, the statement added. "It is with deepest regret and concern that some Taliban leaders were seen in the videos visiting training camps." However, first Vice President Amrullah Saleh in a tweet said, "Mullah Bradar did three things in Karachi. He visited the wounded Taliban terrorists at a government hospital who were there without any visa, went to a training facility to inspire the terror cadets and thanked the government of Pakistan for generous support to the Taliban to this point. "The intensification of violence is due to failure of peace talks in Qatar that were significantly unsuccessful to bear any fruits to at least lower the level of violence.[27]

Pakistan's intelligence agencies are supporting the ISIS terrorist networks in various districts of the country. The country has a long history of promoting terrorism in the name of Pakistan's geostrategic interests. Author Gordon Thomas stated that, Pakistan sponsored terrorist groups in the Indian state of Jammu and Kashmir, funding, training and arming them in their war of attrition against India". However, Mr. Stephen Schwartz noted several terrorist groups were receiving support from Pakistani army, and the ISI. Afghanistan is not the only state where Pakistani supports terrorist groups. The country is also supporting terrorists in Kashmir. Moreover, Military dictator, General Musharraf admitted that his army trained militant groups to fight India in Kashmir, and his government had turned a blind eye. Musharraf said: "Inter-Services Intelligence directorate (ISI) cultivated the Taliban after 2001 because Karzai's government was dominated by non-Pashtuns, who are the country's largest ethnic group, and by officials who were thought to favour India.

The Daesh prodigy in 2015 provoked and agitated Pakistan's landscape, while a video message from the Hafsa Madrassa in Islamabad surfaced, in which students of the madrassa invited the Daesh Chief Abu Bakar al-Baghdadi to Pakistan to teach a lesson to the Pakistan army. After this video appeared in print media, Daesh declared its presence in the country. There are speculations that The Fauji Foundation of Pakistan army has contributed more than 5,000 retired army soldiers and officers in the army of the ISIS terrorist groups. Major retired Agha Amin a Lahore-based Defence analyst, revealed that Pakistani fighters went to Syria and Iraq with the support of the army and government. The army, Agha Amin said, allowed General Hamid Gul to take former Pakistani soldiers to Iraq and Syria. In 2014, a three member Daesh delegation reached Pakistan from Syria, The delegation was headed by Zubair Al Kuwaiti and included Uzbek Commander Fahim Ansari and Sheikh Yusuf from Saudi Arabia (Akbar 2015). They met Pakistan's based terrorist groups.

Daily Khabrain, Pakistan's Urdu newspaper (29th December, 2015) reported the statement of former Foreign Minister of Pakistan Sardar Asif Ahmed Ali on December 29, 2015, the newspaper reported that some Pakistani travel agents were recruiting youth to fight in the Middle East. However, Senator General Rtd. Abdul Qayyum demanded action against the travel agents. Genral Abdul Qayyum also said that women were being exported for sex trade. Another Senator Javed Abbasi told the Senate that there were 17 illegal networks involved in exporting youth to the Middle East and these networks are making profits to the tune of 927 million dollars.[28] Dr. Yunis Khushi (ISIS in Pakistan: A Critical Analysis of Factors and Implications of ISIS Recruitments and Concept of Jihad-Bil-Nikah-26 June 2017) exposed relationship of government authorities and the Islamic terrorist State in Pakistan:

"A sort of high level game is going on, on the political, foreign policy and law-enforcement levels regarding the presence of ISIS in Pakistan. The politicians, Foreign Ministry, Interior Ministry, and Law Enforcement Agencies are singing different tunes regarding the presence, recruitments and migration of jihadis or mujahids and jihadi wives from Pakistan to Syria to join the ISIS. It seems that publicly, the Pakistani Government has refused Saudi Government to send Pakistani armies to Saudi Arabia to fight against Houthi rebels, but silently some private groups have been allowed to recruit youth to join Saudi Armies to fight against Houthis and also against ISIS, which are a major threat against not only Saudi Empire, but also against Arab Emirates and other Middle Eastern Kingdoms. The recruitments for ISIS have been going on in Pakistan for the past more than three years, but the Foreign and the Interior Ministries of Pakistan have been constantly denying the presence and activities of ISIS in Pakistan. Law Enforcement agencies have very recently arrested many people from Lahore, Islamabad, Karachi and Sialkot who were associated with ISIS networks. Men have been recruited as jihadis or mujtahid's and women as jihadi wives to provide sexual needs of fighters who are fighting in Syria, Iraq and Afghanistan. Many women, impressed and convinced through brainwashing with the concept of Jihad-Bil-Nikah, got divorce from their Pakistani husbands and went to marry a Mujahid of ISIS for a certain period, came back gave birth to the child of Mujahid, and remarried their former husband. Some decide to continue that marriage for rest of their lives".[29]

However, Sex business in Pakistan's Sial Kot district, and parts of Bahawal Pur, Rahim Yar Khan and Central Punjab, and the involvement of different groups and individuals in its raised important questions that why Pakistan and its army support the ISIS group in Syria and Iraq, and wht the women brigade of the ISIS army was allowed to recruit women in Sial Kot district? Dr. Yunis Khushi has highlighted this illegal business in his paper and noted that the ISIS terrorist group is paying something around RS. 50,000 to 60,000 per month to every warrior, which is a hefty amount for an unemployed youth suffering in unemployment, poverty and inflation here in Pakistan:

"All of this is being done to obtain worldly wealth and later eternal life in Heaven because ISIS is paying something around RS. 50,000 to 60,000 per month to every warrior, which is a hefty amount for an unemployed youth suffering in unemployment, poverty and inflation here in Pakistan, which is ruled by corrupt ruling elite for the past 68 years and masses only got poverty for being true Muslims and patriot Pakistanis. Most secret and law-enforcement agencies have behaved like a silent bystander to the activities of ISIS in the country. Is this an unofficial channel of providing soldiers to provide the Saudi demands for fighters to fight on behalf of Saudi armies in Yemen and Syria? Whose interests are being protected by the Minister for Interior by his constant denial of the presence of ISIS in the country? Is he afraid of opening his mouth against ISIS? Is he instructed by his bosses to keep his mouth shut? Has he been paid huge sums of Riyals for keeping his mouth shut? Why is Sharif Government closing its eyes to the reality of ISIS in Pakistan? Is Sharif family obliging Saudis as close allies and relatives? Is Sharif family repaying the debt for the 1.5 billion US dollars that was given by the Saudi Government? Is some sort of underground large scale recruitment going on for Saudi Empire? This paper will also try to find answers to different responses of the different State institutions and find answer to the question of "why has government adopted attitude of indifference and taken different position on this serious issue? Also why do youth opt for becoming paid warriors away from their homeland on the foreign lands fighting the war that is not theirs, and why do women and girl are driven crazy to accept the concept of Jihad-Bil-Nikah, leave their husband along with their young children and go to the Syrian war front to become the wives of blood thirsty mujahedeen who do not believe in the words like mercy or forgiveness and have no respect for human life, human dignity, modesty and honor of women and do not believe in human rights of anyone except for themselves"?[30]

On 19 June 2019, ToloNews reported former Indian ambassador to Afghanistan, Amar Sinha, affirmation of allegation against Pakistan that Daesh permanently remained a tool of the Pakistani army. The army fabricated it to put pressure on the Afghan government. Talking to TOLOnews, the former Indian envoy said: "that assessments which are carried out by the Afghan institutions have found that over 70 percent of Daesh fighters are coming from Pakistan's tribal regions. "Now the thing is, is it the new version of Taliban when the Taliban gets reintegrated, mainstreamed? Is this new terror grouping another instrument of Pak[istan] military policy? My hunch is yes. But I guess more research will have to be done both intelligence agencies and we have to look carefully at the origin, at the source of funding and the source of support," he explained. Sinha confirmed that some Indian citizens had also joined Daesh, adding that the Afghan government extradited some of these militants back to their home country. Pakistan has always denied claims of supporting or sponsoring Daesh in Afghanistan"[21]

However, in February 2018, Voice of America reported warning of Russian government that the US army turning Northern Afghanistan into a "resting base" of international terrorism and a "bridgehead" for establishing its "destructive" caliphate in the region. "The "international wing of Daesh" is spearheading the effort of terrorists spilling over the borders of Syria and Iraq and moving worldwide, asserted Russian Ambassador to Pakistan, Alexey Dedov". However, he said: "With clear connivance, and sometimes even with direct support of certain local and outside sponsors, thousands of militants of various nationalities are consolidating under the banners of Daesh there (in northern Afghanistan), including jihadis from Syria and Iraq," Dedov told a seminar in Islamabad. Moreover, Iranian military General also alleged that the U.S. was transferring ISIS militants to Afghanistan to fuel regional instability and justify its presence in the region[22]

In 2019, there were speculations that the Islamic State gained foothold in Baluchistan to train its fighters. On 18 September 2019, in his Samaa News analysis, Roohan Ahmad noted developments of Daesh recruitment in Pakistan: "The Islamic State militant group has named a former Karachi police constable Daud Mehsud the leader of its newly created Wilayah Pakistan, after separating Pakistan from its Khorasan province. Mehsud was a munshi or constable at Karachi's Quaidabad police station, one of them said, requesting anonymity because he is not authorized to speak to reporters. "Previously, he was based in Afghanistan," he added. It is believed that he has moved to Balochistan after Daesh formed its Wilayah Pakistan in May 2019. The official said that there is no direct link between Daesh's Pakistan group and the group's central leadership in Iraq and Syria. According to him, the decisions are made in Syria or Iraq and conveyed to Pakistan through Khorasan (Afghanistan). Mehsud has a history. He started out with the proscribed Tehreek-e-Taliban Pakistan group led by the group's slain leader Hakimullah Mehsud and rose in the ranks to its Karachi chief under Mullah Fazlullah. He had to leave Pakistan after law-enforcement agencies geared up an operation against militant groups. In 2017, Mehsud left the TTP and pledged allegiance to the then Daesh's Khorasan group. According to DIG Goraya, Mastung, Quetta, Kalat, Khuzdar and Lasbela were the most affected parts. These areas are used as a "transit, lodging and boarding point," he added. "Some presence [was] also reported in Bolan and Dera Murad Jamali," the CTD official said".[23]

On 17 may 2019, the Nation reported establishment of the ISIS branch in Pakistan.[24] The newspaper noted the ISIS announcement that it has established its branch in Baluchistan. Since its establishment on May 2015, the group claimed its activities in Balochistan. "The state of Pakistan has been claiming that there's no organized presence of Daesh in the country and that some local militant groups have allied them with IS after their parent organizations were dismantled in the military and intelligence-based operations. However, Daesh has succeeded in proving its footprint by not only carrying out several attacks in the volatile north-western Balochistan but also making some hits in relatively much secure areas of the country. A senior government official insisted that Daesh doesn't have its own infrastructure and recruits in Pakistan; rather, it hires and uses local militants who were associated with different militant outfits in the past. "This means IS has no direct presence in the country [as it is trying to portray by announcing its chapter in Pakistan]," the newspaper reported.[25]

On 23 December 2017, a Pakistani political leader said that following the collapse of the Daesh (ISIS or ISIL) terrorist group in Syria and Iraq, the US government was equipping Daesh militants in border areas of Pakistan with weapons. Speaking to the Tasnim News Agency, Shabir Hussein Sajedi, a member of the Majlis Wahdat-e-Muslimeen (MWM), a Shiite political organization, said the activities of Daesh have increased in northwestern Pakistan. He added that the terror group is recruiting members on Pakistani soil and is beginning some movements in the country. He further warned that the US is providing Daesh terrorists with weapons and other military equipment in border areas.[26] However, on 01 January 2020, Tribal News Network reported the surrender of women and children of Daesh fighters from merged tribal district to Jalalabad authorities:

"In a video released by the official media center of the Nangarhar government, it can be seen that Pakistani relatives have come to receive the women and children of Daesh militant group fighters. The video states that a center for families of surrendered Daesh fighters was formed in Jalalabad city where they were provided all facilities. It says that the legitimate 50 women and 76 children of Daesh fighters were to be handed over to their

Pakistani relatives on Thursday after verification. Afghan officials say the women and children coming from Afghanistan hail from Tirah Valley, Orakzai, Bajaur and Peshawar. An elderly person in the video says he has come to receive three women and four children of his family. He says these women had gone to Afghanistan five years ago. Afghan officials claim that thousands of Daesh fighters had come to Afghanistan from tribal districts of Pakistan and they also brought their wives and children later. They were living in areas under the control of the militant group in Nangarhar. Malik Usman, a tribal elder from Jalalabad, told media after a Jirga that women and children will only be handed over to their family members from Pakistan. In November 2019, Afghan President Ashraf Ghani had announced in Jalalabad that the family members of the fighters will be handed over to their Pakistani relatives through a tribal Jirga".[27]

Hamid Karzai in June 5 2015, condemned establishment of the Islamic State of Khorasan in Afghanistan that this was a new unwelcomed development. The Islamic States (ISIS) is not an Afghan born body-transported from Syria and Iraq. Pakistan has created enough, enough mischief and when I say Pakistan, I mean the Pakistani military and intelligence, not the people. They're as much victims as we are – the Pakistani people – in the hands of the same agencies in Pakistan. So not the Pakistani people. The Pakistani military and intelligence must stop creating excuses for the promotion of terrorism". Karzai said. On 31 May 2015, Afghanistan Times reported anger of civilian population about the intelligence sharing deal between National Directorate of Security (NDS) and Pakistan's spy agency Inter-Services Intelligence (ISI). Venting their anger, over 600 protesters took to the streets in the capital of central Kapisa province and condemned the NDS-ISI deal, asking the government to revoke it. The protest demonstration was organized by civil society group, Rond Sabz. The Memorandum of Understanding (MoU) between the National Directorate of Security (NDS) and the Pakistani spy agency, Inter-Services Intelligence (ISI) was widely criticized by MPs, civil society groups and politicians.[28]

On 23 May, 2015, Afghanistan Times noted criticism of National Security Council on signing of MoU between NDS, ISI. The NSC said that only draft of the MOU has been signed between the National Directorate of Security (NDS) and Pakistani spy agency, the Inter-Services Intelligence (ISI). Mr. Najib Manalai, spokesman for the NSC, while talking to newsmen said that the two countries have only inked draft of the MOU. He added that the draft was signed to layout ground for the technical process of the deal. "The deal would be credible once political agreement was reached between the two countries and it was signed by the chairman of NDS and DG ISI," Manalai said. Moreover, on 22 May 2015 the deal was termed a Pakistan's interference in Afghanistan. National Solidarity Party of Afghanistan (NSPA) warned that the memorandum of understanding (MoU) between the National Directorate of Security (NDS) and Pakistani intelligence agency officially created window to Pakistan's interference in Afghanistan. Having pointed to the fact of intelligence sharing the NSPA said that according to the MoU, the window was created for Pakistan's Inter-Services Intelligence (ISI) to implement its goals which it wanted to reach in Afghanistan. "One of the main parts of the MoU includes joint combat of the two spy agencies against 'separatism'. It comes as there is no 'separatist' movement in Afghanistan; however, it is Pakistan that is faced with separatism challenge from the past.[29]

Therefore, joint fight against separatism finds meaning only in Pakistan. What will be the consideration of NDS from stepping towards joint war against separatism?" the NSPA warned. NSPA also warned about the joint combat operation. On 20 May 2015, Afghanistan Times reported revocation of intelligence sharing deal between Pakistan and Afghanistan. Hamid Karzai, reacted to signing of the intelligence sharing accord between Kabul and Islamabad and asked immediate nullification of it by Afghan government, his office said on Wednesday. The office of the former president issued a statement calling on the national unity government leaders to cancel the agreement immediately. The statement further added that the former President has also urged the leaders of the unity government to restrain from signing agreements that are against the national interests of the country. The signing of the agreement has sparked uproar among the current and former Afghan officials with reports suggesting that the NDS chief Rahmatullah Nabil opposed to ink the agreement. The newspaper reported. The NDS spokesman Haseeb Sediqi said the Memorandum of Understanding (MoU) signed with Pakistanwas not against the national interests of the country and the agreement was concluded based on previous mutual cooperation between the two nations. The former spy chief, Amrullah Salehsaid that the agreement was more dangerous and shameful than recognizing the Durand Line as an international boundary. He termed the MoU a one-sided deal that betrayed the trust and sacrifices of the Afghan National Security Forces (ANSF).[30]

On 5 June, 2015, Afghanistan Times reported Mr. Amrullah Saleh's criticism of the intelligence sharing agreement. Analyst, Sadiq Naqvi noted in his article: "The central issue is the definition of peace. For Pakistanis and the Taliban, peace would eventually mean ceasefire. For us, peace means politics without guns and violence. If the Taliban lay down their arms they become like any other bunch of loud clerics without influence in society. So violence is their identity. They won't give it up easily. Pakistan has come a long way. Pakistan has gone through three stages, strategically. Stage one (2001 to 2004) was deceptive cooperation with the Americans and Afghanistan. Stage two (2004 to 2009) was massive support for the Taliban to help them de-hibernate and re-emerge. I call this a strategic denial stage. Stage three (2009 to 2014) was a gradual strategic confession of 'Yes, we are with the Taliban'. Now it is the last stage and I call it strategic pricing and marketing. Now they say, 'We are with the Taliban and here is the price if you want us to bring them to the table'. It is a hefty price. For the past several years, the Afghans held Pakistan responsible for a lot of things going wrong domestically – especially the violence and their support to the Taliban. This view was endorsed by India as well. How does this square with these renewed attempts to reach out to Pakistan? I don't know the deep Indian thinking but I suspect and reckon India may share some of our concern. But India is a massive regional power. India has crossed critical mass and can't be bullied by Pakistan. We are still prey to the bullying tactics of Pakistan.[31]

However, on 22 May 2017, Afghan security forces seized a Pakistani bus carrying 6,250 kilograms of Ammonium Nitrate, which is used in making Improvised Explosive Device (IED) in eastern Nangarhar province, official said. The explosives packed bus was seized in Marko Bazzaar area of Ghani Kheil district, sharing borders with Pakistan. The provincial governor office in a media statement, said that the seized explosives materials were hidden in 125 bags. Nangarhar was burning at the hand of Islamic State (IS), also known as Daesh terrorist group, and security officials warned that Pakistan supporting them to carry its evil activities in the province. Security officials showed concern that some elements in the region, including Pakistan's Inter-Services Intelligence (ISI) are supporting militant group. In the past, provincial officials said that majority of fighter loyal to Daesh militant operating in Nangarhar province are Pakistani nationals and receiving command from ISI. Documents recovered from Daesh insurgents revealed that they had come from Pakistan to fight under the name of Islamic State terrorist group. On 19 April, 2018, Chairman and Chief Executive Officer (CEO) of Kainaat Group of Companies (KGC), Afghan analyst, Mohammed Gul Sahibbzada has highlighted Pashtoon Tahfooz Movement in the context of Pakistan war against Pashtoon of

Pakistan and Afghanistan. He also noted Pakistan's support to Taliban and the ISIS in Afghanistan to further its foreign policy goals:

"Pakistan military establishment wanted to repeat their policy for Afghan Mujahideen adopted in 1980s, where ISI had murdered almost the entire genre of traditional and secular leaders of Afghanistan and under the name of resistance and jihad, created and supported religious figures and established religious political organizations. It was this policy whereby Dr. Najeebullah's government was toppled and more than seven religious, political organizations were shepherded into Afghanistan where they started fighting each other. It was a smartly choreographed move by Pakistan and the aim was to destroy whatever was standing as institutions in the country so that Pakistan will remain in control of the country. The result was bloodshed, anarchy, civil war and hundreds of thousands of civilian deaths. You cannot organize people without genuine leaders, and there was no genuine leader in ISI plan. All were created. Though international community and US government was in support of the struggle of Afghans against the then United States of Social Russia (USSR) for their so called campaign of liberation of Afghanistan, but they did not notice the undercurrent and hidden agenda of Pakistan as to what will happen after USSR is defeated. There were many other ramifications of US policy of apathy and indifference towards Afghanistan after the Soviets were gone. For example, Osama Bin Ladin was operating in the open along with groups supported by US government and Pakistani military in Afghanistan. He was stationed in Paktika province fighting Soviet forces. Bin Ladin had established a worldwide network of connections with Islamists around the globe whereby he used to attract money and fighters in order to buttress guerrilla ranks in the war against Soviets. After the defeat of Soviet forces, US government and ISI did not dismantle these jihadist organizations, and let them operate free in Afghanistan with their global connections intact. It was this blunder of US policy makers which allowed Usama Bin Laden to establish terrorist training camps in Afghanistan and which were openly supported by ISI of Pakistan for training fighters for guerrilla war in Kashmir against India. And the 9/11 attack was planned and organized out of these camps in Afghanistan, and by the same people who had established highly sophisticated global network of sympathizers"[32]

Chapter 11

Pakistan Army and the Pashtun Tahafooz Movement

I n May 2016, for example, an attack on a military post in the Teti Madakhel area of North Waziristan triggered a manhunt by troops who rounded up the entire population of a village. An eyewitness who watched the operation from wheat field nearby and whose brother was among those detained told the BBC that the soldiers beat everyone with batons and threw mud in children's mouths when they cried. A pregnant woman was one of two people who died during torture, her son said in video testimony. At least one man remains missing". (Muhammad Ilyas Khan, BBC News, Dera Ismail Khan, 02 June 2019).

The Pashtun Tahafooz Movement is the only well banded together movement that created awareness within the Pashtun communities about the atrocities and war crimes of Pakistan army in FATA and Waziristan. However, it started long marches, and rallies to divert the attention of international community towards the forced disappearances of its workers and leaders by the agencies. Frequently, they used social media as a bridge of communication. Originally, its demands included the release of missing persons and an end to extra-judicial killings of Pashtuns, stopping humiliation of passengers at security checkpoints, and removal of landmines in FATA.[1] On 13 January 2018, Naqeebullah Mehsud was kidnapped and killed in a fake police encounter in Karachi.[2] The PTM is the latest manifestation of decades of Pashtun protest against state brutalities. Its origin can be traced back to 2014 when student leaders of Gomal University in the Khyber Pakhtunkhwa (KP) province were propelled into activism to protect the rights of Pashtuns[3] The PTM is a nonviolent movement led by Manzoor Pashteen against the alleged enforced disappearances, extra-judicial killings, as well as the mistreatment of the Pakhtun community by security forces. Madiha Afzal (07 February 2020) interviewed leaders of PTM for her book in Lahore, highlighted the PTM demand in her book:

"The movement alleges grave human rights violations by Pakistan's military against Pashtuns in the country's northwest. It says that Pashtuns have been the target of violence at the hands of both the Taliban and the Pakistani military for two decades. The movement claims that the military has killed innocent civilians in its operations against the Pakistani Taliban, and that it needs to answer for "missing persons." It also contends that Pashtuns are regularly harassed at checkpoints and treated with suspicion, and that landmines continue to make their lives insecure. These complaints festered for years before the movement was officially created in 2018. In 2015, while conducting interviews for my book, I met Pashtun students in Lahore who told me that the army's ongoing, multi-year military operation—Zarb-e-Azb—was not what it seemed from outside the tribal areas. The PTM demands a truth and reconciliation commission to address claims of extrajudicial killings and missing persons. The movement also claims that the military supported Pakistani Taliban (also known as Tehreek-e-Taliban Pakistan, or TTP) militants, and its leaders have said—most explosively — that after the military claims to have decimated the Pakistani Taliban in Zarb-e-Azb, "the Taliban are being allowed to return" to the tribal areas in a "secret deal with the military."[4]

Torture and humiliation in Waziristan couldn't undermine Talibanization, extremism, and terrorism, it alienates citizens from the state. Manzoor never targeted Pakistan army, and never killed a single soldier of security forces; he is fighting for the fundamental rights of the residents of Waziristan and FATA regions. On 11 February 2019, in his New York Times article, PTM leader Manzoor Pashteen gave an account of his struggle for the recovery of kidnapped Pashtun activists by Pakistan's military establishment: "The government ignored us when these militants terrorized and murdered the residents. Pakistan's military operations against the militants brought further misery: civilian killings, displacements, enforced disappearances, humiliation and the destruction of our livelihoods and way of life. No journalists were allowed into the tribal areas while the military operations were going on. Pashtuns who fled the region in hopes of rebuilding their lives in Pakistani cities were greeted with suspicion and hostility. We were stereotyped as terrorist sympathizers. I was studying to become a veterinarian, but the plight of my people forced me and several friends to become activists. In January 2018 Naqeebullah Mehsud, an aspiring model and businessman from Waziristan who was working in Karachi was killed by a police team led by a notorious officer named Rao Anwar. Mr. Anwar, who is accused of more than 400 extrajudicial murders, was granted bail and roams free. Along with 20 friends, I set out on a protest march from

Dera Ismail Khan to Islamabad, the capital. Word spread, and by the time we reached Islamabad, several thousand people had joined the protest. We called our movement the Pashtun Tahafuz Movement or the Pashtun Protection Movement".[5]

Mr. Manzoor Pashteen holds responsible Pakistan army for the disinformation campaign against his movement, and complained that agencies also concocted stories of the involvement of RAW and NDS in his campaign for the recovery of kidnapped men, women and children from the custody of the police and agencies. He, however, accused the army and police for the killing of his workers. PTM leader also lamented military establishment and the police for the harassment of social media activist, and the arrest of Alamzaib Khan Mehsud, activist Hayat Preghal, and Gulalai Ismail: "The military unleashed thousands of trolls to run a disinformation campaign against the P.T.M., accusing us of starting a "hybrid war." Almost every day they accuse us of conspiring with Indian, Afghan or American intelligence services. Most of our activists, especially women, face relentless online harassment. A social media post expressing support for our campaign leads to a knock from the intelligence services. Scores of our supporters have been fired from their jobs. Many activists are held under terrorism laws. Alamzaib Khan Mehsud, an activist who was gathering data and advocating on behalf of victims of land mines and enforced disappearances, was arrested in January. Hayat Preghal, another activist, was imprisoned for months for expressing support from our movement on social media. He was released in October but barred from leaving the country and lost his pharmacist job in Dubai, his sole source of income. Gulalai Ismail, a celebrated activist, has been barred from leaving Pakistan. On Feb. 5, while protesting against the death of Mr. Luni, the college teacher and P.T.M. leader, she was detained and held incommunicado in an unknown place for 30 hours before being released. Seventeen other activists are still being detained in Islamabad".[6]

On 17 February 2020, the Print published yell of Gul Bukhari against the ISI wing of Pakistan Embassy in the UK. Gul Bukhari complained that the ISI wing was sniffing for her home address in London. "I am at a loss, I can't understand what is it about me that fascinates the Pakistani government or makes it obsess over me so much. I left Pakistan in December 2018 and am leading a quiet life in the UK. Yet, the establishment hasn't stopped hounding me. Just a few days ago, a friend sent me some screenshots of Pakistani media channel ARY and asked what the case against me was, and what 'dehshatgardi' I had done. I was stunned. I asked around if these were fake screenshots. "No, Gul, this is breaking news on ARY right now," I was told. According to the news, Pakistan's Federal Investigation Agency (FIA) had sent a notice, asking me to appear before it and explain myself. And if I fail to do so, I would be slapped with charges under cybercrime and anti-terror laws, my properties in Pakistan would be seized, and I would be extradited via the Interpol". Gul said.[7]

Gul Bukhari also kicked up the fuss that the PTI government requested the UK government to expel her from London as soon as possible. The PTI government wrote directly to the government in the UK, hoping that action will be taken against her here, but the UK government does not prosecute asylum seekers, and the PTI government cannot force the UK government in any case because Gul Bukhari is a human rights activist: "The Pakistan Tehreek-e-Insaf (PTI) government wants the UK to take action against me under the country's hate speech and anti-terrorism laws. And the Pakistani establishment, according to journalist Ali Shah, has sent this letter to 10 Downing Street, the Foreign Office, the Home Office, and to the local police. It was another shock to me. As reported by the journalist, the language used in the letter (which I haven't seen yet) contained typical fauji terms like "inimical activities", and seeks an investigation into my "lifestyle". Having realized it may not be successful in bringing me back to Pakistan via the FIA, the Imran Khan regime wrote directly to the government in the UK, hoping that action will be taken against me here. I am wondering if those in power in Pakistan think the UK government is as big a duffer as they are. Yes, we have Boris Johnson at the helm here but he is not the one and all. Murtaza spat out his Coke laughing while reading the letter, but the serious concerns are these: they are hounding me; slapping me with made-up charges or trying to get that done by the UK government; the Inter-Services Intelligence (ISI) wing of the Pakistan embassy in the UK is trying to sniff out my residential address. They are trying anything and everything...I was in their safe house and under their control in 2018 when they asked me if I would toe their line if they put me on prime time TV. I said no. Then they asked me again in the car (when they were taking me back home after my abduction) and also threatened me with my son's life, "Aitchison jata hai na (he goes to Aitchison, doesn't he?)", they said, referring to his school. "Uss ko kuchh ho gaya toh hum se na gila karna (if something happens to him, then don't complain to us)." I replied, "No, you must be out of your minds." They literally threatened to kill my son" Gul Bukhari grumbled.[8]

Having commented on her tearful complaints against Pakistan Embassy in London, prominent journalist Aurang Zeb Khan Zalmay (17-02-2020) in his Facebook account criticized agencies for their campaign against Pakistani human rights activists in Britain and Europe: "The Pakistani monster is constantly following and intimidating journalists and human-rights activists across Europe and Middle East. This project to hound rights-activists was launched by Gen. Bajwa on his official visit to Pakistan High Commission in London in Jun 2019. Since that day the Pakistan's embassies in Europe and their spies and stooges are active to stop vioces of the voiceless. However, they attacked one of our friends in Rottardam in front of his home. They can't intimidate us with their cowardice and cheap tactics, they are in self-deception, and we will never give up our peaceful rights activism".[9]

The PTM activist, Gulalai Ismail was also accused of treason, but human rights defenders said allegations were bogus and she was being targeted for highlighting abuses committed by Pakistan's military. Notwithstanding her arrival in New York, she still lives in consternation. She was arrested and harassed by intelligence agencies to change her opinion on the war crimes of the army in FATA and Waziristan, but she strongly refused to become reticent. In his New York Times article, Jeffrey Gettleman (19 September, 2019) reported that Gulalai Ismail had been advocating the rights of raped women, kidnapped and tortured Pashtuns, Punjabis and Balochs since years: "Her account of being chased out of the country does not help the government's efforts to win diplomatic support at a time when the economy is tanking and Pakistan is begging the world to censure India for its recent moves on Kashmir, a disputed territory claimed by both Pakistan and India. It has taken Ms. Ismail some time to feel safe even in New York, she said, but she has begun to meet with prominent human rights defenders and the staffs of congressional leaders."I will do everything I can to support Gulalai's asylum request," said Senator Charles Schumer, Democrat of New York. "It is clear that her life would be in danger if she were to return to Pakistan." Pakistani security officials said they had suspected for some time that Ms. Ismail had slipped through their fingers. "Our guys have been after her, by all means, but she is not traceable," said a Pakistani intelligence agent who spoke on the condition of anonymity, citing intelligence protocols. "She has gone to a place beyond our reach.".......Ever since she was, Ms. Ismail has been speaking out about human rights abuses, focusing on the plight of Pakistani women and girls who suffer all kinds of horrors including forced marriages and honour killings. In January, she aired accusations, on Facebook and Twitter, that government soldiers had raped or sexually abused many Pakistani women. She has also joined protests led by an ethnic Pashtun movement that Pakistan's military has tried to crush. Pakistani officials have accused Ms. Ismail of sedition, inciting treason and defaming state institutions".[10]

While Gulalai reached New York, her father also suffered torment due to his daughter's campaign for the rights of oppressed Pakistani citizens. According to the CIVICUS, systematic attacks against the PTM with scores of peaceful protesters arbitrarily arrested, detained and prosecuted on spurious charges, while protests by the PTM have been obstructed by security forces. In his interview with CIVICUS, Professor Mohammed Ismail said: "I have been targeted because of my daughter's activism. In May 2018, my daughter Gulalai Ismail, a women's rights activist, visited South Waziristan, an area on the border with Afghanistan, which was once a hub for international terrorism. Residents of the area have been complaining that the Pakistani army was protecting the militants, killing peaceful citizens and destroying their property".Gulalai Ismail was arrested three times, harassed and mentally tortured by FIA in Islamabad. Her name was put on ECL but her arrest in Islamabad Press Club enraged journalist and intellectual community across Pakistan. The CIVICUS analysis of her struggle to save lives of innocent women and children noted her pain and industrious struggle. Some newspapers also published stories about her zeal and pluckiness. Gulalai led a protest in Islamabad against police brutality and misconduct and spoke up about sexual harassment of women and girls of tribal areas. Due to her activism, the government brought two criminal cases against Gulalai for attending gatherings of the PTM, but these were quashed by the courts:

"Gulalai visited an area named Khaisoor along with a group of women human rights activists. Women and girls shared their stories about sexual harassment by army personnel. Gulalai assured them that she would highlight their situation and work on the issue of sexual harassment of women and girls in conflict areas. In May 2019, a nine-year-old girl whose parents had been internally displaced from tribal areas experiencing conflict was raped and killed in Islamabad, the capital of Pakistan. The police refused to file a first information report (FIR) of the incident, and instead abused and harassed the father and brother of the child in the police station. Gulalai led a protest in Islamabad against police brutality and misconduct and spoke up about sexual harassment of women and girls in tribal areas and of the internally displaced population from tribal areas. Due to her activism, the government brought two criminal cases against Gulalai for attending gatherings of the PTM, but these were quashed by the courts. On 12 October 2018, Gulalai was arrested at Islamabad Airport by the Federal Investigation Agency (FIA) on her arrival from London and her name was put on the Exit Control List (ECL), which bans her from travelling outside the country. In February 2019, Gulalai was picked by security agencies at the Islamabad Press Club while she was attending a protest for the release of PTM activists, but her name was not on the list of people arrested and she went missing for 36 hours. She was produced and released by the Pakistani army after the Prime Minister of Pakistan interceded".[11] PTM was helped by social media in circulating its messege across the globe.[12] Without the help of the social media and international press, information about the military operation in Waziristan was inaccessible. prominet scholar and journalist Daud Khattak (Foreign Policy, 30 April 2019) in his well-written analysis of Pashtun Tahafuz Movement (PTM) has noted some aspects of PTM's challenges in demanding justice for families whose relatives were kidnapped by the army:

"Pashtun Protection Movement came to prominence in early 2018 in Waziristan, a remote outpost along Pakistan's rugged border with Afghanistan. Although the grievances PTM tapped into—discrimination against tribal people, violence by the Taliban, and military presence in the area—were long-standing, the trigger for the group's recent explosion was the extrajudicial killing of an aspiring model and artist from Waziristan in the city of Karachi in January 2018. Despite a media blackout—the major news channels have refrained from covering PTM gatherings or running interviews with its leadership, allegedly because of bullying and arrests by the intelligence agencies—Pashteen's protest is gaining ground. In February 2018, the PTM staged a sit-in in Islamabad, which was followed by more protests against the military in all major Pakistani cities. In February this year, for example, hundreds of young men and women marched in Lahore, the country's second-largest city, to demand freedom of expression, respect for the country's constitution, and civil rights. The name of their rally— Shehri Tahafuz March, or Citizen Protection March—was homage to PTM. And in April, tens of thousands of people demonstrated under the PTM banner in the North Waziristan city of Miran Shah".[13]

The agencies intercepted all newspapers and electronic media from reporting PTM's protests across Pakistan. Tehrik Insaf's government has a turbulent relationship with media under Imran Khan, elected as Prime Minister with strong backing from the military. Journalists are living in a climate of consternation and suppression. Scholar and journalist Daud

Khattak also noted some incidents of kidnapping of PTM leaders and workers by Pakistani intelligence agencies. He also documented statement of General Ghafoor, in which he accused PTM leadership of getting money from Indian and Afghan intelligence agencies:"In early February, for example, Ammar Ali Jan, a college teacher and PTM supporter, was picked up by law enforcement agencies from his house in Lahore in the middle of night on charges of supporting the PTM. In response, dozens of Punjab-based activists launched a social media campaign for his release. A few days after his release, Jan explained his ordeal in an op-ed. He clarified that he is not an ethnic Pashtun but has supported the PTM in its broader struggle against human rights violations.Facing widespread protest, the Pakistani military has resorted to its old playbook and condemned the PTM and other emerging movements as "fifth-generation warfare"—that is, hybrid warfare against the state. Meanwhile, the military has also linked Pashteen and others to foreign governments and intelligence agencies. Addressing a news conference on April 29, Pakistani military spokesman Maj. Gen. Asif Ghafoor accused the PTM leadership of getting money from Indian and Afghan intelligence. "But tell us how much money did you get from the NDS [Afghan National Directorate of Security] to run your campaign?" he asked. "How much money did RAW [India's Research and Analysis Wing] give you for the first dharna [sit-in] in Islamabad?"[14]

General Raheel Sharif protected terrorists, and accommodated them in guest houses, and ordered the killing and kidnapping of young men, women and children, and used sophisticated weapons in North Waziristan. He never allowed maimed, disabled and mutilated children to treat their wounds, or leave the region safely. Extrajudicial killings in FATA and Waziristan by his forces and illegal torture of children and women by his cronies caused permanent consternation and schezopherenic diseases in North Waziristan. More than 1,000 women and girls were kidnapped, and 2,000 tribal leaders have been disappeared by the army in FATA and Waziristan since 2004. Reftworld in its recent report highlighted cases of torture, humiliation, ill-treatment and unlawful arrest and detention in Pakistan: "Irrespective of the "war on terror", the people of Pakistan suffer widespread violations of their civil and political rights. In Pakistan, torture and ill-treatment are endemic; arbitrary and unlawful arrest and detention are a growing problem; extrajudicial executions of criminal suspects are frequent; well over 7,000 people are on death row and there has recently been a wave of executions. Discriminatory laws deny the basic human rights of women and of minority groups. To this dismal human rights record, Pakistan's actions in the "war on terror" have added a further layer of violations. Hundreds of people suspected of links to al-Qaeda or the Taleban have been arbitrarily arrested and detained. Scores have become victims of enforced disappearance (for a definition see section 6); some of these have been unlawfully transferred (sometimes in return for money) to the custody of other countries, notably the USA. Many people have been detained incommunicado in undisclosed places of detention and tortured. Their families, distressed about the lack of information on the whereabouts and fate of their loved ones, have been harassed and threatened when seeking information. The right to habeas corpus has been systematically undermined as state agents have refused to comply with court directions or have lied in court. The fate of some of the victims of arbitrary arrest, detention and enforced disappearance has been disclosed – some have been charged with criminal offences unrelated to terrorism, others have been released without charge, reportedly after being warned to keep quiet about their experience, while some have been found dead".[15]

Journalist, M. Ilyas Khan (Uncovering Pakistan's secret human rights abuses, M Ilyas Khan, BBC News, Dera Ismail Khan, 02 June 2019) has confirmed atrocities of Pakistan army in his BBC News report: "In May 2016, for example, an attack on a military post in the Teti Madakhel area of North Waziristan triggered a manhunt by troops who rounded up the entire population of a village. An eyewitness who watched the operation from wheat field nearby and whose brother was among those detained told the BBC that the soldiers beat everyone with batons and threw mud in children's mouths when they cried. A pregnant woman was one of two people who died during torture, her son said in video testimony. At least one man remains missing".[16]Human Rights Commission of Pakistan in its report "State of Human Rights in 2018" noted the scourge of enforced disappearances in Pakistan and reported the statement of Sardar Akhtar Mengal of the BNP-M, who warned that the situation in Naya Pakistan didn't changed as 235 people, including nine women gone missing from Balochistan:

"Families had received 45 dead bodies during the period from 25 July to 30 October 2018 and as many as 5,000 people are still reportedly missing from Balochistan. According to him, people were afraid to register FIRs if any of their families went missing because, if they did, they received threats from law enforcement agencies. Sardar Akhtar claimed that human rights activists, nationalists, and anyone who raised the issue of enforced disappearances on social media were also picked up by intelligence agencies. In their Bi-annual Report 2018, The State of Baluchistan's Human Rights, the Baloch Human Rights Organization and Human Rights Council of Balochistan said they had received 'partial reports' of 541 cases of enforced disappearances in the first half of the year. In the majority of cases 'the persons were picked up by security forces from their homes, in front of the entire families and villagers'. According to Amnesty International in March, the UN Working Group on Enforced or Involuntary Disappearances had more than 700 pending cases from Pakistan. Addressing a press conference at the Quetta Press Club in April, Hamida Baloch, sister of missing Saghir Baloch, appealed to the government of Pakistan, the Supreme Court, the Human Rights Commission of Pakistan, and civil society to raise their voice for the safe recovery of her brother. Saghir, a student of BS Political Science at the University of Karachi, went missing on 20 November 2017.[17]

In April 2019, Al Jazeera reported Pakistan army allegations against PTM leaders that it received fund from foreign intelligence services, warning its leaders that "their time is up". Major General Asif Ghafoor, speaking at a press conference at the military's headquarters in Rawalpindi levelled allegations that the Pashtun Tahafuz Movement (PTM) had been funded by RAW and NDS: "The way they are playing into the hands of others, their time is up," he said. "No one will be hurt and nothing illegal will be done. Everything will be done according to the law. Whatever liberties you could take, you have taken." General Ghafoor said. PTM leaders denied the charges, saying they were ready to present the group's accounts before parliament or other accountability bodies to be examined. "These accusations are being levelled against us only because we are demanding accountability," said Mohsin Dawar, a PTM leader and Member of Parliament, on the floor of Pakistan's National Assembly hours after Ghafoor's press conference. "We want accountability for targeted killings, for extrajudicial killings, for missing persons, people who have been held without charge or crime by the government. Whenever anyone speaks of these issues, they are accused of being foreign funded, "he said.[18]

However, Pakistani army attacked PTM workers near the border of Afghanistan, leaving at least three people dead and scores wounded. Leaders of the Pashtun movement said they exercised their right to protest peacefully, but the military saw the movement as being propped up by foes of the state and accuses neighbouring Afghanistan and India of trying to stir up unrest with support of the movement in areas straddling the Afghan border. "You have enjoyed all the liberty that you wanted to," Maj. Gen. Asif Ghafoor, the military spokesman, warned P.T.M. leaders in a news conference. However, on 01 May 2019, Zahid Hussain noted General Ghafoor warning and the army bitterness against Pashtuns: "Notwithstanding the conscious efforts of some elements to turn to chauvinism, the movement has so far remained peaceful, and there have not been incidents of any violence in its protest rallies, which is quite a rare phenomenon in Pakistani politics. The move to turn it into an anti-state movement can only be criticized, and the use of force would fuel negative propaganda. There is no denying the sacrifices rendered by Pakistan's security forces in eliminating militancy and bringing the former tribal areas into the national mainstream. It is wrong to blame the security establishment for everything that has gone wrong in the strife-torn region. But any attempt to suppress the protests will only widen alienation. It may be true that in this age of hybrid war, hostile foreign intelligence agencies are exploiting discontent for their own vested interests. But the inept handling of the situation will only help their agenda. Any rash action could be disastrous for the country. Warnings of the sort given at the briefing can only make people angrier. It is an issue that must be dealt with politically. The prime minister has taken the right approach in handling the problem. The allegation of foreign funding is very serious and no state can tolerate foreign meddling in its internal matters. There is an urgent need to investigate the matter and action must be taken if the charges are substantiated. More important, however, is that the blackout of the PTM should be lifted. The Senate committee has done a right thing by hearing the PTM leaders. This kind of dialogue must continue. Rational dialogue is the only way out of the problem".[19]

Pakistan army needs to adopt new strategy of counterinsurgency, instead of killing and kidnapping innocent people in Pakistan. This policy of oppression and humiliation will turn the region into an endless war, and foreign involvement will also challenge the authority of the state. On 30 May 2019, Human Rights Watch demanded the investigation of the North Waziristan atrocities: "Pakistan authorities should impartially investigate the deaths of at least three people during violence between Pashtun activists and the army in North Waziristan on May 26, 2019, Human Rights Watch said. Both the army and supporters of the Pashtun Tahaffuz Movement (PTM), which campaigns for the rights of ethnic Pashtuns in the former tribal areas bordering Afghanistan, accuse the other of initiating a clash at a military checkpoint at Khar Kamar. In addition to the deaths, several people, including soldiers, were injured. "The uncertainty surrounding the deaths at Khar Kamar requires a prompt, transparent, and impartial investigation by Pakistani authorities," said Brad Adams, Asia director. "Upholding the rule of law is critical for maintaining security and protecting human rights in North Waziristan." The incident arose during a protest at the checkpoint by local residents following the arrest of two men after a military search operation. The search operation was in response to two attacks on army personnel, on May 6 and May 24, that killed one soldier and injured three others. A key PTM leader, Mohsin Dawar, told the media that as the group's elected representative, he and his supporters had gone to meet the demonstrators at the checkpoint. Dawar said that while he was meeting with the protesters, soldiers opened fire without provocation. After the incident, the army issued a statement that a group led by Dawar and Ali Wazir, another leader of the Pashtun group attacked the military checkpoint to force the release of a suspected terrorist facilitator. "In exchange of fire," the statement said, "three individuals who attacked the post lost their lives and 10 got injured." The prime minister's office endorsed the military's statement. The authorities registered a criminal case against Wazir and eight other PTM members who have been arrested. On May 27, the army issued a statement that five more bodies were found close to the area where the clash occurred"[20]

Pakistan's Armed Forces have been implicated in torture and other ill-treatment cases of individuals detained over the past decade of so called counter-insurgency operations in Waziristan and FATA. As the state practices have moved away from traditional counterinsurgency operations to sporadic clashes with local population since 2014, security and law and order situation is consecutively deteriorating in the region. With this shift in focus, Amnesty International became increasingly concerned about the treatment of detainees. Charles Pierson in his Wall Street Journal article noted the killing of 20 truck drivers by Pakistan army: "Only three months ago, the Journal reported on an army massacre of unarmed civilians. This earlier story quoted local residents, three of them named, who told how an army unit ordered more than 20 men out of a restaurant in North Waziristan and then killed them execution style. No trial, no jury. The restaurant owner said that the men killed were truck drivers"[21] Raheel Sharif inflicted huge fatalities on civilian population in North Waziristan. His army kidnapped women and children, and humiliated tribal leaders. On 02 May 2019, Kunwar Khuldune Shahid in his analysis noted the resentment of Gen Ghafoor and the army against Pashtuns:

"Pakistan Army's spokesperson, Major General Asif Ghafoor, has warned the leadership of the Pashtun Tahaffuz Movement (PTM) that their "time is up." Ghafoor dedicated most of his press conference on April 29 to the PTM–a nationalist movement dedicated to safeguarding the rights of the Pashtun community–accusing the group of receiving funds from Indian and Afghan intelligence agencies. While Ghafoor failed to substantiate his allegations, he laid the onus of disproving the Army's claims against the PTM on the movement's leadership. He put forth a questionnaire for the PTM, demanding answers regarding the group's responsibilities in the tribal areas, their overseas activities, collaborators in Kabul and New Delhi, narrative against the military, and income sources. At the same time, Ghafoor categorically told the media not to invite the movement's leadership on their channels to answer his own questions, amid the continued blanket ban on covering the PTM. In the same press conference, the spokesperson had earlier said with a straight face that the Army does not tell the media what to air and what not to air. When Member of the National Assembly (MNA) Mohsin Dawar, a PTM leader, tried to respond to the Army spokesperson's questions, his speech was cut short by the NA speaker. But there was enough time for Dawar to express his readiness for accountability, asking the military establishment if it could similarly come clean. On April 26, the PTM's elected MNAs from Waziristan, Dawar and Ali Wazir, weren't allowed to hold a press conference at the Islamabad Press Club, where they were going to address similar accusations that Prime Minister Imran Khan had levelled against them during a rally in the Orakzai tribal district on April 19. The Pakistan state habitually touts any emerging ethno-nationalist movements as a threat to national unity, remaining completely oblivious to the reality that it is actually through addressing valid grievances, like the ones that the PTM has taken up, that the state can overcome centrifugal forces and maintain its integrity".[22]

The army strived to undermine the leadership of Pashtuns in Waziristan but failed, and clefts appeared within the army ranks. Jaibans Singh in his analysis of the Pashtun Tahafooz Movement noted responses of Pashtun leaders and activists to the former ISPR Chief tweets: "DG-ISPR's comments, especially on the missing persons, created a twitter storm: "The whole presser was horrendous. But this was the OMG moment. This confession will sink the military image. He is admitting to crime against humanity on television, OMG," wrote well known journalist, Gul Bukhari, in a tweet after the press conference. Screenshot of Pakistani Journalist Gul Bukhari's tweet in response to DG-ISPR Maj. Gen. Asif Ghafoor's admission that Pakistan Army has been responsible for missing Pakistani citizens. Gulali Ismail, a well known Human Rights Activist from Khyber Pakhtunkhwa tweeted, "I consider this Press Conference not an attack on PTM, but an attack on the Parliament of Pakistan, an attack on the Democracy of Pakistan and an attack on the Constitution of Pakistan PTMZindabad." In fact, there are thousands of tweets on the same line with PTMZindabad which, by now, must be giving nightmares to the Pakistan Army. They are also generating debates on the role of social media across the country. It will not come as a surprise if the DG-ISPR is soon transferred from the post. It is now apparent that the PTM and its leadership are not going to be cowed down by the usual pressure tactics of the Pakistan Army based on rising of anti-National, anti-Islam bogeys. These calls for accountability of the actions taken by the Army are going to increase and also envelope other trouble torn areas of the country like Balochistan and Pakistan Occupied Kashmir (POK)".[23]

On 14 January 2020, the News International reported leaders of Pakistan's political parties to work with Pashtun Tahafuz Movement (PTM) for the protection of the rights of Pakhtuns. PTM chief Manzoor Pashteen at a public rally in Bannu announced the formation of a jirga to convince Pakhtun leaders to collectively work for Pakhtuns rights. Jamaat-e-Islami (JI) leader Senator Mushtaq Ahmad Khan told The News that he had raised the problems being faced by Pakhtuns at the highest forum in the country. "Pakhtuns rights are being violated at every level in Pakistan, adding that their undisputed rights provided in the Constitution were made disputed," he added. He said that he all parties' conference would be convened on January 29, 2020.[24] Senator Mushtaq Ahmad Khan also said that he had raised the issues of net hydel profit, gas and others. He said Khyber Pakhtunkhwa was denied the rights to use its gas resource, which had been ensured in article 158. "They are making their own interpretation of this article to deny our rights," Mushtaq said. Jamiat Ulema-e-Islam-Fazl (JUI-F) leader Maulana Attaur Rehman said that they could respond on the possibility of cooperation after the PTM leaders present their demands. "The party leaders could take a decision on whether or not to work with PTM when we meet them and know their position," he added.[25] PTM held the public gathering in Bannu after a break of seven months and reiterated its demand of de-mining of the erstwhile FATA, end to enforced disappearances and constitution of truth and reconciliation commission.[26]

However, Mohsin Dawar, a leading member of Pashtun Tahafuz Movement (PTM) and Pakistani parliamentarian, termed the PTM rally in Bannu as a bigger success, adding that participation of thousands of Pashtuns in the rally showed that Pashtuns want their rights and could not remain silent. Mohsin Dawar said that since the starts of the PTM, a number of issues faced by Pakhtun in Pakistan have been resolved: "Cases of forced disappearances as well as violence in tribal districts reduced and PTM is getting more attention. However, he added, When the pressure is reduced they (Security forces) will yet again resort to their old ways".[27] Talking to Radio Ashna, Dawar added that the Bannu meeting was according to their expectations. Other political parties have not organized such a huge gathering in the region.[28] "Our issues would automatically be resolved if they properly implement the constitution of the Pakistan," Dawar argued, and said: "We would continue our non-violent protests and would keep pressurizing the government to accept the PTMs' demands," He said. Before the Banu PTM conference, on 22 Fabruary 2019, Senator Farhatullah Babar in his Friday Times analysis argued that the military culture of torture must undermine. He also noted that new legislation will limit the right of free trial, and the army will be operating with impunity:

"Due to conflict zones in Balochistan and erstwhile tribal areas, new legislation limiting the right to free trial, opaque detention centers under control of the military and increasing reliance on so called 'doctrine of exceptionalism' has blurred focus on the culture of impunity of torture in Pakistan. However, two recent developments should help return our focus on this issue and can serve as a catalyst for criminalizing torture and ending the widespread impunity of the crime in the country. First, a recent Peshawar High Court verdict overturning scores of convictions awarded by military courts on grounds that suggested questionable ways of confessions extracted possibly under torture. Second, a report jointly prepared by the National Commission of Human Rights (NCHR) and Justice Project of Pakistan (JPP) on systematic torture by police in Faisalabad over a seven-year period covering three different administrations. Although Pakistan signed the Convention against Torture (CAT) in 2008 and also ratified it in 2010, it has still not made domestic legislation that defines and criminalizes torture. Pakistan's official report to the third Universal Periodic Review (UPR) in 2017 of its human rights record, referring to articles of the Constitution and penal laws, claimed that torture had already been eliminated and no one was tortured in the country. Referring to the Extradition Act, the official report claimed fool proof guarantees against handing over suspects to other parties who could subject them to torture. 1,424 cases of torture and other forms of cruel, inhuman and degrading treatment by the police were documented. No official inquiry was launched by any government body into any of these cases."[29]

However, Maj General Asif Ghafoor's irresponsible tweets, comments and conferences against the Pashtun nation left a black contemptuousness blot on the face of Pakistan army that the army only represents a club of Punjabi Generals. Gen Asif Ghafoor acted like a vandal and warlord that put the army in ordeal by challenging the Pushtun nation of Pakistan. The fact is, his resentment against Pashtuns, and his immature statement issued from the flat form of ISPR couldn't attract civil society in Pakistan. His past history and lose character show that he has often been swimming in contaminated water where he adopted an abusive language. A man of the shameless character created numerous controversies while his childlike statements and tweets caused misunderstanding between Pakistan army and the Pashtun population across the border. On 15 January 2020, he shamelessly warned Pashtun nation that Pakistan army will butcher their children again. These and other artless statements and tweets forced GHQ to replace him by Maj General Babar Iftikhar.[30]

Domestic and foreign media, intellectuals, think tanks, and literary forums are critical of the unconstitutional operations and actions of Pakistan's armed forced and the ISI in North Waziristan, Khyber Pakhtunkhawa and Baluchistan. Pakistan army and ISI treat residents of Waziristan and Baluchistan like enemies, kill and arrest them with impunity. Their houses are being destroyed, and set to fire and their businesses are looted and plundered. Newspapers reported the army spokesman announcement of controlling Miramshah town, while he didn't disclosed war crimes of rogue military units who killed thousands, kidnapped women and girls and looted their businesses. In 2018, traders and owners of petrol pumps, shops and markets in Miran Shah and Mir Ali of North Waziristan Agency (NWA) demanded the government to stop re-construction work on the bazaars and allow them to rebuild the damaged markets, shops, and petrol pumps by themselves. On 08 September 2016, Daily Times reported: "All North Waziristan Petroleum Owners Association President, Sirajuddin, Vice President, Property Association of Miran Shah and Mir Ali along with owners of petrol pumps, representatives of various trade bodies, and tribal elders gathered for a news conference at press club. Thousands of protesters attended anti-military protests overnight in northwestern Pakistan after activists from a rights group were killed when soldiers fired at their demonstration." According to Radio Free Europe, members of the Pashtun Tahafuz Movement (PTM) representing ethnic Pashtuns protested in major cities across the region late on May 27, chanting slogans against the army and demanding the release of their leaders.

There is a lot of disinformation about the military operation in North Waziristan, where children were also killed by rogue military units In Punjab the ISI also encourage violence against democratic governments. On 15 August, 2015, Pakistani Minister resigned after alleging the former head of ISI encouraged violent street demonstrations to unseat the government. The comments of Mushahidullah Khan once again exposed fragile balance between civilian government and military. He alleged that a civilian intelligence agency (IB) had recorded former Inter-Services Intelligence (ISI) chief Lieutenant-General Zaheer-ul-Islam instructing protesters to cause chaos. The tape had been played to the prime minister and chief of army staff, Khan said. He said he had not personally heard it. The ISI, driven by the Pakistan Armed Forces, (Ehsan Sehgal-19 September, 2017) ignores the supreme constitutional rule of a democratic head of the state, under which even the Armed Forces themselves fall. This is not only a violation of the constitution, but also a rejection of the civilian leadership.

Pakistan's interference in Afghanistan causes pain and consternation and its financial and military support to the Taliban terrorist group prompted destruction, poverty, and displacement. According to a detailed comment of Daily Outlook Afghanistan newspaper: (08 June, 2021)"Taliban occupied residential houses in order to fight against Afghan security forces. There the locals, mainly Pashtuns, complained against the Taliban militant fighters. According to them, the Taliban insurgents occupy their houses as well as schools forcefully. They collect food and money from locals with the barrel of gun. The death of civilians does not matter for the Taliban fighters......Destruction of their houses and death of their family members are not significant for the militants. That is, the Taliban use locals as human shields. In case the Afghan soldiers attack residential areas, which could lead to civilian casualties, the Taliban will say out loud that Afghan soldiers do not respect humanitarian law and kill ordinary people". On 07 June 2021, Afghanistan Times in its editorial page noted atrocities of Taliban and the ISI supported groups:"The Taliban are not irresolute even to carry out car bomb attacks and the government is trying to overplay the collapse of the districts as a tactical retreat of the Afghan security forces. What is more worrisome is that the militants have been gaining territorial gains around the country. "Many Afghan leaders had repeatedly said that the key to peace in Afghanistan is in the hands of the U.S. and Pakistan. If the policy is changed, there should be some practical actions, like the Pakistani authorities should force the Taliban to engage in meaningful talks with Afghan peace members, and also agree to a comprehensive ceasefire". Afghanistan Times noted.

Pakistani and international media have reported numerous cases of forced disappearance in Punjab, Sindh, Baluchistan and Khyber Pakhtunkhawa. Writers, bloggers, journalists, politicians, and members of parliament have been kidnapping and disappeared by intelligence agencies since 2001. Pakistan and international human rights groups are struggling to find clue of their place of incarceration but failed. All kidnapped and forcibly disappeared men, women, and children are being kept in army field units prisons where media access is denied. Amnesty International (Pakistan: Enduring Enforced Disappearances-27 March 2019) in its report noted challenges faced by journalists, bloggers and activists:

"In April 2017, Hidayatullah Lohar, school teacher (headmaster), blacksmith and political Sindhi activist was forcibly disappeared from the school where he taught. He was taken away in a "double-cabin grey coloured" vehicle by men in police uniform and civilian clothes. Since then the authorities have refused to disclose his whereabouts. Despite the presence of eye-witnesses, his family had to petition the Larkana High Court to order the area police station to register the First Information Report. Hidayatullah Lohar is one of Sindh's "missing persons". His family have been patiently seeking truth and justice through the courts and on the streets of Pakistan since his disappearance.....Enforced disappearances have long been a stain on Pakistan's human rights record. Despite the pledges of successive governments to criminalize the practice, there has been slow movement on legislation while people continue to be forcibly disappeared with impunity......The groups and individuals targeted in enforced disappearances in Pakistan include people from Sindhi, Baloch, Pashtun ethnicities, the Shia community, political activists, human rights defenders, members and supporters of religious and nationalist groups, suspected members of armed groups, and proscribed religious and political organizations in Pakistan"[31]

Families of disappeared people have been threatening of dire consequences by spy agencies and Rangers in all four provinces. Amnesty international (Pakistan: Enduring Enforced Disappearances-27 March 2019) in its report documented maroonness of mothers and daughters of incarcerated Pakistanis: "While marching against enforced disappearances, Sasui and SorathLohar have spent Eids in hunger strike camps outside the Karachi Press Club with other families of the "missing persons", as the victims of enforced disappearance are commonly referred to in Pakistan. In May 2018, during a violent dispersal of the protest they were part of in Sindh, Sasui says she was assaulted by a law enforcement officer. In November 2018, a peaceful march of the missing persons of Sindh was interrupted repeatedly by the Sindh Rangers and by officials in plain clothes – who are thought to be from the intelligence agencies. On 12 January 2019, Sindh

Rangers attempted to detain one of Lohar's sons, Sanghaar Lohar, without search warrants, from his mobile shop in Karachi. The sisters and mother resisted and raised enough noise to gather neighbors and managed to halt the detention. The video evidence of the entire incident shows men in uniform claiming that their brother was involved in wrongdoing, without specifying any allegations or charges".[32]

Relatives of all disappeared people are in pain and trouble. There sons and daughter have kidnapped by intelligence agencies, and they are not allowed to meet in secret prisons: "Associate Asia Director, Patricia Gossman (End Pakistan's Enforced Disappearances: Prime Minister Imran Khan Should Back Promises with Accountability-Human Rights watch 22 March 2021) in her analysis noted the grievances of disappeared families: International human rights law strictly prohibits enforced disappearances, the detention of an individual in which the state denies holding the person or refuses to provide information on their fate or whereabouts. In addition to the grave harm to the person, enforced disappearances prompt continuing suffering for family members. In January, the Islamabad High Court, after hearing a petition on a disappearance case from 2015, ruled that the prime minister and his cabinet were responsible for the state's failure to protect its citizens "because the buck stops at the top." The court called enforced disappearances "the most heinous crime and intolerable."[33]

Notes to Chapters

Introduction: The ISI War Crimes and Murder of Civilian Culture of Intelligence in Pakistan

1. The Diplomate, August 24, 2021

2. Arie Perliger (August 18, 2021)

3. On August 3, 2021, the Kabul Times

4. Former Canadian Ambassador to Afghanistan, Mr. Alexander

5. Modern diplomacy, on August 29, 2021

6. On August 14, 2021 Afghanistan Times reported that the situation in Afghanistan was deteriorating rapidly- thousands of people fled their homes and were seeking resettlement in capital Kabul and some major cities due to fierce fighting going on between the Afghan security forces and Taliban.

7. August 08, 2021, Afghanistan Times

8. Amit Chaturvedi, of Hindustan Times-31 August, 2021

9. The Times of London, 06 August 2021

10. Ibid

11 A leaked UN document said the Taliban were intensifying the search for anyone who may have worked with the US or NATO

12. The Murder of History, K.K Aziz.

13. Ibid

14. Pakistan. Living with Nuclear Monkey. Musa Khan Jalalzai, 2018 India

15. Christiaan Menkveld, (Understanding the complexity of intelligence problems. Institute of Security and Global Affairs, Leiden University, The Hague, the Netherlands-2021).

16. Dawn Newspaper, March 1999.

17. GeoTV 2008

18. 07 June 2013 the end of PPP government. Dawn

19. 28 July 2017, Nawaz Sharif war disqualified in fake case by a Pakistani court.

20. The News International news story, 2018 The ISI War Crimes and Murder of Civilian Culture Of Intelligence

21. Christian Menkveld, (Understanding the complexity of intelligence problems. Institute of Security and Global Affairs, Leiden University, The Hague, the Netherlands-2021).

22. Ibid

23. Pakistan: Living with a Nuclear Monkey, Musa Khan Jalalzai

24. Ibid

25. Ibid

26. Intelligence Bureau (IB) in the Limelight: Apparent Tussle between Agencies-October 3, 2017

27. The growing 'tug-of-war' between Pakistan's spy agencies: Conflict between the civilian Intelligence Bureau (IB), and the military's Inter-Services Intelligence (ISI) is at boiling point, with the former accused of overstepping constitutional bounds, Asia Times. 04 October, 2017, The Sunday Guardian. 06 September, 2020. On 13 February 2015, General Musharraf admitted that he had instructed the ISI to recruit suicide bomber and organize attacks against Afghan army and government institutions to force the Karzai administration to close unnecessary diplomatic presence of India in Afghanistan. Pakistan Institute for Conflict and Security Studies (Intelligence Bureau (IB) in the Limelight: Apparent Tussle between Agencies-October 3, 2017).

28. F.M. Shakil in his article (The growing 'tug-of-war' between Pakistan's spy agencies. Former terrorist leader and member of TTP spokesman Ehsanullah Ehsan revealed that Pakistan army asked him to lead death a squad. On 13 August 2020, he revealed that Pakistani authorities had given him a hit list of people who they would like to be killed in Khyber Pakhtunkhwa. Daily Times reported his confession audio, in which he admitted: "I was asked to lead a death squad and accept killing of the listed the list people from Khyber Pakhtunkhwa and Pashtuns from all walks of life including journalists. In the audio, he talked about his conversations with ISI and the parleys that took place. Ehsanullah Ehsan (Liaqat Ali) was a former spokesman of Tehreek-e-Taliban Pakistan (TTP) and Jamaat-ul-Ahrar. In April 2017, Inter-Services Public Relations (ISPR) Director-General Asif Ghafoor announced that Ehsan had surrendered himself to Pakistan's security agencies. In early February 2020, Ehsanullah claimed that escaped from the custody of Pakistani Agencies. Daily Times.

29. *The Sunday Guardian* (06 September, 2020) reported Mr. Ehsanullah Ehsan conversation with Taliban leader Mullah Wali-ur-Rahman: "Maulana Waliur-Rehman took a letter out of the envelope and gave it to me and told me to read it. I opened the letter and read it aloud.

30. *The Sunday Guardian* (06 September, 2020).

Summary: The Failure of CIA, ISI and NATO Intelligence Agencies to Prognosticate the Collapse of Afghan State and Government

1. *Friday Times*, Mr. Najam Sethi's, editorial, 30 August, 2021

2. Alexander Cooley, August 23, 2021

3. Najmuddin Shaekh-Dawn, 09 September 2021

4. *Hindustan Times,* 05 September 2021, Shashi Shekhar

5. Rezaul H Laskar August 27, 2021-*Hindustan Times*

6. Pervez Amirali Hoodbhoy, 11 September, 2021 *Dawn*

7. P. Michael McKinley. We All Lost Afghanistan: Two Decades of Mistakes, Misjudgements, and Collective Failure, 16 August, 2021

8. Andrew Mumford. Joe Biden and the future of America's foreign policy: By withdrawing from Afghanistan so determinedly, Biden has firmly pressed the 'reset' button. Andrew Mumford, 01 September, 2021.

9. Military Times analysis. August 17, 2021

10. Lara Seligman. Kabul's collapse followed string of intelligence failures, Politico.com.16 August 2021

11. Patricia Gossman, (How US-Funded Abuses Led to Failure in Afghanistan-06 July 2021

12. Ibid

13. Tom Blanton, Claire Harvey, Lauren Harper, and Malcolm Byrne "The US National Security Archive's Briefing book-772, Washington, D.C., August 19, 2021.

14. Gerry Hassan (Afghanistan, "Forever Wars" And the Reality of Empire State Britain-The National, 31 August 2021

15, Joydeep Bose Hindustan Times (08 September 2021

16. 03 September, 2021, Tehran Times

17. Ibid

18. Daily Dawn newspaper on 09, 09 2021

19. 08 September 2021, Human Rights Watch report

20. *The Express Tribune*

21. Professor of Philosophy, Public Policy and Governance, University of Washington, Michael Blake (17, August 2021

22. John Walsh (Biden exits Afghanistan, heads in the wrong direction: The US has learned nothing from 20 years of war, Asia Times, 08 September 20201.

Chapter 1: Pakistan's Intelligence Agencies: Stakeholders, Crisis of Confidence and lack of Modern Intelligence Mechanism

1. The Intelligence War in Afghanistan, Musa Khan Jalalzai, Vij Publishing 2019

2. Ibid

3. Pakistan: Living with a Nuclear Monkey. Musa Khan Jalalzai, Vij Publishing 2018

4. The European Asylum Support Office.16 October 2018

5. Florina Cristiana Matei and Carolyn Halladay-2019

6. Pakistan army brass meets amid political turmoil, 01 September, 2014, https://www.rediff.com/news/report/pakistan-army-brass-meets-amidpolitical-turmoil/20140901.htm

7. Musa Khan Jalalzai, Pakistan: Living with a Nuclear Monkey, Vij Books, Delhi, 2018, pp. 1, 2 and.

8. Ibid.

9. Musa Khan Jalalzai, Pakistan: Living with a Nuclear Monkey, Vij Books, Delhi, 2018

10. The crisis of Indian intelligence. Musa Khan Jalalzai, Daily Times, 08 September 2016

11. Assistant Sub-Inspector (ASI) of IB, Malik Mukhtar Ahmed Shahzad, who filed a petition before the Islamabad High Court (IHC) requesting it to refer the matter to the Inter-Services Intelligence (ISI) for a thorough probe.

12. Ibid

13. Musa Khan Jalalzai, 2018,

14. 24 June 2021, the ISI directed FIA

15. 04 November 2013, Dawn reported recommendations of the Senate Standing Committee on Human Rights

Chapter 2: Militarization of Intelligence, Dematerialization of Civilian Intelligence and a War of Strength between the Military and Civilian Spy Agencies

1. Financial Times-12 January 2012

2. 01 July 2013, Dawn newspaper

3. Dawn newspaper on 07 March, 2013

4. Musa Khan Jalalzai, 2015

5. Pakistan's Inter-Services Intelligence Contributes to Regional Instability. Global Security Review, Alexandra Gilliard-Jun 7, 2019, and the Challenges

of Civilian Control over Intelligence Agencies in Pakistan, Frederic Grare, 18 December 2015. Book Chapter: Bangladesh Institute of Law and International Affairs.

6. John. R. Schmidt, ISI Wrongfully Accused of Killing Journalist? Also Pakistan's Supreme Court told military and intelligence agencies to stay out of politics, Agence France-Presse, 07 Feb, 2019Agence France-Presse, 07 February 2019

7. Digital Desk of Sentinel (19 September, 2020) has noted multirole stories of the ISI in Pakistan, and quoted journalist's Declan Walsh book to uncover misgivings of the agency approach to national security and neighbouring states.

8. Ibid

9. Alamedas papers, 26 January 2020, Dawn newspapers

10. Ibid

11. Ibid

12. Express Tribune newspaper (26 April, 2017)

13. Dawn 06 October, 2016

14- Dawn 14 October 2016

15. 12 October 2016, DAWN newspaper

16. October 2016, a columnist for Dawn newspaper, Cyril Almeida, wrote a front-page story about a rift between Pakistan's civilian and military leaderships over militant groups that operate from Pakistan but engage in proxy war against India and Afghanistan.

17. 10 June 2017, the Wire

18. Scholar Frederic Grare (18 December 2015)

19. Pakistan: Living with Nuclear Monkey. 2018

20. Ibid

21. 06 October 2016, Dawn newspaper reported an unprecedented warning of civilian government to the military leadership of a growing international isolation of Pakistan and sought consensus on several key actions by the state.

22. Ayaz Amir (daily Dawn. 22 September 2006

23. Ibid

24. 07 May 2018; Javid Ahmad

Chapter 3: The ISI Director Generals, War Criminals and Pilferers

1. Amit Chaturvedi, of Hindustan Times-31, 2021 has quoted the daily Mail letter narrating the presence of those in the court who committed crimes.

2. Research Fellow, Institute for Conflict Management, Ajit Kumar Singh noted that 'though just two weeks have passed since the Taliban returned to power in Kabul, fear among masses, as expected, has spread like wildfire across Afghanistan, forcing thousands to run towards the Hamid Karzai International Airport in Kabul, to escape a dreaded future.

3. Shaun Gregory (ISI and the War on Terrorism. Studies in Conflict & Terrorism Volume: 30 Issue-12, December 2007

4. On 12 March, 2021 (ToloNews) journalist Haseeba Atakpal once more defined the role of ISI in the Afghan conflict

5. Former terrorist leader and member of TTP spokesman Ehsanullah Ehsan revealed that Pakistan army asked him to lead death a squad. On 13 August 2020, he revealed that Pakistani authorities had given him a hit list of people who they would like to be killed in Khyber Pakhtunkhwa. In an audio, he claimed that after some time of his surrender he was given the list of prominent voices in order to facilitate Pakistan in eliminating rogue elements.

6. Journalist and Analyst, Kunwar Khuldune Shahid, The diplomat--April 20, 2020

7. The Sunday Guardian (06 September, 2020

8. Ibid

9. Musa Khan Jalalzai, 2018 India,and F. M. Shakil, "The growing 'tug of war' between Pakistan's Spy Agencies", Asia Times, October 4, 2017, http://www.atimes.com/article/growing-tugwar-pakistans-spy-agencies/.

10. M. Ilyas Khan (Uncovering Pakistan's secret human rights abuses, BBC News, Dera Ismail Khan, 2 June 2019.

11. 16 August 2015, DW news

12. 15 August 2015, BBC

13. Analyst Shekhar Gupta (25 May 2018)

14 Abbas Nasir, "Pakistan's Intelligence Agencies: The inside Story"

15. Pakistan Press International on 15 May 2005, reported the PPP reference against the ISI DG Lieutenant General Javed Nasir.

16. G Parthasarathy, Rogue army runs the show-11 January, 2003, The Pioneer

17. In an interview with the BBC in August 2015, Senator Mushahidullah Khan claimed that an audio tape obtained by the Intelligence Bureau was played during a meeting between Prime Minister Nawaz Sharif and Raheel Sharif

18. 19-Aug-04, Asia Times

19. 30 September 2020, Express Tribune

20. Daily Express Tribune's News Desk (November 13, 2020) reported Nawaz Sharif's attack against the miltablishment and ISI for their alleged plot to him from power

21. Musa Khan Jalalzai, 2018

22. Dr Niaz Murtaza. Dawn. 22 October, 2019

23. 02 August 2018, Dawn Newspaper reported anxiousness of the three-member bench, headed by Chief Justice of Pakistan Mian Saqib Nisar.

24. The TTP commander Ehsanullah Ehsan (ISI chief begged for Taliban's help in Kashmir, September 6, 2020) who escaped from a safe house operated by the Pakistan army reveals how Pakistan army and the ISI demanded help of various terror groups to target Indian and US forces.

25. Joint Intelligence Directorate", National Counter Terrorism Authority NACTA Pakistan, Government of Pakistan, https://nacta.gov.pk/jointintelligence-directorate-jid/.

26. Former ISI Chief, Lt. General. Asim Munir has also been playing the role of vandals and DAKO mafia group by using the ISI officer to terrify business communities in Pakistan. The NEWintervention in its heart-touching report about the corruption and vandalism of former Chief of Inter-Services Intelligence (ISI) exposed the real face of Pakistan army and the ISI's sarcastic Director Generals. The news Intervention reported a blatant bribery case of Gujranwala's District senior commander and former ISI Chief, Lt. General. Asim Munir who immediately demanded Rs. 90 crore in extortion money from the CEO of Master Tiles. Former ISI Chief Lieutenant-General Asim Munir had previously held the privileged positions of DG ISI and DG Military Intelligence (MI).

27. In his letter to Prime Minister Imran Khan Sheikh Mahmood Iqbal, CEO Master Tiles (News Intervention-June 5, 2021) described all the details of what the ISI Chief had told him and his subsequent request for Rs 90 crore in extortion money.

28. On 07 October, 2017, in his Tweet, Hashim Azam called Lt Gen Rizwan Akhtar as a "butcher of hundreds of Mohajirs & a corrupt General.

29. Moreover, on 12 March, 2021, PTI news reported allegations of Mian Nawaz Shrif against the army that his daughter Maryam was being threatened, New Delhi Times, 25 September 2017

Chapter 4: The ISI, Military Establishment and an Inefficacious Intelligence Infrastructure

1. 2019, BBC report

2. 19 March 2012, the News International

3. The Nation 2019

4. Masud Ahmad Khan, Targeting state institutions, the nation April 05, 2021

5. Prominent analyst and writer, Farhatullah Babar in 10 July 2012 moved a bill to control ISI or bring it under democratic control.

6. 10 July 2012, the News International

7. 16 May 2014, the News International

8. 16 May 2014, the News International reported the Intelligence Bureau (IB) proposal of oversight law to watch performance of intelligence agencies

9. 25 July 2015, the News

10. 28 February 2018, Umar Cheema of the News International Lahore

11. Ibid, Omer Cheema

12. Middle East Institute, November 3, 2020

13. 11 July 2013, the News International

14. Ibid

15. Ibid

16. 09 January, 2021, Times of India

Chapter 5: The ISI Atrocities, Military and political Stakeholders, Crisis of Confidence and lack of Modern Intelligence Technique

1. Rai Mansoor Imtiaz (14 November 2019

2. Ibid

3. Intelligence war in Afghanistan, 2018

4. Florina Cristiana Matei and Carolyn Halladay-2019

5. Ibid

6. Ibid

7. Dr. Julian Richards, an author of four books and a number of papers and book chapters on a range of security and intelligence issues have contributed a chapter on Pakistan's intelligence agencies in the book (The Image of the Enemy: Intelligence Analysis of Adversaries Since 1945.

8. Prem Mahadevan research paper. 2011

9. Janani Krishnaswamy. 2013

10. Pakistani Writer and analyst Muhammad Taqi. 13 March 2019

11. Military analysts Sanjeeb Kumar Mohanty and Jinendra Nath Mahanty, 04 October 2011

12. Sanjeeb Kumar Mohanty and Jinendra Nath Mahanty

13. Grant Holt and David H. Gray in their paper, Winter-2011

14. Rajesh Bhushan, 12 January 2019

15. Dr Bidanda M Chengappa noted some aspects of ISI relationship with Afghan Mujahedeen.

16. Ibid

17. Dr Bidanda M Chengappa

18. Analyst Taha Siddiqui, 06 May 2019

19. 01 August 2001, Indian analyst B.Raman

20. Dr Bidanda M Chengappa

21. Abbas Nasir. Herald, January 1991

22. Ibid

23. Dr. Bidanda M. Chengappa

24. 01 August 2001, Indian analyst B.Raman

25. Dr. Bidanda M. Chengappa

Chapter 6: Dematerialization of Civilian Intelligence and a War of Strength between the ISI and the IB

1   Musa Khan Jalalzai, 2018, op. cit. p. 174.

2   F. M. Shakil, "The growing 'tug of war' between Pakistan's Spy Agencies", Asia Times, October 4, 2017, http://www.atimes.com/article/growing-tugwar-pakistans-spy-agencies/.

3   Abbas Nasir, "Pakistan's Intelligence Agencies: The Inside Story", op. cit.

4   Hassan Abbas, op. cit.

5   Musa Khan Jalalzai, 2018, op. cit. pp. 165-167.

6.   Dr Niaz Murtaza. Dawn. 22 October, 2019

7.   Joint Intelligence Directorate", National Counter Terrorism Authority NAC-TA Pakistan, Government of Pakistan, https://nacta.gov.pk/jointintelligence-directorate-jid/.

8.   Musa Khan, The Afghan Intel Crisis: Satellite State- War of Interests and the Blame Game, Algora Publishing, New York, 2017, p.133.

9.   New Delhi Times, 25 September 2017

10. On 22 July, 2018, Mr. Justice Shaukat Aziz Siddiqui levelled serious allegations against ISI that the agency's interference in judicial affairs badly affected independence of judiciary, Dawn newspaper, Pakistan.

11. Ibid

12. Supreme Judicial Council No. 347 of 2018. Inquiry against Mr. Justice Shaukat Aziz Siddiqui. LEAP-Pakistan in Case Reports, October 16, 2018

13. Ibid

14. Ibid

15. IHC judge sacked for accusing ISI of interference, Malik Asad, Dawn 12 October 2018

16. Ibid

17. Dr. Faqir Hussain, 30 April 2019, Pakistan Today

18. Global Village, 21 October 2018

19. Musa Khan Jalalzai, 2018, op. cit., p. 133.

20. Ibid.

21. The Challenges of Civilian Control over Intelligence Agencies in Pakistan, Frederic Grare, 18 December 2015. Book Chapter: Bangladesh Institute of Law and International Affairs.

22. ISI cultivated Taliban to counter Indian action against Pakistan: Musharraf. Dawn.com February 13, 2015. The Guardian, February 13, 2015

23. Imad Zafar, "Dawn Leaks: A Tweet that Underscored the State within State", The Nation, May 1, 2017, https://nation.com.pk/01-May-2017/ dawn-leaks-a-tweet-that-underscored-the-state-within-a-state.

24. Why Pakistan supports terrorists Groups" Vanda Felbab-Brown, Brookings, January 5, 2018, https://www.brookings.edu/blog/order-fromchaos/2018/01/05/why-pakistan-supports-terrorist-groups-and-why-theus-finds-it-so-hard-to-induce-change/.

25. Issue Brief, N0-3, 2008, Dr. Suba Chandran is Deputy Director of the Institute of Peace and Conflict Studies (IPCS). The Centre for Land Warfare Studies (CLAWS), New Delhi

26. Civilian-military Relations during the Zardari Regime (2008-2012) in Pakistan, internal and external factors. A Dissertation Submitted to The School of Politics and International Relations Quiad-i- Azam University Islamabad In Partial Fulfillment of the Requirement for the Degree of Doctor of Philosophy Nasreen Akhtar, 2017

27. Musa Khan Jalalzai, 2018, op. cit., p. 4.

28. Civilian-military Relations during the Zardari Regime (2008-2012) in Pakistan, internal and external factors. A Dissertation Submitted to The School of Politics and International Relations Quiad-i- Azam University Islamabad In Partial Fulfillment of the Requirement for the Degree of Doctor of Philosophy Nasreen Akhtar, 2017

29. Causes of Military Intervention in Pakistan: A Revisionist Discourse Muhammad Hassan. http://pu.edu.pk/images/journal/studies/PDF-FILES/Article-3_V_12_No_2_Dec11.pdf

30. National Security Committee agrees to recalibrate foreign policy, initiate economic partnerships", February 28, 2019, Dawn, https://www.dawn. Com/news/1392089.

31. Musa Khan Jalalzai, 2018, op. cit., p. 4.

32. New Internationalist, 01 July 2007

33. Is the mullah-military nexus crumbling? Mubashir Zaidi, Dawn. 11 November 2013

34. Pervez Hoodbhoy, "Mainstreaming Jihad: Why Now?", Dawn, December 16, 2017, https://www.dawn.com/news/1376805.

35. Reuters, 22 November 2008

36. Civilian-military Relations during the Zardari Regime (2008-2012) in Pakistan, internal and external factors. A Dissertation Submitted to The School of Politics and International Relations Quiad-i- Azam University Islamabad In Partial Fulfillment of the Requirement for the Degree of Doctor of Philosophy Nasreen Akhtar, 2017

37. The Armed Forces in the Muslim World, Italian Institute for International Political Studies.2014

38. Contemporary Pakistan: Political System, Military and Changing Scenario. Dr. Nitin Prasad. Vij Books India Pvt Ltd, 20 February, 2016

39. Dawn, Pakistan's Supreme Court in 2012 remarked that the entire state machinery.

40. Ibid

41. Samson Simon Sharaf, the Nation 03 August, 2012

42. ISI Wrongfully Accused of Killing Journalist? Washington's vengeful accusations lead us one step closer to war with Islamabad. John R. Schmidt, The National Interest, July 11, 2011.

43. Dhruva Jaishankar, Foreign Policy, 15 February 2019

44. ISI Wrongfully Accused of Killing Journalist? Washington's vengeful accusations lead us one step closer to war with Islamabad. John R. Schmidt, the National Interest, July 11, 2011.

45. Amir Hamza Marwan October 2015, PP-25

46. The CIA, the ISI and the Next Bin Laden. The man next in line to lead al-Qaeda has close ties to the ISI. Almost as close as the ties between the ISI and the CIA, John R. Schindler, May 12, 2011

Chapter 7: The Challenges of Civilian Control over Intelligence Agencies, Democratic Governments, Military Establishment and a

War of Strength

1. *Financial Times*-12 January 2012

2. Musa Khan Jalalzai, 2015, op. cit., p. 111.

3. The intelligence and agencies of Pakistan (Part I), By Ali K Chishti, 11 February 2011

4. Musa Khan Jalalzai, 2015, op. cit., p. 111.

5. The Challenges of Civilian Control over Intelligence Agencies in Pakistan, Frederic Grare, 18 December 2015. Book Chapter: Bangladesh Institute of Law and International Affairs.

6. Pakistan's Supreme Court tells military and intelligence agencies to stay out of politics, Agence France-Presse, 07 Feb, 2019Agence France-Presse, 07 February 2019

7. Ibid

8. Ibid

9. 26 January 2020, daily Dawn

10. Ibid

11. Ibid

12. Privacy International, July 2015

13. The Intelligence War in Afghanistan, Musa Khan Jalalzai, 2019, Vij Publishing India

14. Privacy International, July 2015

15. Economic Times, 25 July 2019

16. Dhruv C. Katoch, "Pakistan's Armed Forces: Impact on the Stability of the State", Journal of Defence Studies, Volume 5, Number 4, 2011, p. 72.

17. Pakistan's Inter-Services Intelligence Contributes to Regional Instability. Alexandra Gilliard December 18, 2018

18. Dawn newspaper, 06 October 2016,

19. Ibid

20. Ibid

21. Musa Khan Jalalzai, 2015, op. cit., p. 111.

22. Ibid.

23. Alok Bansal, "radicalisation of Pakistani Armed Forces", CLAWS, June 28, 2011, https://www.claws.in/624/radicalisation-of-pakistani-armed-forcesalok-bansal.htm.

24. Yunis Khushi, "Pakistan's Internal and External Enemies", Annals of Social Sciences & Management studies, Volume 1, Issue 4, 2018, p. 1.

25. Ibid

26. The Intelligence War in Afghanistan, Musa Khan Jalalzai, 2019, Vij Publishing India

27. Ibid

28. Pakistan's Inter-Services Intelligence Contributes to Regional Instability. Alexandra Gilliard On December 18, 2018

29. The Intelligence War in Afghanistan, Musa Khan Jalalzai, 2019, Vij Publishing India

30. Ibid

31. Dawn, 29 September 2017

32. Ibid

33. Frontier Post, May 18, 1994

34. Dawn, 25 April, 1994

35. Azaz Syed, 28 September 2018

36. The Intelligence War in Afghanistan, Musa Khan Jalalzai, 2019, Vij Publishing India

37. Ibid

38. Ibid

39. Ibid

40. 26 September 2017, Dawn newspaper

41. Ibid

42. *Economic Times*, 26 September 2017

43. Ibid

44. Ibid

45. Ibid

46. Ibid

47. *Dawn* Newspaper, 26 September 2017

48. 30 September 2017, Abhinandan Mishra article

49. *Sunday Guardian*, 30 September 2017

50. Ibid

51. Cyril Almeida's principled patriotism - Times of India, 17 February 2017

52. On April 29, 2019, Major General Asif Ghafoor, the spokesman of Pakistan army's Inter-Services Public Relations (ISPR) department, expressed his institution's dissatisfaction over the government's probe into the leak that put military and the civilian government on a collision course. Daily Dawn.

53. General Ghafoor Twitter, Dawn, 29 April 2017

54. Scholar Frederic Grare Paper, 18 December 2015

55. The News International, November 27, 2013

56. Pakistan: Living with a Nuclear Monkey, Musa Khan Jalalzai, 2018, Vij Publishing, India

57. BBC, 02 June 2019

58. New book offers important insights on Pakistani military: The launch of acclaimed author Shuja Nawaz' latest work 'The Battle for Pakistan' was blocked by the authorities. Imad Zafar, Asia Times, 31 December 2019.

59. Ibid

60. Ibid

61. Pakistan: Living with a Nuclear Monkey, Musa Khan Jalalzai, 2018, Vij Publishing, India

62. Ibid

63. Mapping Pakistan's internal dynamics Implications for State Stability and Regional Security. Mumtaz Ahmad, Dipankar Banerjee, Aryaman Bhatnagar, C. Christine Fair, Vanda Felbab-Brown, Husain Haqqani, Mahin Karim, Tariq A. Karim, Vivek Katju, C. Raja Mohan, Matthew J. Nelson, and Jayadeva Ranade, Te National Bureau of Asian Research, February 2016.

64. Dawn Leaks: A tweet that shows a "State within a State". Who is at the helm of affairs in Pakistan? Every single sane person knows it. It is a fact that the civilian governments in Pakistan are always dependent on the defence establishment's mandate rather than depending on the mandate of the masses. Imad Zafar, May 1, 2017

65. Scholar Frederic Grare, 18 December 2015

Chapter 8: The ISI and Miltablishment War against Journalists, Bloggers, and Social Media Anchors

1. The US Department of State in its report, Country Reports on Human Rights Practices: Pakistan-2020, March 30, 2021

2. Ibid

3. *The Friday Times*, 04 June 2021

4. Amnesty International (Pakistan: Enduring Enforced Disappearances-27 March, 2019

5. Jaffer A. Mirza in his article (The Diplomat) noted Pakistan's anti-Shia policies, but conversely, Nasrullah Baloch (Ending Pakistan's epidemic of enforced disappearances-Al Jazeera 9 Mar 2021)

6. Research Associate, Institute for Conflict Management, Tushar Ranjan Mohanty (Balochistan: Violent Retaliation-16 Jun 2020

7. Research Analyst at Manohar Parrikar Institute for Defence Studies and Analyses, Dr. Nazir Ahmad Mir. Abysmal Human Rights Situation in Baluchistan-20 May 2020

8. Dawn newspaper (27 April, 2014

9. 06 June 2014, Dawn newspaper

10. The Print-01 June, 2021

11. Dawn newspaper 02 June, 2021

12. BBC News 2021

13. May 05, 2020. People Dispatch

Chapter 9: Military Courts, Fair Trials Violations, Confessions without Adequate Safeguards against Torture, Rough-Handling of Prisoners, and Denial of Public Hearing

1. Twenty-points National Action Plan (NAP) approved by Parliament, The News International, 24 December 2014

2. A perspective on Military Courts. Mohsin Raza Malik. 22 January, 2019

3. Dr. Muhammad Zubair, 28 January 2019

4. Military Courts in Pakistan: Will they return? What are the implications? D. Suba Chandran, National Institute of Advanced Studies (NIAS) Strategic Forecast, 11, December 2017.

5. Watchdog: Pakistan's Military Courts 'Disaster' for Human Rights. Ayaz Gul. January 16, 2019

6. On 16 January 2019, International commission of jurists deeply criticised the illegal function of military courts in Pakistan.

7. On 12 January 2019, Dr. Mehdi Hasan, Chairperson of the Human Rights Commission of Pakistan (HRCP) expressed grave concern at the government's decision to table a bill in favour of extending the tenure of military courts, which were otherwise due to end their term, Press release of the Human Rights Commission of Pakistan (HRCP). 12 January 2019.

8. Dawn, 06 Mar, 2017

9. Amnesty international in its report, 27 March 2019

10. Pak Army's confession of enforced disappearances.19 May 2019, Rahim Baloch

11. General Ghafoor admitted in a Press conference on 29 April, 2019

12. Ibid

13. Imad Zafar. Asia Times, 17 September 2019

14. January 2018, Human Right Watch Report

Chapter 10: The Political and Military Involvement of Inter-Services Intelligence in Afghanistan

1. Bin Ladin, Palestine and al-Qa'ida's Operational Strategy. Asaf Maliach. Middle Eastern Studies, Vol. 44, No. 3 (May, 2008), pp. 353-375

2. Intelligence war in Afghanistan, Musa Khan Jalalzai, 2018, Vij Books India

3. Ibid

4. Disrupting the ISI-Taliban relationship: A Principal-Agent Approach. Hollingsworth, Christopher L. and Sider, Joshua, 2018- Monterey, CA; Naval Postgraduate School. http://hdl.handle.net/10945/61387

5. Ibid

6. The Afghan Intel Crisis, Musa Khan Jalalzai, 2017, New York USA

7. Ibid

8. The National Insterest, 07 May 2018; Javid Ahmad's article

9. The Afghan Intel Crisis, Musa Khan Jalalzai, 2017, New York USA

10. Pakistan: Living with a Nuclear Monkey, Musa Khan Jalalzai, Vij Publishing, India, 2018

11. Dr. Bidanda M. Chengappa Research paper, The ISI Role in Pakistan's Politics-2001. Military governments, the ISI and political hybridity in contemporary Pakistan: from independence to Musharraf, Kunal Mukherjee, 07 Apr 2017.

12. 19 September 2019, Afghan human rights activist Bilal Sarwary accused Inter-Services Intelligence (ISI) of providing institutional support to terrorist groups operating in Afghanistan.

13. Pakistan's Secret War Machine: Pakistani intelligence has mainstreamed terrorism and political violence in the region. Javid Ahmad, May 07, 2018

14. Ayaz Amir (daily Dawn. 22 September 2006

15. My Life with the Taliban, Mullah Abdul Salam Zaeef, and Alex Strick Van Linschoten (Editor), 01 Jul 2011, C Hurst & Co Publishers Ltd.

16. The ordeal of Mullah Zaeef, Ayaz Amir, Dawn, September 22, 2006

17. 26 September 2016, Tolonews reported Deputy Chief of Afghanistan's Strategic and Scientific Research Center, Aimal Liyan, allegations against ISI.

18. Chris Alexander (Ending Pakistan's proxy war in Afghanistan. Chris Alexander (March 2021)

19- Dr. Adrian Hänni and Lukas Hegi (Pakistani Godfather: (The Inter-Services Intelligence and the Afghan Taliban, 1994-2020, Small War Journal Tuesdat, 04 February, 2013)

20. PTI Washington on April 16, 2021

21. Ibid

22. The Project syndicate, 08 June 2021

23. 25 July, 2010, journalist Declan Walsh

24. The Guardian newspaper, February 2015

25. Human Rights Watch in its report (2021

26. Ibid

27. Afghan Foreign Ministry

28. 31 May 2015, *Afghanistan Times*

29. 23 May, 2015, *Afghanistan Times*

30. 20 May 2015, *Afghanistan Times*

31. 5 June, 2015, *Afghanistan Times*

32. 19 April, 2018, Afghan analyst, Mohammed Gul Sahibbzada

Chapter 11: Pakistan Army and the Pashtun Tahafooz Movement

1. Rights Movement in Pakistan Vows to Continue Its Protests, VOA News, May 13, 2018

2. Naqeebullah was killed in 'fake encounter', had no militant tendencies: police inquiry finds, Imtiaz Ali, Dawn newspaper, January 20, 2018

3. Impact of the Pashtun Tahafuz Movement on Pakistan's. takshashila.org. S Ramachandran, 2018

4. Madiha Afzal (07 February 2020) interviewed leaders of PTM for her book in Lahore.

5. On 11 February 2019, in his New York Times article, PTM leader Manzoor Pashteen gave an accout of his struggle for the recovery of kinapped Pashtun

activists by Pakistan's military establishment. The Military Says Pashtuns Are Traitors. We Just Want Our Rights: Pakistan's powerful military is trying to crush a nonviolent movement for civil rights. Manzoor Ahmad Pashteen. 11 February 2019.

6. Ibid

7. The Print, 17 February 2020, the Print published yell of Gul Bukhari, a Pakistani human rights activist. Gul Bukhari complained that the ISI wing of Pakistan embassy in UK was sniffing for her home address in London.

8. Ibid

9. On 17-02-2020, prominent journalist Aurang Zeb Khan Zalmay in his facebook comment criticised Pakistani agencies for their campaign against Pakistani human rights activists in Britain and Europe.

10. In his New York Times article, Jeffrey Gettleman reported that Gulalai Ismail had been advocating the rights of raped women, kidnapped and tortured Pashtuns, Punjabis and Balochs since years. New York Times, 19 September, 2019.

11. On 12 October 2018, Gulalai was arrested at Islamabad Airport by the Federal Investigation Agency (FIA) on her arrival from London and her name was put on the Exit Control List (ECL), which bans her from travelling outside the country. In February 2019, Gulalai was picked by security agencies at the Islamabad Press Club while she was attending a protest for the release of PTM activists, but her name was not on the list of people arrested and she went missing for 36 hours.

12. The CIVICUS analysis of her struggle to save lives of innocent women and children noted her pain and industrious struggle. Some newspapers also published stories about her zeal and plcukiness.

13. Journalist Daud Khattak, Foreign Policy, 30 April 2019

14. Ibid

15. Pakistan: Human rights ignored in the "war on terror". Pakistan Human rights ignored in the "war on terror", Refworld. www.refworld.org . Journalist, M. Ilyas Khan (Uncovering Pakistan's secret human rights abuses, M Ilyas Khan, BBC News, Dera Ismail Khan, 02 June 2019.

17. Human Rights Commission of Pakistan report: "State of Human Rights"2018

18. Al Jazeera, April 2019

19. Dawn. 01 May 2019, Zahid Hussain article

20. Pakistan: Investigate North Waziristan Deaths: Uphold Rights of Region's Pashtun Population. Human Rights Watch, 30 May 2019.

21. Charles Pierson in his Wall Street Journal, Pakistani Army. 31, 2014

22. Pakistan Declares War on Pashtun Nationalism: The Pakistani military is trying to sound the death knell of the Pashtun Tahaffuz Movement. By Kunwar Khuldune Shahid, the Diplomat--May 02, 2019

23. Pashtun Tahafuz Movement: The game changer for Pakistani politics, Jaibans Singh, June 2019

24. 14 January 2020, the News International

25. Ibid

26. Ibid

27. PTM is on a peaceful quest to free all Pakistanis from oppression: The Pakistani state's repeated attacks on us only strengthen our resolve. Mohsin Dawar. Al Jazeera, 6 Dec 2019.

28. PTM will continue pressurizing government for Pakhtuns' rights: Dawar, Syhoon New, 16 February, 2010

29. *Friday Times*, 22 February 2019, Senator Farhatullah Babar

30. 15 January 2020, General Ghafoor shamelessly humiliated Pashtun nation that Pakistan army will butcher their children again.

Bibliography

Ahady Anwar-ul-Haq. 1991. Conflict in post-soviet-occupation Afghanistan. Journal of Contemporary Asia, Vol. 21, No. 4

Abbas, Hassan 2015. Pakistan's Drift into Extremism: Allah, the Army, and America's War Terror. Abingdon: Routledge.

Afzal, Madiha 2018. Pakistan under Siege: Extremism, Society, and the State. Washington, DC: Brookings Institution Press.

Ahmed, Shamila Kouser, 2012, July. The Impact of the "War on Terror": On Birmingham's Pakistani / Kashmiri Muslims' Perceptions of the State, the Police and Islamic Identities. (Doctoral Thesis, University of Birmingham, Birmingham, United Kingdom). http://etheses.bham.ac.uk/id/eprint/3635

Ali, Murad, 2012.The Politics of Development Aid: The Allocation and Delivery of Aid from the United States of America to Pakistan. Doctoral Thesis, Massey University, Palmerston North, New Zealand. URL: http://hdl. handle.net/10179/3418

Ahmed, Khaled. 2016, Sleepwalking to Surrender: Dealing with Terrorism in Pakistan. Haryana: Viking. Ataöv, Türkkaya (2018): Kashmir and Neighbors: Tale, Terror, Truce.

Abingdon: Routledge. Barfield, Thomas. 1996. 'The Afghan Morass', Current History, Vol. 95, No. 597.

Andrew, Christopher M. and Jeremy Noakes. 1987. Intelligence and International Relations, 1900-1945. Exeter: Exeter University Press,

Ashman, Harold Lowell. 2009. Intelligence and Foreign Policy: A Functional Analysis. Salt Lake City: Ashman, 1974. Association of the Bar of the City of New York, Committee on Civil Rights The Central Intelligence Agency: Oversight and Accountability. New York,

Abshire, David. 2001, "Making the Pieces Fit: America Needs a Comprehensive National Security Strategy." American Legion Magazine,

Ackerman, Wystan M. 1998,"Encryption: A 21st Century National Security Dilemma." International Review of Law, Computers & Technology.

Andersen, Per, Richard Morris, David Amaral, Tim Bliss, & John O'Keefe 2006. The Hippocampus Book, Oxford: University Press.

Anderson, Alan Ross, & Nuel D. Belnap, Jr. 1975 Entailment: The Logic of Relevance and Necessity, Princeton University Press, Princeton.

Anderson, John R. (1983) The Architecture of Cognition, Cambridge, MA: Harvard University Press.

Anderson, John R., & Gordon H. Bower,1973 Human Associative Memory, Washington, DC: Winston.

Anderson, John R., & Gordon H. Bower, 1980 Human Associative Memory: A Brief Edition, Hillsdale, NJ: Erlbaum.

Anderson, John R., & Lebiere, C. 1998. The atomic components of thought, Mahwah, NJ: Erlbaum.

Adams, Thomas K. "Future Warfare and the Decline of Human Decisionmaking." Parameters, Winter 2001/2002, v. 31, no. 4

Adler, Emanual. "Executive Command and Control in Foreign Policy: The CIA's Covert Activities," Orbis, fall 1979, v. 23, no. 3

Agrell, Wilhelm. Sweden and the Dilemmas of Neutral Intelligence Liaison. Journal of Strategic Studies, August 2006, v. 29, no. 4

Aid, Matthew M. "All Glory is Fleeting: SIGINT and the Fight against International Terrorism." Intelligence and National Security, Winter 2003, v. 18, no. 4

Ast, Scott Alan. Managing Security Overseas: Protecting Employees and Assets in Volatile Regions Boca Raton; FL: CRC Press, 2010.

Ataov, Türkkaya 2018: Kashmir and Neighbors: Tale, Terror, Truce. (Routledge Revivals). Abingdon: Routledge.

Afghanistan Analyst Network (Osman, B.) 18 October 2019, The Islamic State in 'Khorasan': How it began and where it stands now in Nangarhar, 27 July 2016, https://www.afghanistan-analysts.org/the-islamic-state-inkhorasan-how-it-began-and-where-it-stands-now-in-nangarhar/,

Amnesty International, Pakistan: Enduring Enforced Disappearances, 27 March 2019,https://www.amnesty.org/en/latest/research/2019/03/pakistan-enduring-enforceddisappearances/, accessed 15 July 2019

Azam, M., Javaid, U, 2017, The sources of Militancy in Pakistan, in: Journal of the Research Society of Pakistan, Volume No. 54, Issue No. 2 http://pu.edu.pk/images/journal/history/PDF-FILES/13-Paper_54_2_17.pdf, accessed 24 July 2019.

Baloch, H., Peace Talks, ISKP and TTP--The Future in Question, 6 May 2019, ITCT (Islamic Theology of Counter Terrorism), https://www.itct.org.uk/wp-content/uploads/2019/05/Peace-Talks-ISKP-andTTP.

Bell, Paul M. P. 2007, Pakistan's Madrassas – Weapons of Mass Instruction? (Master's Thesis, Naval Postgraduate School, Monterey, United States). URL: http://hdl.handle.net/10945/3653

Bennett, John T. 2014, Bend but Don't Break: Why Obama's Targeted-Killing Program Challenges Policy and Legal Boundaries but Rarely Breaches them. (Master's Thesis, Johns Hopkins University, Baltimore, United States). http://jhir.library.jhu.edu/handle/1774.2/37221

Badalic, Vasja, 2019 The War against Civilians: Victims of the "War on Terror" in Afghanistan and Pakistan.(Palgrave Studies in Victims and Victimology). Cham: Palgrave Macmillan / Springer Nature. DOI: https://doi.org/10.

Bergen, Peter L.; Rothenberg, Daniel (Ed.) 2015, Drone Wars: Transforming Conflict, Law, and Policy. New York: Cambridge University Press.

Bergen, Peter L.; Tiedemann, Katherine (Eds.), 2013, Talibanistan: Negotiating the Borders between Terror, Politics, and Religion. Oxford: Oxford University Press. Brooke-Smith, Robin (2013): S

Bayly, C. A. 1996, Empire and Information: Intelligence Gathering and Social Communication in India: 1780-1880. NY: Cambridge University press,.

Bazan, Elizabeth B. 2008. The Foreign Intelligence Surveillance Act: Overview and Modifications. New York: Nova Science Publishers,

Bailey, David, 1997, A Computational Model of Embodiment in the Acquisition of Action Verbs, Doctoral dissertation, Computer Science Division, EECS Department, University of California, Berkeley.

Baillie, Penny, 2002 The Synthesis of Emotions in Artificial Intelligence, PhD Dissertation, University of Southern Queensland.

Baker, Mark C. 2003 Lexical Categories: Verbs, Nouns, and Adjectives, Cambridge University Press, Cambridge.

Baldwin, J.F. 1986 Automated fuzzy and probabilistic inference, Fuzzy Sets and Systems, vol 18,

Ballard, Dana H., Mary M. Hayhoe, Polly K. Pook, & Rajesh P. N. Rao 1997 Deictic codes for the embodiment of cognition, Behavioral and Brain Sciences 20, 723-767.

Bar Hillel, Yehoshua, 1954 Logical Syntax and Semantics, Language 30, 230-237.

Beck, Melvin. 1984. Secret Contenders: The Myth of Cold War Counterintelligence. New York, NY: Sheridan Square Publications,

Beichman, Arnold. 1984. "The U.S. Intelligence Establishment and Its Discontents." IN Dennis L. Bark (ed.) To Promote Peace: U.S. Foreign Policy in the Mid-1980s. Stanford, CA: Hoover Institution Press, Stanford University,

Bazai, Fida Muhammad, 2016 Pakistan's Responses to the United States' Demands in the War against the Taliban and Al-Qaeda. (Doctoral Thesis, University of Glasgow, Glasgow, United Kingdom). http://encore.lib.gla.ac.uk/iii/encore/record/C-Rb3258590

Bell, Paul M. P. (2007, March): Pakistan's Madrassas – Weapons of Mass Instruction? (Master's Thesis, Naval Postgraduate School, Monterey, United States). URL: http://hdl.handle.net/10945/3653

Bennett, John T. 2014 Bend but Don't Break: Why Obama's Targeted-Killing Program Challenges Policy and Legal Boundaries but Rarely Breaches them. (Master's Thesis, Johns Hopkins University, Baltimore, United States). http://jhir.library.jhu.edu/handle/1774.2/37221

Bhattacharya, Sandhya S. 2008 The Global Impact of Terror: 9/11 and the India-Pakistan Conflict. (Doctoral Thesis, Pennsylvania State University, State College, United States https://etda.libraries.psu. edu/catalog/7900

Barrett, David M. "Glimpses of a Hidden History: Sen. Richard Russell, Congress, and Oversight of the CIA." International Journal of Intelligence and Counterintelligence, Fall 1998, v. 11, no. 3, p. 271-298.

Barry James A. "Managing the Covert Political Action: Guideposts from Just War Theory." Studies in Intelligence, 1992, v. 36, no. 5 https://www.cia.gov/library/center-for-the-study-of-intelligence/kentcsi/docs/v36i3a05p_0001.htm

Barry, James A. Bridging the Intelligence-Policy Divide. Studies in Intelligence, 1994, v. 37, no. 5. https://www.cia.gov/library/center-for-the-study-of-intelligence/kentcsi/docs/v37i3a02p_0001.htm

Basile, James F. Congressional Assertiveness, Executive Authority and the Intelligence Oversight Act: A New Threat to the Separation of Powers. Notre Dame Law Review, 1989, v. 64, no. 4

Beres, Louis Rene. On Assassination, Preemption, and Counterterrorism: The View from International Law." International Journal of Intelligence and Counterintelligence, Winter 2008, v. 21, no. 4

Bhattacharya, Sandhya S. 2008, The Global Impact of Terror: 9/11 and the India-Pakistan Conflict. (Doctoral Thesis, Pennsylvania State University, State College, United States). https://etda.libraries.psu. edu/catalog/7900

Clarke, Ryan 2011, Crime–Terror Nexus in South Asia: States, Security and Non-State Actors. (Asian Security Studies). Abingdon: Routledge.

Coll, Steve, 2018 Directorate S: The C.I.A. and America's Secret Wars in Afghanistan and Pakistan. New York: Penguin Press.

Dorronsoro, Gilles. 2012. 'The transformation of the Afghanistan-Pakistan border', in under the drones: Modern lives in the Afghanistan-Pakistan Borderlands. Harvard University Press

Cassirer, Ernst,1942 Zur Logik der Kulturwissenschaften, translated by S. G. Lofts as The Logic of the Cultural Sciences, Yale University Press, New Haven.

Cattell, R. G. G., & Douglas K. Barry, eds. 1997, The Object Database Standard, ODMG 2.0, Morgan Kaufmann, San Francisco, CA.

215

Ceccato, Silvio. 1961 Linguistic Analysis and Programming for Mechanical Translation, Gordon and Breach, New York.

Ceccato, Silvio,1964 Automatic translation of languages, Information Storage and Retrieval 2:3, 105-158.

Chafe, Wallace L. 1970 Meaning and the Structure of Language, University of Chicago Press, Chicago.

Chamberlin, Don, 1996 Using the New DB2, Morgan Kaufmann Publishers, San Francisco.

Cruickshank, Paul, 2013, Al Qaeda. (5 Vols.). (Critical Concepts in Political Science). Abingdon: Routledge.

Canfield, Robert L. 1992. 'Restructuring in Greater Central Asia: Changing Political Configurations', Asian Survey, Vol. 32, No. 10.

Drumbl, Mark A. 2002. 'The Taliban's 'other' crimes', Third World Quarterly, No. 23.

Daily Times, Police service-challenges and reforms, 6 October 2018,https://daily-times.com.pk/306595/police-service-challenges-and-reforms/,

Daily Times, Reforming the judicial system, 8 March 2019,https://dailytimes.com.pk/362536/reforming-the-judicial-system/, accessed 17 October 2019

Dawn, 2009: Southern Punjab extremism battle between haves and have-nots, 21 May 2011 https://www.dawn.com/news/630651, accessed 21 July 2019

David, G.J. 2009. Ideas as Weapons: Influence and Perception in Modern Warfare. Washington, DC: Potomac Books,

DCAF Intelligence Working Group, Intelligence Practice and Democratic Oversight – a Practitioner's View. DCAF, Occasional paper no. 3. August 2003.

Dehaene, Stanislas, 2014 Consciousness and the Brain, New York: Viking.

DeJong, Gerald F.1979 Prediction and substantiation, Cognitive Science, vol. 3,

DeJong, Gerald F. 1982 An overview of the FRUMP system, in W. G. Lehnert & M. H. Ringle, eds., Strategies for Natual Language Processing, Erlbaum, Hillsdale, NJ,

Deledalle, Gerard, 1990 Charles S. Peirce, Phénoménologue et Sémioticien, translated as Charles S. Peirce, An Intellectual Biography, Amsterdam: John Benjamins.

de Moor, Aldo, Wilfried Lex, & Bernhard Ganter, eds. 2003 Conceptual Structures for Knowledge Creation and Communication, LNAI 2746, Berlin: Springer.

Deng, Li, & Dong Yu, 2014 Deep Learning: Methods and Applications, Foundations and Trends in Signal Processing.

Dennet, Daniel C. 1987 The Intentional Stance, MIT Press, Cambridge.

Dennet, Daniel C. 1995 Darwin's Dangerous Idea: Evolution and the Meanings of Life, Simon & Schuster, New York.

Dennet, Daniel C. 1996 Kinds of Minds, New York: Basic Books.

Dearth, Douglas H. 1992, Strategic Intelligence and National Security: A Selected Bibliography. Carlisle Barracks, PA: U.S. Army War College Library, http://handle.dtic.mil/100.2/ADA256389

Dearth, Douglas H. and R. Thomas Goodden. 1995. Strategic Intelligence: Theory and Application. 2nd ed. Carlisle Barracks, PA: U.S. Army War College Library

Der Derian, James. 1992. Antidiplomacy: Spies, Terror, Speed and War. Cambridge, MA: Blackwell,

Diamond, John. 2008.The CIA and the Culture of Failure: U.S. Intelligence from the End of the Cold War to the Invasion of Iraq. Stanford, CA: Stanford Security Series,

Dawn, Military courts cease to function today, 31 March 2019,https://www.dawn.com/news/1472947, accessed 3 July 2019

Dawn, Military Courts part of National Action Plan: PM Nawaz, 30 December 2014https://www.dawn.com/news/1154046, accessed 20 July 2019

Diplomat, July 2019,The, Taking Stock of Pakistan's Counterterrorism Efforts, 4 Years After the Army Public School Attack, 21 December 2018, https://thediplomat.com/2018/12/taking-stock-of-pakistanscounterterrorism-efforts-4-years-after-the-army-public-school-attack/,

Economic Times (The), US asks Pakistan to act against Haqqani network, other terror groups, 27 February 2018, https://m.economictimes.com/news/defence/us-asks-pak-to-act-against-haqqaninetwork-other-terror-groups/articleshow/63096010.cms, accessed 17 June 2019

Express Tribune, The Army launches Operation Radd-ul-Fasaad against terrorists across the country,22 February 2017, https://tribune.com.pk/story/1335805/army-launches-country-wide-operationterrorists/, accessed 30 July 2019

Einstein, Albert, 1921 The Meaning of Relativity, Princeton University Press, Princeton, NJ, fifth edition, 1956.

Einstein, A., H. A. Lorentz, H. Weyl, & H. Minkowski, 1923 The Principle of Relativity, Dover Publications, New York.

Einstein, Albert, 1944 Remarks on Bertrand Russell's Theory of Knowledge, in P. A. Schilpp, ed., The Philosophy of Bertrand Russell, Library of Living Philosophers.

Eklund, Peter W., Gerard Ellis, & G. Mann, eds. 1996 Conceptual Structures: Knowledge Representation as Interlingua, LNAI 1115, Berlin: Springer,

Express Tribune (The), Blast hits Hazara community's shoe market in Quetta, 6 August 2019, https://tribune.com.pk/story/2029583/1-least-two-martyred-13-injured-quetta-market-blast/

Elahi, N. 2019 Terrorism in Pakistan: The Tehreek-e-Taliban Pakistan (TTP) and the Challenge to Security. London: I.B. Tauris.

Fair, C. Christine 2014 fighting to the End: The Pakistan Army's Way of War. Oxford: Oxford University Press.

Fair, C. Christine 2018 In their Own Words: Understanding Lashkar-e-Tayyaba. London: Hurst.

Farwell, James P. 2011 The Pakistan Cauldron: Conspiracy, Assassination & Instability. Dulles: Potomac Books.

Feldman, J. A. 1981. A connectionist model of visual memory. In Hinton, G. E. and Anderson, J. A., editors, Parallel Models of Associative Memory, chapter 2. Erlbaum, Hillsdale, NJ.

Fukushima, K. 1975. Cognitron: A self-organizing multilayered neural network. Biological Cybernetics, 20:121–136.

Feigenbaum, Edward A., & Pamela McCorduck, 1983. The Fifth Generation, Addison-Wesley, Reading, MA. Brain and Language 89, 385-392.

Feldman, Jerome A. 2006 From Molecule to Metaphor: A Neural Theory of Language, MIT Press, Cambridge, MA.

Feldman, Jerome, & Srinivas Narayanan,2004 Embodied meaning in a neural theory of language, Brain and Language 89, 385-392.

Feldman, Jerome, Ellen Dodge, & John Bryant,2009. Embodied construction grammar, in B. Heine & H. Narrog, eds., The Oxford Handbook of Linguistic Analysis, Oxford: University Press.

Fellbaum, Christiane, 1998. WordNet: An Electronic Lexical Database, MIT Press, Cambridge, MA.

Feynman, Richard, 1965 The Character of Physical Law, Cambridge, MA: MIT Press.

Glatzer, Bernt. 2002. 'Centre and Periphery in Afghanistan: New Identities in a Broken State', Sociologus, winter issue.

Goodson, Larry. 1998. 'The Fragmentation of Culture in Afghanistan', Alif: Journal of Comparative Poetics, No. 18, Post-Colonial Discourse in South Asia.

Goodson, Larry P. 1998 'Periodicity and intensity in the Afghan War', Central Asian Survey, Vol. 17, No. 3.

Goudarzi, Hadi. 1999. 'Conflict in Afghanistan: Ethnicity and Religion', Ethnic Studies Report, Vol. XVII, No. 1.

Harpviken, Kristian Berg. 1997. 'Transcending nationalism: the emergence of non-state military formations in Afghanistan', Journal of Peace Research, Vol. 34, No. 3.

Haqqani, Husain, 2018 Reimagining Pakistan: Transforming a Dysfunctional Nuclear State. Noida: HarperCollins India.

Hayes, Louis D. 2016 The Islamic State in the Post-Modern World: The Political Experience of Pakistan. Abingdon: Routledge.

Hiro, Dilip, 2012 Apocalyptic Realm: Jihadists in South Asia. New Haven: Yale University Press.

Hussain, Rizwan, 2005 Pakistan and the Emergence of Islamic Militancy in Afghanistan. Aldershot: Ashgate.

Hinsley, F.H. and Richard Langhorn. 1985, Diplomacy and Intelligence during the Second World War: Essays in Honour of F.H. Hinsley. Cambridge, NY: Cambridge University Press

Hitchcock, Walter T. 1991, The Intelligence Revolution: A Historical Perspective: Proceedings of the Thirteenth Military History Symposium, U.S. Air Force Academy, Colorado Springs, Colorado, October 12-14, 1988. Washington, DC: U.S. Office of Air Force History,

Haaparanta Leila, 1994, Charles Peirce and the Drawings of the Mind, in Histoire Épistémologie Langage 16:1, 35-52.

Harris, Kathryn E. 2015, Asymmetric Strategies and Asymmetric Threats: A Structural-Realist Critique of Drone Strikes in Pakistan, 2004-2014. (Master's Thesis, Virginia Polytechnic Institute and State University, Blacksburg, United States).http://hdl.handle.net/10919/64516

Hoyt, Melanie Raeann, 2014, Decembe. A Game of Drones: Comparing the U.S. Aerial Assassination Campaign in Yemen and Pakistan. (Master's Thesis, Angelo State University, San Angelo, United States).http://hdl. handle. net/2346.1/30273

Hubbard, Austen, 2016, A Study on the Relationship between Security and Prosperity in Pakistan. (Master's Thesis, Angelo State University, San Angelo, United States). URL: http://hdl.handle.net/2346.1/30604

Hussain, Syed Ejaz, 2010, Terrorism in Pakistan: Incident Patterns, Terrorists' Characteristics, and the Impact of Terrorist Arrests on Terrorism. (Doctoral Thesis, University of Pennsylvania, Philadelphia, United States). https://repository.upenn.edu/edissertations/136

Hoffman, Bruce. Lessons of 9/11. Santa Monica, CA: RAND, 2002. http://www.rand.org/pubs/testimonies/CT201/index.html

Hussain, Safdar, and Muhammad Ijaz Latif. 2012. 'Issues and Challenges in Pakistan-Afghanistan Relations after 9/11', South Asian Studies, Vol. 27, No. 1.

Hussain, Shabir, and Syed Abdul Siraj. 2018. 'Coverage of Taliban conflict in the Pak–Afghan press: A comparative analysis', International Communication Gazette.

ICG. 2014. 'Resetting Pakistan's Relations with Afghanistan', International Crisis Group.

Iqbal, Khalid. 2015. 'Natural Allies: TurkeyPakistan-Afghanistan', Defence Journal, Vol. 18. No. 8.

Inderfurth, Karl F. and Loch K. Johnson. 1988, Decisions of the Highest Order: Perspectives on the National Security Council. Pacific Grove, California: Brooks/Cole,.

Ibrahimi, S. Yaqub. 2017. 'The Taliban's Islamic Emirate of Afghanistan (1996–2001): 'War-Making and State-Making' as an Insurgency Strategy', Small Wars & Insurgencies, Vol. 28, No. 6.

Intelligence Services and Democracy. Geneva, Switzerland: Geneva Centre for Democratic Control of Armed Forces, 2002.

Iran: Intelligence Failure or Policy Stalemate? Washington, DC: Georgetown University, Institute for the Study of Diplomacy, 2005. http://www12.georgetown.edu/sfs/isd/Iran_WG_Report.pdf

Jinnah Institute. 2013. 'Sources of Tension in Afghanistan & Pakistan: Perspectives from the Region

Johnson, Thomas H. and M. Chris Mason. 2008. 'No Sign until the Burst of Fire: Understanding the Pakistan-Afghanistan Frontier', International Security, Vol. 32, No. 4.

Jaffrelot, Christophe (Ed.), 2016, Pakistan at the Crossroads: Domestic Dynamics and External Pressures.

(Religion, Culture, and Public Life). New York: Columbia University Press.

Jamal, Arif, 2009, Shadow War: The Untold Story of Jihad in Kashmir. New York: Melville House.

Jan, Faizullah, 2015, The Muslim Extremist Discourse: Constructing Us versus Them. Lanham: Lexington Books.

Jalalzai Musa Khan. May 2018, Pakistan: Living with a Nuclear Monkey, Vij Books India Pvt Ltd, Darya Ganj New Delhi, India,

Judah, Tim. 2002. 'The Taliban Papers', Survival, Vol. 44, No. 1.

Jaffrelot, Christophe, 2016, Pakistan at the Crossroads: Domestic Dynamics and External Pressures. New York: Columbia University Press.

Jalalzai Musa Khan, 22 September, 2015. The Prospect of Nuclear Jihad in Pakistan: The Armed Forces, Islamic State, and the Threat of Chemical and Biological Terrorism. Algora Publishing, Riverside, New York, USA. ISBN-10: 1628941650. ISBN-13: 978-1628941654.

Jan, Faizullah, 2015, The Muslim Extremist Discourse: Constructing Us versus Them. Lanham: Lexington Books.

Kalia, Ravi, 2016, Pakistan's Political Labyrinths: Military, Society and Terror. Abingdon: Routledge.

Kapur, S. Paul, 2017, Jihad as Grand Strategy: Islamist Militancy, National Security, and the Pakistani State. New York: Oxford University Press.

Khalilzad, Zalmay. 1996. 'Afghanistan in 1995: Civil War and a Mini-Great Game', Asian Survey, Vol. 36, No. 2.

Khan, Ijaz. 1998. 'Afghanistan: A geopolitical study', Central Asian Survey, Vol. 17, No. 3.

Magnus, Ralph H. 1998. 'Afghanistan in 1997: The War Moves North', Asian Survey, Vol. 38, No.2.

Maley, William. 1997. 'The Dynamics of Regime Transition in Afghanistan', Central Asian Survey, Vol. 16, No. 2.

Malik, Iftikhar Haider, 2005, Jihad, Hindutva and the Taliban: South Asia at the Crossroads. Karachi: Oxford University Press.

Malik, Jamal, 2008, Madrasas in South Asia: Teaching Terror? (Routledge Contemporary South Asia Series, Vol. 4). Abingdon: Routledge.

Murphy, Eamon, 2013, The Making of Terrorism in Pakistan: Historical and Social Roots of Extremism. (Routledge Critical Terrorism Studies). Abingdon: Routledge.

Murphy, Eamon, 2019, Islam and Sectarian Violence in Pakistan: The Terror Within. Abingdon: Routledge.

Maloney, Sean M. 2015. 'Army of darkness: The jihadist training system in Pakistan and Afghanistan, 1996-2001', Small Wars & Insurgencies, Vol. 26, No. 3.

Mukhopadhyay, Dipali. 2012. 'The Slide from Withdrawal to War: The UN Secretary General's Failed Effort in Afghanistan, 1992', International Negotiation, Vol. 17, No. 3.

Nester, William, 2012, Hearts, Minds, and Hydras: Fighting Terrorism in Afghanistan, Pakistan, America, and Beyond – Dilemmas and Lessons. Dulles: Potomac Books.

Nielsen, Thomas Galasz; Syed, Mahroona Hussain; Vestenskov, David, 2015, Counterinsurgency and Counterterrorism: Sharing Experiences in Afghanistan and Pakistan. Copenhagen: Royal Danish Defence College.

Ollapally, Deepa M. (2008): The Politics of Extremism in South Asia. Cambridge: Cambridge University Press.

Odom, William E. 2003, Fixing Intelligence: For a More Secure America. New Haven: Yale University Press, 2003.

Odom, William E. 2004, Fixing Intelligence: For a More Secure America. 2nd ed.New Haven, CT: Yale University Press, 2004.

Odom, William E. et al. 1997, Modernizing Intelligence: Structure and Change for the 21st Century. Fairfax, VA: National Institute for Public Policy,

Olmsted, Kathryn S. 1996, Challenging the Secret Government: The PostWatergate Investigation of the CIA and FBI. Chapel Hill: University of North Carolina Press,

Olmsted, Kathryn Signe. 1993, Challenging the Secret Government: Congress and the Press Investigate the Intelligence Community, 1974-76. Dissertation. Davis, CA: University of California, Davis.

Pande, Aparna, 2018, Routledge Handbook of Contemporary Pakistan. Abingdon: Routledge.

Rais, Rasul Bakhsh. 2000. 'Afghanistan: A Forgotten Cold War Tragedy', Ethnic Studies Report, Vol. XVIII, No. 2.

Rieck, Andreas. 1997. 'Afghanistan's Taliban: An Islamic Revolution of the Pashtuns' in Orient, Vol. 38, No. 1.

Roy, Olivier. 1992. 'Political elites in Afghanistan: rentier state building, rentier state wrecking', International Journal of Middle East Studies, No. 24.

Rashid, Ahmed, 2008, Descent into Chaos: The United States and the Failure of Nation Building in Pakistan, Afghanistan, and Central Asia. New York: Viking.

Rashid, Ahmed, 2012, Pakistan on the Brink: The Future of America, Pakistan, and Afghanistan. New York: Viking.

Riedel, Bruce, 2011, Deadly Embrace: Pakistan, America, and the Future of the Global Jihad. Washington, DC: The Brookings Institution Press.

Riedel, Bruce, 2013, Avoiding Armageddon: America, India, and Pakistan to the Brink and Back. (Brookings Focus Books). Washington, DC: Brookings Institution Press.

Rubin, Barnett R. 2000. 'The Political Economy of War and Peace in Afghanistan', World Development, Vol. 28, No. 10.

Rubin, Barnett R. 1999. Afghanistan under the Taliban', Current History, Vol. 98, No. 625.

Rubin, Barnett R. 1994. Afghanistan in 1993: abandoned but surviving'Asian Survey, Vol. 34, No. 2.

Schmidt, John R. 2011, The Unraveling: Pakistan in the Age of Jihad. New York: Farrar, Straus and Giroux.

Shah, Sikander Ahmed, 2015, International Law and Drone Strikes in Pakistan: The Legal and Socio-Political Aspects. Routledge Research in the Law of Armed Conflict

Sharma, Surinder Kumar; Behera, Anshuman, 2014, Militant Groups in South Asia. New Delhi: Pentagon Press.

Sheikh, Mona Kanwal, 2016, Guardians of God: Inside the Religious Mind of the Pakistani Taliban. New Delhi: Oxford University Press.

Saikal, Amin. 1996. 'The UN and Afghanistan: A Case of Failed Peacemaking Intervention', International Peacekeeping, Vol. 3, No. 1.

Shahrani, M. Nazif. 2002. 'War, Factionalism, and the State in Afghanistan', American Anthropologist, Vol. 104, No. 3.

Schneider, Erich B. 2013, Balancing the Trinity: U.S. Approaches to Marginalizing Islamic Militancy in Pakistan. Master's Thesis, Naval Postgraduate School, Monterey, United States. http://hdl.handle. net/10945/39008

Shabab, Asma (2012, May): Marketing the Beard: The Use of Propaganda in the Attempt to Talibanize Pakistan. Master's Thesis, University of Southern California, Los Angeles, United States. http://digitallibrary.usc. edu/cdm/ref/collection/p15799coll3/id/38217

Shah, Abid Hussain, 2007,The Volatile Situation of Balochistan – Options to Bring it into Streamline. Master's Thesis, Naval Postgraduate School, Monterey, United States. http://hdl.handle.net/10945/10280

Siddique, Osman, 2013, Rational Irrationality: Analysis of Pakistan's Seemingly Irrational Double Game in Afghanistan. Master Thesis, University of Oslo, Oslo, Norway. https://www.duo.uio.no/ handle/10852/37342

Shahrani, M. Nazif. 2001. 'Resisting the Taliban and Talibanism in Afghanistan: Legacies of a Century of Internal Colonialism and Cold War Politics in a Buffer State', Perceptions: Journal of International Affairs, Vol. 5, No. 4.

Shahrani, M. Nazif. 2000. 'The Taliban Enigma: Person-Centered Politics & Extremism in Afghanistan', ISIM Newsletter, Vol. 6.

Tankel, Stephen, 2013, Storming the World Stage: The Story of Lashkar-e-Taiba. Oxford: Oxford University Press.

Topich, William J. 2018, Pakistan: The Taliban, Al Qaeda, and the Rise of Terrorism. Praeger Security International. Santa Barbara: Praeger.

Tripathy, Amulya K.; Pandit, D. Santishree; Kunjur, Roshni, 2016, Understanding Post 9/11 Cross-Border Terrorism in South Asia: U.S. and other Nations' Perceptions. New Delhi: Ess Ess Publications.

Tarzi, Shah M. 1993. 'Afghanistan in 1992: A Hobbesian State of Nature', Asian Survey, Vol. 33, No. 2.

Verkaaik, Oskar, 2004, Migrants and Militants: Fun and Urban Violence in Pakistan.Princeton Studies in Muslim Politics. Princeton: Princeton University Press.

Vandenbroucke, Lucien S. Perilous Options: Special Operations as an Instrument of U.S. Foreign Policy. New York: Oxford University Press,

Violia, Marc Anthony. 1993. A Spy's Résumé: Confessions of a Maverick Intelligence Professional and Misadventure Capitalist. Lanham, MD: Scarecrow Press

Volkman, Ernest. 1989. Secret Intelligence. New York: Doubleday,

Von Hassell, Agostino. 2006. Alliance of Enemies: The Untold Story of the Secret American and German Collaboration to End World War II. New York: Thomas Dunne Books,

Williams, Brian Glyn. 2014. 'Afghanistan after the Soviets: From jihad to tribalism', Small Wars & Insurgencies, Volume 25, Issue 5-6.

Webel, Charles; Tomass, Mark, 2017, Assessing the War on Terror: Western and Middle Eastern Perspectives. Contemporary Terrorism Studies. Abingdon: Routledge.

Woods, Chris, 2015, Sudden Justice: America's Secret Drone Wars. London: Hurst.

Yasmeen, Samina, 2017, Jihad and Dawah: Evolving Narratives of Lashkar-e-Taiba and Jamat ud Dawah. London: Hurst.

Yusuf, Moeed, 2008, Insurgency and Counterinsurgency in South Asia: Through a Peacebuilding Lens. Washington, DC: United States Institute of Peace Press.

Zaidi, Syed Manzar Abbas, 2016, Terrorism Prosecution in Pakistan. USIP Peaceworks, No. 113 https://www.usip.org/publications/2016/04/terrorism-prosecution-pakistan

Zaidi, Syed Manzar Abbas, 2016, Reconstituting Local Order in Pakistan: Emergent ISIS and Locally Constituted Shariah Courts in Pakistan. (Brookings Local Orders Paper Series, Paper 4). https://www. brookings.edu/research/reconstituting-local-order-in-pakistan-emergent-isis-and-locally-constitutedshariah-courts-in-pakistan

Index

About the Author

Musa Khan Jalalzai is a journalist and research scholar. He has written extensively on Afghanistan, terrorism, nuclear and biological terrorism, human trafficking, drug trafficking, and intelligence research and analysis. He was an Executive Editor of the Daily Outlook Afghanistan from 2005-2011, and a permanent contributor in Pakistan's daily *The Post*, *Daily Times*, and *The Nation*, *Weekly the Nation*, (London). However, in 2004, US Library of Congress in its report for South Asia mentioned him as the biggest and prolific writer. He received Masters in English literature, Diploma in Geospatial Intelligence, University of Maryland, Washington DC, certificate in Surveillance Law from the University of Stanford, USA, and diploma in Counter terrorism from Pennsylvania State University, California, the United States.

CPSIA information can be obtained
at www.ICGtesting.com
Printed in the USA
BVHW030916071021
618411BV00001B/30